# The Complete Idiot's Reference Card

## 15 Frequently Asked Questions Concerning Personality

1. **Q.** Are we born with our personalities?

   **A.** No. The biological component is only one aspect of our personalities.

2. **Q.** Why are our beliefs important?

   **A.** They signify the meaning we attribute to biology and environmental factors.

3. **Q.** How is learning related to our personalities?

   **A.** Through modeling and reinforcement, we learn to think, feel, and act in certain ways.

4. **Q.** What is self-actualization?

   **A.** The fulfillment of our need to become ourselves to the fullest.

5. **Q.** Are psychological tests that measure personality valid?

   **A.** Tests used by psychologists have undergone extensive study to demonstrate their reliability and validity. Tests in magazines and on the Internet often have not undergone a rigorous validation process.

6. **Q.** What are personality traits?

   **A.** The relatively enduring aspects of our personalities, such as the qualities of being outgoing or sensitive.

7. **Q.** What is the difference between a trait and a state?

   **A.** A trait is an enduring characteristic, while a state is a relatively temporary condition.

8. **Q.** What is the impact of having low self-esteem?

   **A.** Low self-esteem affects how we think about ourselves, how we think of others, and what we think other people will say about us.

9. **Q.** What is a personality disorder?

   **A.** It is a relatively enduring pattern of thinking, feeling, and acting that differs significantly from what is typical in society.

10. **Q.** Is there such a thing as an addictive personality?

    **A.** This is very controversial, and the debate is ongoing. Some people feel that there is, while others say addiction is a learned behavior.

11. **Q.** How does personality affect your choice of profession?

    **A.** It can affect your choice of work setting, level of interaction with others, and types of jobs you find interesting.

12. **Q.** Does your personality affect your parenting style?

    **A.** Yes, it affects the examples you set for your children and what types of behavior you reward in them.

13. **Q.** Can you change your personality?

    **A.** You can change certain aspects of your personality.

14. **Q.** Can changing your personality affect your health?

    **A.** Research shows that by making personality changes, you can improve your physical health.

15. **Q.** Where can you get more information about these frequently asked questions?

    **A.** All of these subjects, and many more, are covered right here in this book.

alpha
books

## 10 Things That Affect Personality

1. Biology
2. Genetics
3. General health
4. Living environment
5. Modeled behavior
6. Reinforcement
7. Schemas
8. Core beliefs
9. Assumptions
10. Automatic thoughts

## 10 Personality Disorders

1. Paranoid
2. Schizoid
3. Schizotypal
4. Antisocial
5. Borderline
6. Histrionic
7. Narcissistic
8. Avoidant
9. Dependent
10. Obsessive-Compulsive

# THE COMPLETE IDIOT'S GUIDE®TO

# Personality Profiles

*by Allen R. Miller, Ph.D., and Susan Shelly*

**alpha
books**

Macmillan USA, Inc.
201 West 103rd Street
Indianapolis, IN 46290

A Pearson Education Company

**Publisher**
*Marie Butler-Knight*

**Product Manager**
*Phil Kitchel*

**Managing Editor**
*Cari Luna*

**Acquisitions Editor**
*Randy Ladenheim-Gil*

**Development Editor**
*Doris Cross*

**Production Editor**
*Billy Fields*

**Copy Editor**
*Fran Blauw*

**Illustrator**
*Jody P. Schaeffer*

**Cover Designers**
*Mike Freeland*
*Kevin Spear*

**Book Designers**
*Scott Cook and Amy Adams of DesignLab*

**Indexer**
*Tonya Heard*

**Layout/Proofreading**
*Angela Calvert*
*Mary Hunt*

# Contents at a Glance

# Contents

# Foreword

The study of personality has fascinated people from the time of the Ancient Greeks. I am pleased to introduce this book, which covers many aspects of personality and change. Authors Allen Miller and Susan Shelly delve into some fairly complex ideas and explain them in everyday language.

A recurring theme in the book, along with Dr. Aaron Beck's cognitive therapy, is the schema-focused approach to personality. The schema approach recognizes the biological and environmental contributions to personality. It expands upon the research and clinical findings of cognitive-behavior therapy and is consistent with the constructivist view that we create our own realities. The ideas and practices of various theoretical and clinical approaches are integrated into schema-focused therapy.

Much has been written for the professional community about personality characteristics and how to change them. It is exciting that this book presents many ideas known within the professional community in a format suited to the layperson. In contrast to the idea suggested in the book's title, there are no "Idiots." The authors treat with sensitivity and respect all kinds of people with all kinds of characteristics.

The book is presented in six parts. Part 1 explains different ideas about where personality comes from and the role of beliefs in personality. Part 2 of the book focuses on psychological tests that are used to assess personality and makes suggestions for the best use of the myriad self-administered questionnaires available at newsstands, on bookshelves, and on the Internet. Part 3 includes an in-depth discussion about schemas, the role of personality traits, and early environmental influences on personality profiles. It also contrasts relatively enduring personality traits and temporary moods such as depression and anxiety. Personality disorders as defined by the American Psychiatric Association are the focus of Part 4. The way beliefs affect relationships, job performance, and parenting skills is described in Part 5. Part 6 is about change. Temporary mood states and enduring personality characteristics can be changed, although it may require time and patience on the part of the person who desires to change. Examples compiled from actual cases illustrate how a change in beliefs can affect emotions and behavior, and vice versa. Instructions and worksheets that you can use on your own are drawn from schema and cognitive therapy.

In summary, this book covers a lot of material about personality and change. It contains many examples to explain difficult concepts and to illustrate how to change. The ideas presented here are based on solid research and clinical practice. I recommend this book to those who want a better understanding of how personality is developed, how it is maintained, the pervasive role of personality in our lives, and how to improve the quality of life by changing personality.

Jeffrey E. Young, Ph.D.

Jeffrey E. Young, Ph.D., is founder and director of the Cognitive Therapy Centers of New York and Connecticut. He is also on the faculty of the Department of Psychiatry at Columbia University. Using well-known procedures and materials he has developed over the past 18 years, he has trained thousands of cognitive therapists at workshops throughout the world. He has published widely on cognitive therapy and has co-authored several books, including Reinventing Your Life, a self-help book based on his schema-focused approach.

# Introduction

The fascinating topic of human personality is multifaceted and can be dealt with on many levels.

We can talk about it as a health-related issue, as there's evidence that your personality directly impacts your mental and physical condition. We can discuss it as a social issue, for personality affects how people act and behave within our communities.

Personality can be dealt with on a spiritual level, a practical one, or a scientific one. The subject of personality is widely encompassing and has intrigued people for thousands of years. Throughout human history, we've tried to unlock the secrets of personality and get a better understanding of the ways in which all people are alike, and all of us have differences that make each of us unique and individual.

We may never understand every piece of the personality puzzle, but we've certainly come a long way in learning what makes us think, believe, and act in the ways we do. We're also getting better all the time at diagnosing and treating personality disorders—making life, if not pleasant, more bearable for thousands of sufferers.

Come along now and learn about personality—the subject that has mystified and intrigued men and women for thousands of years. Let's get started.

## How to Use This Book

The Complete Idiot's Guide to Personality Profiles is divided into six parts.

**Part 1, "What Is Personality?"** gives you an overview of personality. It introduces core beliefs and explores some of the best-known and respected theories regarding personality. You'll see which of the theories are still relevant today and get an idea of how they overlap and differ from one another. You'll also meet some of the people who most influenced the field of psychology by their theories and beliefs.

**Part 2, "Tests, Tests, and More Tests,"** takes a look at psychological tests and what they're used for. This part explores the development of these tests and the standards to which professional psychological tests are held. You'll learn about the differences between professional and nonprofessional tests, and you'll find out which professional tests are the best known and most enduring.

You'll also get some suggestions for finding nonprofessional tests, along with some cautions about using them.

**In Part 3, "Personality Characteristics,"** you'll find out about personality traits and how they influence our views and actions. We look at the issue of self-esteem and give you some suggestions for fostering positive esteem in yourself and others.

You'll also find out more about schemas—the cognitive processes we use to process and store assumptions and beliefs. A lot goes on in our brains all the time: It's fascinating to dig a little bit and find out what, and how, it all works.

This part also deals with moods, or temporary conditions, such as depression and anxiety.

**Part 4, "Personality Disorders,"** examines the issue of addiction and the argument about whether it's a disease or learned behavior. Personality disorders are divided into three clusters of behavior: eccentric, dramatic, and fearful.

The eccentric behaviors include the paranoid, schizoid, and schizotypal personality disorders. Antisocial, borderline, histrionic, and narcissistic personality disorders are the dramatic behaviors; and the cluster of disorders known as fearful behavior contains avoidant, dependent, and obsessive-compulsive disorders.

**In Part 5, "For Love and Money,"** you'll learn how your personality affects nearly every aspect of your life. You might be surprised at the extent to which your personality figures into your love life and how much it affects your career. It also largely determines the type of mom or dad you are, or will be, and explains why some people are better parents than others.

**Part 6, "Personality and Change,"** examines the processes of changing our automatic thoughts, behaviors, and even core beliefs. These changes aren't always easy, but those who really want to change and believe they have the ability to do so, very often can be successful in altering various aspects of their personality.

When you finish this book, you'll have a better understanding of your beliefs and attitudes, where they come from, and how they affect your life.

# Extras

In addition to the information in the chapters, you'll find bits and pieces of information and wisdom throughout this book. These snippets, known as sidebars, make the book not only more readable, but more personal and relevant. Here's what to look for:

### Personality Parlance

Here you'll find the authors' take on concepts, terms, and ideas as they apply to understanding personality.

**Don't Go There!**

These are warnings that point out misconceptions and snares that could trip you up as you endeavor to understand people's personalities—and your own.

**Personality Pointer**

These include tips or bits of information to enhance your knowledge and understanding of issues related to personality.

**Notes and Quotes**

Here you'll find interesting historical and statistical tidbits.

# Acknowledgments

The authors would like to thank the many people who provided time, information, and resources for this book. Especially, we thank our editors at Macmillan Publishing, Randy Ladenheim-Gil, Doris Cross, and Billy Fields. Special thanks also go to Bert Holtje of James Peter Associates for his warmth, humor, and understanding, and to Mike, Sara, and Ryan McGovern.

Dr. Miller would especially like to acknowledge and thank the following people: Aaron Beck, M.D., and Albert Ellis, Ph.D. greatly influenced my understanding of cognitive theory and therapy. Schema-focused cognitive therapy, developed by Jeffrey Young, Ph.D., has been a great help in my efforts to tie together the otherwise disparate aspects of my education. The training and supervision I received at the Beck Institute was an extraordinary learning experience. Judith Beck, Ph.D., Cory Newman, Ph.D., and Kevin Kuelwein, Psy.D. were especially supportive in helping me to transform theory into practice, and I am grateful.

I am equally appreciative to all the people who have allowed me to know the intimate details of their personalities. What I have learned from them has provided a basis for my own understanding and description of personality. Many people have supported me while I worked on this book, including Patti Bush, Bob Ortmyer, and Dorene Anderson, who most notably helped me to keep up with daily responsibilities.

A special thank you goes to Carol Turkington, who provided me with this opportunity. And, most important of all are Wanda and Katie, who tolerate me and enhance my life every day. Thank you!

## Trademarks

# Part 1

# What Is Personality?

*For thousands of years, people have tried to make sense of this thing we call personality. We've marveled at the similarities among people and the great differences as well.*

*Why, people have wondered for centuries, are some people happy, while others are morose and depressed? Why are some timid, while others embrace life to the fullest?*

*Many theories have resulted from our efforts to explain human behavior. In Part 1, we look at some of the major theories of personality—psychodynamic, learning, humanistic, Neo-Freudian, and several others. We also look at some of the lesser known and more bizarre theories of personality.*

*This first part also gives you an overview of the vast topic of personality and how it affects nearly every aspect of our lives.*

*We can't escape the implications of our personalities. The traits and beliefs that we have affect our love lives, our professional lives, the kinds of parents we'll be, and generally, how we look at the world around us.*

# Chapter 1

# The Personality Puzzle

## In This Chapter

➤ Defining the broad issue of personality

➤ Examining some theories of personality

➤ The uses and challenges of psychological tests

➤ Looking at personality development

➤ Personality's impact on our relationships and careers

➤ Changing your personality—Not easy, but it can be done

The subject of human personality is a fascinating one, to say the least. And with good reason. Personality affects everything we humans endeavor to do. It's absolutely central to our humanity.

So exactly what is this thing called *personality* that's intrigued and baffled scholars, doctors, scientists, and other curious folks for centuries?

We know that our personalities are what make us unique individuals. But why? How are our personalities determined? What is it that makes some of us so different from others? Are we born with a certain personality, or do we develop our personalities over time? Are we stuck with the personalities we have, or can we change them?

## What Is Personality, and Why?

While it's easy to talk about personality (we do it all the time), it's extremely difficult to know exactly how personality is formed and how it affects our lives.

Why are some people outgoing, while others are introverted? Why are some folks optimistic and happy, while others are sure the world will end tomorrow and they'll be the first casualties?

What makes some people generous and eager to help, while others are reluctant to part with a dollar for a homeless person?

**Personality Pointer**

Theories are not absolutes. There's always room for speculation and question when it comes to personality, and we're constantly learning more about the issues pertaining to it.

The complexity of the personality issue is what makes it so challenging and intriguing. There are many, many theories regarding personality. While doctors, researchers, and others gather as much evidence as possible to support these theories, we can't consider any theory completely indisputable.

The study and understanding of personality is important to everyone because it affects us all. We all are impacted by the personalities of the people around us. Think about it.

If your first encounter of the day is with someone who is upbeat and cheerful, you'll probably find yourself in a better mood than if that encounter is with a decidedly unpleasant, grouchy person who berates you at every opportunity.

Have you ever met a person who was so incredibly inspiring or warm that you felt you somehow were changed by that person? If so, you've experienced the power of personality.

Consider the implications of living with different personality types. As long as we interact with others, we'll be affected by their personalities.

In this book, we explore many aspects of personality. We look at how personality is shaped and how it affects our lives. We examine how personality is studied, evaluated, and tested, and how it can be changed. And we talk about personality disorders and some of the problems people encounter along the way.

This first chapter looks at what we mean when we discuss the issue of personality, and it provides an overview of some of the topics that are covered in greater detail later in the book.

The subject of personality is huge, with many varying opinions and schools of thought. While we do our best to give you many different viewpoints of personality, ultimately, the subject matter in this book reflects our opinions and findings. Let's get started.

# Pieces of the Puzzle

The word *personality* has many different meanings. A personality can be a well-known person, such as in "David Letterman is a popular TV personality."

"Personality" also has a legal meaning, concerning the capacity, condition, and state of individuals. Or it can be used to describe a person, such as in "Janet has a great personality."

Primarily, though, at least for the purposes of this book, personality is defined as the relatively fixed parts of what and who each of us is. It's the collection of particular traits and qualities of behaviors and beliefs that make a person an individual. It's who we are and how we interact with the world. Physical, environmental, and genetic factors all contribute to our personalities.

**Personality Parlance**

Your **personality** is the reflection of the traits, qualities, and beliefs that make you unique—the relatively fixed parts of what and who you are.

## *Body Basics*

We all exhibit our personalities in many ways. The things we do physically often are indicators of personality. The ballerina who devotes her entire life to dancing, for instance, tells us much about her personality through her physical activities.

Someone who hugs a lot tells us something of his personality through his actions. Someone who physically hurts another person also exemplifies his personality.

A person's physical appearance, and how others react to it, can affect his or her personality.

Rosa has been extremely overweight her entire life. Although she's basically a warm, thoughtful person, she acts standoffish and defensive toward others. Why? Because she's gotten the message loud and clear from others that she's fat. She's too big. She's not socially acceptable. Rosa's self-image has been damaged and shaped from the messages she's been given, and her defensive behavior is a result.

Society constantly gives us messages that we interpret, and some of those messages can be quite cruel. We react to those messages, and our behavior reflects the reaction.

On the other hand, a positive physical appearance also can shape one's personality. Jack's a great-looking guy, and he's been getting that message for all of his 24 years. Wherever he goes, Jack gets noticed. People want to get to know him—not because he's clever or kind, but simply because he resembles a young god. Things come easily to Jack because of his looks.

Jack's self-image can't help but be affected by how others treat him, and his self-image affects his personality.

### Notes and Quotes

We knew a young woman who had freckles on every visible part of her body. Of course, everyone she met felt compelled to comment or joke about her freckles. She grew extremely self-conscious and uncomfortable about them and took to wearing long pants and long-sleeved shirts whenever she went out—even in the middle of the hottest summers. Eventually, she became so upset that she pretty much stopped going out at all. Her self-consciousness, caused by the messages she got from others, affected her personality.

While physical factors are important, they're not the only pieces of the personality puzzle. Certainly, environmental factors affect our personalities tremendously.

## Circumstances and Surroundings

A child growing up in war-torn Bosnia, for instance, definitely has a different view of the world than a child growing up in the American heartland. A teenager who lives in a home where he's beaten regularly by his alcoholic father has a different outlook than one living with a loving, supportive family.

What we expect from life, and many of our behaviors, are founded on the beliefs that evolve from our experiences.

### Notes and Quotes

Children who are labeled early on as "learning disabled" often grow up with self-images that reflect that label, even if they overcome their learning problems later in life.

Picture yourself somewhere that you consider safe and nurturing. You'll feel relaxed in that place and able to act pleasantly and lovingly toward others. Now picture yourself in a situation that is terribly threatening and unsafe. You'd most likely behave in a very defensive manner, or in another way to compensate for your fear.

People have widely varying experiences during their lives, and we get very different messages from other people and the world.

Some of us are told as children that we look good, are well behaved, intelligent, and have the brightest futures ahead of us. Others are told that we're no good and we'll never amount to anything.

Messages like these largely determine our self-images and self-esteem. They shape what we think of ourselves and what we think we're capable of doing. And they affect the way we approach other people, situations, and tasks.

## Genetic Factors

Genetics is another important factor in our personalities. As we learn more and more about personality and personality disorders, it becomes clear that some traits are at least partially predisposed. It's a fascinating subject, and one we deal with later in the book. As you can see, the definition of personality is not a simple one. There are many factors to consider when thinking about or discussing personality.

# Theories of Personality

You've probably figured out by now that this topic of personality is complex and not always clear-cut. A big reason for that complexity is that there are, and always have been, many varying *theories,* or beliefs, concerning personality.

Throughout history, humans have tried to figure out why they and others are the way they are. Why do some people seem similar to one another, while others are so different? Why do some people succeed, while others with comparable back-grounds and upbringing fail? Why are some people more self-confident, or happier, or lazier, or meaner than others?

Over the centuries, hundreds of theories have been developed to explain why people are how they are, and why they're different from one another. Let's look at a few of those theories:

**Personality Parlance**

A **theory** is one step up from a hypothesis, which *is* a supposi-tion. A theory is supported by facts and data that have been collected using a formal testing process called the *scientific method.* Although theories are supported by facts and data, they are not considered to be infallible.

➤ Early Greeks believed that a person's character was dependent on the presence—or absence—of certain substances in the body.

➤ *Phrenology* asserts that the shape and size of a person's head account for mental abilities and personal characteristics.

➤ *Morphology* states that a person's temperament is dependent on the form and shape of his or her body.

➤ Many Japanese people still believe that blood type determines the type of per-sonality a person has. It's not uncommon to hear Japanese people asking each other what type of blood they have in order to get an idea of the other's person-ality.

➤ All kinds of books and charts attribute certain personality traits to people depending on the zodiac sign under which they were born. Someone born under the Gemini sign, for instance, is supposed to be bright and quick witted, very expressive, and eager to learn. We know the zodiac theory doesn't always hold true, but lots of people believe it anyway.

Theories such as these were—and in some cases still are—based on a variety of observations and experiences. Today's theories concerning personality are based on evidence, but even the most modern theories are not considered to be absolutely, without-a-trace-of-a-doubt true. Again, that's because they're theories, not absolutes.

It's also important to understand that no single theory can fully explain the concept of personality. Many theories overlap and intertwine. We look more closely at some of the major modern theories in upcoming chapters.

The people who come up with fact-based theories concerning personality (or anything else, for that matter) are called *theorists.*

Scientific theories must be based on reliable and valid research conducted over a period of time. Researchers who study personality often use tests to identify and measure the personality traits or characteristics of their subjects. The results of such tests help them to formulate their theories.

**Don't Go There!**

While most people no longer believe in these theories, some remnants of them are still around. Many people stereotype fat people as being jolly. That sort of stereotyping, which directly relates to the morphology theory, is certainly inaccurate—and can be dangerous.

# Testing, Testing: Psychological Tests

Psychological tests are used all the time for many different reasons.

Somebody who opens fire on his classmates, kills her mother because she wasn't allowed to borrow the car, or sets fire to his grandfather's house no doubt will face a great number of psychological tests after being apprehended.

The woman who's a candidate for a job with the FBI or CIA will be given psychological tests to determine whether she's competent to handle the job.

A violent offender certainly should undergo psychological tests before being sentenced to determine his or her mental capacity and state of mind.

These dramatic examples are far from the only uses of psychological tests. In fact, you've probably taken a test or two yourself. For example …

➤ If you've ever completed one of those magazine surveys to find out whether you and your significant other are right for each other, you've taken a type of psychological test.

➤ If your high school or college guidance counselor sat you down and made you answer a lot of questions about what you like to do and how you view the world, you've taken another type of psychological test.

➤ If you've ever undergone counseling, you may have been given a psychological test to help the counselor evaluate your condition.

Psychological tests commonly are used to determine job aptitude, to gauge the suitability of a partner, or to measure problems of personality. Other tests frequently are used for court purposes, such as determining whether someone has the potential to be violent or is likely to relapse. Psychological tests also often are used to measure aptitude and achievement in students.

Obviously, psychological tests are very significant, because we use the results for extremely important decisions.

To ensure that the tests work the way they're supposed to, we need to consider three areas: reliability and validity, interpretation, and application.

**Personality Pointer**

It's important to remember that, while psychological tests can tell us a lot about someone's personality, we can't base diagnosis and treatment on test results alone. Tests are valuable, but they're only one piece of the puzzle.

## Test Reliability and Validity

There's no point in giving somebody a psychological test if you can't trust the results.

The *reliability* of a test refers to being able to depend on the results. If a test is reliable, you'll get basically the same results from the same group of people the first time they take the test, and when they take it again a short time later.

The validity of a test means that it measures what it's supposed to measure. If you're giving somebody a career aptitude test, for instance, you have to be sure the questions will bring responses that will help determine career aptitude.

You can get all sorts of information from a psychological test, but you've got to make sure you get the information you need.

It's important to understand that psychological tests aren't put together casually. Developing reliable and valid tests is a painstaking process, involving many trained professionals. We get into tests and the testing process in much more detail in Part 2, "Tests, Tests, and More Tests," of the book.

## Interpreting Tests

You can have the most reliable and valid psychological tests in the world, but if they're not interpreted properly, they're worthless.

A doctor or researcher must be able to tell exactly what test results mean if those results are to be useful. Psychologists and some other specialists are highly trained to interpret test results, which makes their interpretations more reliable and valid than those of most other people.

And, doctors understand that while test results are important, they're not absolute. Other factors must be considered, such as what's going on in the patient's life at the time the test is taken, and how the patient's test results compare with those of others who have taken the test. Conclusions about a person should never be based solely on test results.

### Don't Go There!

Dozens of psychological tests are available on the Internet, and some of them are quite fun and interesting. If you take them, however, be careful when you start interpreting the results. Test results aren't always what they seem to be, and you shouldn't base any important decisions on your results from these kinds of tests.

## Applying Test Results

If Tom takes a psychological test, and it shows that he has a high score for aggression, what should be done? Should we institutionalize Tom just to be sure his aggression doesn't get the best of him? Or should we leverage his capacity for aggression by training him to be a soldier, a go-get-'em entrepreneur, or a professional football player?

Just because Tom's score for aggression was higher than what's considered normal doesn't mean he'll show up for work the next day with a high-powered rifle.

Test results must be considered as indicators, not absolutes. Tom's score must be evaluated along with other factors, such as his current living circumstances, personal history, and physical health. Other tests or psychological interviews might be necessary to examine the source of Tom's aggression.

Psychological tests are best looked at as just one of the tools professionals use to make their recommendations and determine treatments.

# Personality: A Work in Progress

Those who ponder these sorts of questions have long wondered how a personality develops and is formed. Is it primarily dependent on how we're raised, where we live, or the people with whom we associate? Or are none of those things important?

Some people believe that each of us has a fixed and concrete personality. They believe that a person's personality never changes, from the moment of birth until death. Most professionals consider that view to be a bit old-fashioned, but it's still considered viable by some.

The more modern feeling is that our personalities change and evolve as we move through life. These changes can occur naturally as a result of the normal aging process, or from changes in our *environment* or biology.

One's personality also can be changed deliberately. We get into changing personality in much more detail later in this chapter and in other chapters, but we certainly do know that deliberate change is possible, and that personality disorders often can be managed.

Normally, however, personality develops over a period of time, due to many factors. We believe that environment plays a huge role in how one's personality develops.

Think about a child who is placed into foster care at age two. Would his personality develop in the same manner, regardless of his environment? We don't think so. If the child goes through hell, as some foster (and other) kids do, we don't believe he'll grow up to have the same personality as he would if he'd lived with a loving, supportive, caring family.

Some people feel that personality is largely dictated by genetics, and that we have little control over its development. They think that someone born into a family of alcoholics, for instance, is genetically predisposed to being alcohol dependent.

What if the person is born into an alcoholic family but is raised by another family in which no alcohol or alcoholics are present? Will he still have alcoholic tendencies? We know that not everyone who has an alcoholic parent becomes an alcoholic. But why do some, and not others?

**Personality Parlance**

When talking about **environment,** we're talking about the people, things, and circumstances that surround a person. The environment includes all the factors of one's surroundings.

**Personality Pointer**

Personality changes can be caused by something as subtle as a hormonal change or as dramatic as a serious disease or injury. Many factors can contribute to a personality change.

These things are intriguing to think about but extremely difficult to prove, for obvious reasons. We can't prove that a person would be different if he'd had another sort of upbringing, because we can't go back and do it over.

However, many psychiatrists and psychologists—and we agree—adamantly believe that personality development hinges strongly on environment. We believe that because we see evidence of it all the time.

We often can guess the circumstances under which a patient grew up by looking at his or her current behavior or personality traits.

Some who were severely neglected or abused during childhood, for instance, may be predisposed to feel vulnerable, to expect to be treated badly by others, and to feel there is no escape from their personal hell.

They may feel that they've been abandoned by those they should have been able to trust. Those underlying feelings of abandonment might cause them to desperately seek approval and acceptance from others. Or they may take the offensive—steamrolling over everyone they meet to discourage them from doing something hurtful.

Personality development occurs in many ways, for many reasons. It normally is a gradual, ongoing process. You'll learn a lot more about development and personality changes in later chapters.

## Personality and Relationship Issues

The type of personality you have affects nearly every aspect of your life—including your relationships.

Personality has a big role in whom we choose as partners, how we handle relationships, how we treat our partners, and how we're treated by them.

We hate to be the ones to break it to you, but despite our strongest convictions to the contrary, we often end up choosing partners who are similar to our parents. Alas, we often end up *being* like our parents.

**Don't Go There!**

While it's true that people choose partners who treat them the way they expect to be treated, it's not necessary to do so. If you find yourself choosing partners who abuse you or don't value you, think about consulting a professional to learn how you can change that behavior. No one should be abused or neglected.

This is because our values, beliefs, likes, and dislikes tend to mirror those of our parents. If your parents always stressed education, for instance, and encouraged you to get the best education you possibly could, it's likely that you'll also value education. If, on the other hand, your parents thought working at the Safeway was just fine, and told you repeatedly that college is a waste of time, you're less likely to place a high value on education.

When we start looking at potential partners, we normally are attracted to those who like and value the same things we do. Since our likes and values tend to be similar to those of our parents ... yep, you've got it: Our partners often end up having personalities that are similar to those of good old mom and dad.

On a different level, we choose partners who meet our expectations. If you believe yourself to be a valuable, worthwhile person, and you expect to be treated well by others, you probably will choose a partner who values you and treats you well. On the other hand, if you hold a low opinion of yourself and expect others to abuse you, you're likely to choose someone who doesn't value you and will abuse you.

Personality also affects the relationships you have with friends, co-workers, teachers, and practically everyone else you know.

That's because your personality largely determines how you view others, what you expect from others, and how you treat them. Practically every aspect of the relationships we have with others is affected by our personalities.

# How Personality Affects Your Career

Just as our personalities affect our relationships, they also greatly impact our careers.

We've already discussed the use of psychological tests to determine career aptitude. These tests are designed to describe our personalities and match them with the type of work to which we are best suited. Personality-work matches are based on temperament, likes and dislikes, aptitudes, and abilities. Some tests also predict the types of people we'll best be able to work with. Once those tests have put you on the road to your perfect career, your personality will continue to play a major role in just how far along that road you get.

The ideas and attitudes we've grown up with or have been exposed to later in life greatly affect our interests and work ethic. Our personalities affect not only the work we choose, but how we treat the people we work beside and how we expect them to treat us.

Certain personality types tend to move ahead in work more quickly than others. Some people are miserable in their jobs, while others love their work. All of these things are related to personality.

### Notes and Quotes

We've probably all known people who hate every job they've ever had. They're always blaming somebody else—their boss or co-workers, usually—for problems they encounter in the workplace, and they encounter plenty of them. Is this a result of their personality? Probably.

# Changing Your Personality

By now we've established that our personalities affect just about all aspects of our lives. They cause us, in many instances, to act the way we do; they affect how we treat others and how others treat us; and they play a big part in our careers.

So what if we don't like our personality? Then what? Can we make a list—sort of like New Year's resolutions—vowing to change two personality traits a week for six weeks? Can we turn ourselves into the new-and-improved Charlie or Cheryl? If yes, how do we do so? And if no, where does that leave us? Stuck with our old, lousy personality?

Well, you've already read earlier in this chapter that change is possible. It's not simple, though.

We don't undergo magical transformations like the Beast in Disney's "Beauty and the Beast." Personality changes look more like those of Eliza Doolittle in "Pygmalion" or "My Fair Lady." They require hard work and practice.

We may be able to someday alter our personalities through genetic engineering. At this point, however, perhaps blessedly so, we're not able to manipulate our personalities genetically.

We *can* identify and work toward changing beliefs that affect our thinking and the ways we react to particular situations, however. And we can change the way we act toward others.

Of course, not everyone wants to change his or her personality, even if some say they do. Whether or not people are willing and able to change their personality is a complicated matter.

Often, people will express a desire to change their personality when they feel bad more often or more intensely than they can bear. Feeling bad might mean feeling sad, feeling very angry, experiencing panic attacks, and so forth.

Another reason people might want to change their personality is because the way they've been living is no longer working. This is common with people whose lives are spiraling out of control due to their abuse of drugs or alcohol.

Generally, however, people won't seek to change their personality as long as the distress is tolerable.

People who do seek to change their behavior must be willing to work hard, and they are likely to need professional help. It's not easy, but it can be done.

## Check Yourself Out

Here are several questions to help you reflect on what you've read in this chapter, and perhaps take the information a step or two farther in your own mind:

➤ Briefly summarize what you feel are the most important ways that your personality affects your life.

➤ Describe your attitude toward psychological tests.

➤ What experiences early in your life do you feel may have affected your personality?

➤ How has your personality affected your life so far?

➤ To what extent do you believe it's possible to change your personality?

➤ You might benefit from discussing these questions with another person, or just thinking about them on your own

## The Least You Need to Know

➤ Your personality is the sum of the traits, attitudes, and beliefs that make you the person you are. It's the qualities about you that stay relatively the same.

➤ There are many theories regarding personality; although many are supported by information and facts, none can be proven beyond a doubt.

➤ Psychological tests have many uses, such as determining job aptitude, measuring the suitability of a partner, or determining problems of personality.

➤ Tests must be reliable and valid, as well as properly interpreted and applied, in order to serve their intended purposes.

➤ While some believe that personality is fixed and never-changing, most experts think that personality develops throughout life due to a variety of factors.

➤ Personality affects our relationships, our careers, and many other areas of our lives.

➤ Changing your personality is not easy, but it's possible.

# Chapter 2

# You Are What You Believe

---

**In This Chapter**

➤ Understanding the cognitive/constructivist theory

➤ How early messages shape our beliefs

➤ Different kinds of early messages

➤ Understanding core beliefs and how they affect personality

➤ Recognizing automatic thoughts and attaching meaning to them

---

If you take a minute to think about it, you'll discover that what you believe affects nearly everything about you.

How and what you believe affect what you'll be able to accomplish within your lifetime. Your beliefs affect how you feel about yourself and others, and how you think others feel about you.

Your beliefs shape the way you look at the world and how you react to it.

The fundamental beliefs that you hold serve as links between your biological instincts and your environment. They act as connectors between your physical instincts and what you're taught.

In this chapter, we look at how our beliefs develop. We examine how the beliefs that we come to early in our lives remain with us and shape our perceptions, our dealings with other people, and how we live.

These issues of early beliefs and how they shape our lives are common concepts relating to cognitive therapy. That therapy evolved from two theories: cognitive and constructivist. As you'll see, the theories are closely related.

Let's look at the theories, and then we'll see how they relate to our beliefs and how they affect us.

# The Cognitive/Constructivist Theory

Modern cognitive ideas have their roots in constructivist thinking. Constructivism, which proposes that we all interpret our environments differently, based on our experiences and the things that we learn, stems back to the thinking of Greek philosophers.

Some of these philosophers believed that people's thoughts profoundly affect their personality and how they live. Epictetus, a Greek Stoic philosopher, summed up cognitive thinking when he said, "What disturbs men's minds is not events, but their judgments on events."

How we judge what happens to us allows us to create our own reality. We organize our experiences into cognitive structures called *schemas*.

**Personality Parlance**

The **constructivist theory** states that psychological processes (our thoughts, feelings, and behaviors), are formed according to how we anticipate events. The **cognitive theory** says our beliefs affect our emotions and behaviors, and that our emotions and behaviors affect our beliefs. **Schemas** are cognitive structures with themes that contain our memories, emotions associated with those memories, and our core beliefs surrounding that theme.

The *cognitive theory* says that our beliefs affect our emotions and behaviors, and vice versa.

As you can see, the two theories are similar, each dealing with how we organize our thoughts and beliefs, and how those thoughts and beliefs affect our personalities. Because the two theories are closely tied together, we sometimes lump them together as the *cognitive/constructivist theory*.

New information is assimilated into existing schemas, or if appropriate schemas don't exist, people may create them to accommodate the new information.

There is a rich lineage of philosophers and psychologists who are aligned with cognitive/constructivist thinking. Immanuel Kant, William James, John Dewey, Jean Piaget, and Lev Vygotsky are all associated with constructivist ideas.

A modern-day constructivist, George A. Kelly, gets credit for pinpointing ways in which people respond to the external world. Kelly, who was born in Kansas in 1905 and spent a major part of his career teaching at Ohio State University, said that people react differently to the world around them, and that the differences in their reactions are due to the different constructs they have.

Kelly proposed that people come to anticipate events from past experiences. We tend to think that, if a particular event occurred in a certain manner in the past, it will happen again in the same way.

Kelly cited three ways in which people respond to the external world. The responses are in relation to their constructs:

➤ If Mary's construct doesn't match reality (that is, if what she anticipates doesn't happen), Mary may learn from the experience and change her construct.

➤ If David's construct doesn't match reality, he may try to make reality meet his construct.

➤ If Jessica's construct doesn't match reality, she may choose to act in a very rigid manner. Regardless of what actually occurs, Jessica may insist that her construct is true and correct. If she admits that her construct is different from reality, she will insist that her construct is correct, and that it will match reality the next time a similar event occurs.

Mary, David, and Jessica all respond differently to the external world because each has a different set of constructs related to his or her individual beliefs and early messages.

Psychologists still acknowledge the concept of constructs, and the constructivist theory continues to be seriously regarded today.

# The Social Learning Theory

The social learning theory states that we learn from the things we observe in our environments. What we observe happening around us helps to form our beliefs, and how we perceive our world. The social learning theory ties in with the cognitive theory, which says our beliefs and how we perceive the world affect our emotions and behaviors.

The social learning theory expands on the idea that environment causes behavior. Social learning theorists believe that, while a person's environment does indeed affect how he or she will behave, there are cognitive factors at work, as well. Two people with similar environments often behave very differently. Social learning theorists attribute the difference to how those people interpret their environments, and the beliefs that result from their interpretations.

While learning theorists believe that observable behavior is all that's important to personality (more about that in Chapter 4, "The Learning

**Personality Pointer**

Behaviorists—those who observe and study behavior—say people's environments are what shape and cause their behavior. Behaviorists don't consider factors such as cognitive structures and meaning.

Theory of Personality"), psychologist Albert Bandura, who's credited with fully developing the social learning theory, went a step beyond.

Bandura, born in Mundare, Canada, in 1925, is a respected psychologist who served as president of the American Psychological Association in 1973. Most of his professional career has been spent teaching at Stanford University.Instead of considering only a person's observable behavior, Bandura took into account the interactions among a person's environment, behavior, and psychological processes, and the learning that resulted.

Psychological processes include the following factors:

➤ A person's ability to pay attention

➤ A person's ability to remember

➤ A person's ability to imagine events and their consequences

Bandura thought that a person's environment and behavior were tied in with these psychological processes.

Bandura's consideration of psychological processes separated him from strict behaviorist thinking, which focuses only on observable behavior. Like behaviorists, however, Bandura highly valued the scientific method and the study of observable and measurable activity.

While behaviorists believe that reinforcement will increase the likelihood that a person will perform a desired behavior, Bandura expanded on that concept with his theory of *modeling*.

Bandura's experiments demonstrated that kids learn behavior by watching another person's behavior. Reinforcement, Bandura, asserted, is not necessary.

**Personality Parlance**

**Modeling** is the process of someone observing another person (a model) do something, and then repeating that particular behavior.

Based on research conducted in the 1950s, Bandura concluded that some behavior occurs without any reinforcement. Children, Bandura asserted, eagerly do what they observe others do—no conditioning necessary.

One of Bandura's best-known experiments was the one involving Bobo the clown.

Bobo was one of those plastic, doll-like figures that's weighted at the bottom. When hit, Bobo would pop back up for more.

Bandura set up an experiment where a group of children were gathered to watch an actress (the model) "beat up" Bobo. The actress hit Bobo with a hammer while the children observed. Afterward, the children were put into a playroom with their own Bobo and some hammers. No adults were present in the room.

You can guess what happened. Poor Bobo got beat up again, hammers and all. The children received no reinforcement for their actions. They learned them by observing what the actress had done and repeated her behavior.

Bandura also used the notion of modeling behavior in a therapeutic way. To treat a person with a snake phobia, for instance, he would have the phobic person watch while an actor (a model) approached a snake and pretended to be very much afraid. Eventually, the actor would begin to handle the snake. After observing the actor's behavior, the phobic person would be encouraged to do what the actor had done.

Bandura's research in modeling behavior has been the basis of many arguments against television violence and other issues, and it has been useful for clinical purposes.

Bandura's work with modeling behavior illustrates how learning occurs without reinforcement. This differs from the strict behaviorists, who study reinforcement as the primary way to facilitate learning.

The cognitive/constructivist theory is extremely important. We discuss its uses and applications throughout the book.

**Don't Go There!**

You can tell your children ten thousand times not to smoke cigarettes. But if they see you smoking cigarettes, they're getting the message that it's okay, and it's more likely they'll *repeat* your behavior. If you don't want a kid to engage in a particular behavior, be sure you don't exhibit it.

# Early Messages

What happens to you when you're very young shapes your early beliefs.

As a baby and young child, you receive countless messages that tell you about the world into which you've been born.

The lucky ones—born into loving homes with nurturing, protective caregivers—get the message from the minute they're born that the world is safe and warm. They develop the belief that they'll be cared for, and they grow to expect kindness and love.

In time, of course, even lucky people discover that the world is not always gentle and loving. Their earliest perceptions, however, are of safety and care.

Those who aren't so lucky may be born into very different circumstances.

We've all heard too many horrible stories of babies being shaken, burned, beaten, and sexually abused. We've all read too often about children who are abandoned, neglected, and unwanted.

The children who live their early years in these types of circumstances don't grow up believing that the world is a safe and loving environment. They grow up quite differently—in fear and distrust of the people on whom they must depend.

If you can, imagine knowing that the people who take care of you are also those who hurt you. As a baby or young child, you have no alternative. You can't pick up the phone and ask to be placed in foster care. You're completely dependent on the people with whom you live, who are supposed to care for you and keep you safe.

When that doesn't happen, children learn very early on to fear everyone. They learn that no one should be trusted. If their primary caregivers hurt them, they have no reason to believe that others won't hurt them, as well.

The world is a dark and scary place for these unlucky children, who usually grow up with low self-esteem, often believing that they somehow caused the bad things that have happened to them.

On the other hand, children who grow up with loving, supportive parents who encourage and help them usually develop positive self-images. In time, of course, they come to understand that they'll be faced with problems, and that the world is not a perfect place. Because they've been taught that they're worthwhile and valuable, however, they believe that they can deal with, and probably overcome, the problems that come their way.

The manner in which early beliefs affect us is evident in many situations.

Consider Amy and Sharon. Amy and Sharon both were born with extremely large noses. Sharon learned to believe that she wasn't pretty, that she'd be lucky to ever find somebody who would want to marry her, and that her chances of having a career in television were absolutely nil.

Amy, on the other hand, learned to believe that her extra-large nose made her very special. It made her distinguished-looking, gave her great character, and set her apart from the crowd. While Sharon's family debated about which ancestors may have been responsible for Sharon's large nose, Amy's family ignored Amy's nose, focusing on her talents and strengths, instead.

Sharon and Amy grew up with very different self-perceptions and self-esteem. It's no surprise that Sharon suffered about her nose through adolescence and young adulthood and had it "fixed" at the first opportunity.

Amy, on the other hand, grew up thinking that the worth of people didn't depend on how they looked,

### Notes and Quotes

Most therapists realize that by the time children reach high school age, it's too late to entirely prevent personality problems from occurring. By this time, their beliefs have long been set and are affecting the way they perceive the world and react to it.

but on their abilities, values, and spirit. She felt she'd be able to accomplish whatever she set her mind to. Having a big nose, of course, is trivial compared to the tragic problems of some babies and children. This story does illustrate, however, that our perceptions of who we are and how the world will treat us are shaped very early in our lives.

The things that we're told when we're young—both through words and actions—shape our beliefs, how we see ourselves, and how we view the world.

These messages don't come only from our parents; they filter in from a variety of sources. Early teachers give us messages and help to shape our beliefs. So do babysitters, day-care providers, siblings, members of our extended families, friends, and acquaintances.

**Personality Pointer**

We remember the early messages we get and interpret them to shape our beliefs, about ourselves, other people and the world.

# Reinforcement of Early Messages

After these early messages creep into our minds, they are reinforced until we have little chance of not believing them.

Reinforcement occurs when we get the same messages repeatedly. Parents tell their children over and over again that they're special and precious, and their actions reinforce their words. Or perhaps parents repeatedly tell their children that they're troublesome and a burden. Or even worse, that they're useless and bad.

Regardless of the message, repetition reinforces it until the child hearing it is sure that it's true.

It's important to understand that messages aren't only spoken. A look of disgust at children who are physically misshapen or deformed tells those children as clearly as words would that they are imperfect.

Or a caregiver might tell a child one thing, while doing something else. If a father tells his daughter that she's good and he loves her, but he is sexually abusing her during the same period of time, what do you think the little girl will believe? The father's actions—not his words—are the stronger message he's sending to his daughter.

The father hurting his daughter, while at the same time telling her that he loves her, sends a terribly

**Personality Pointer**

Early messages and how they're reinforced are worth thinking about as we interact with our own or other children. It's pretty staggering to consider the impact that our words and actions can have.

conflicting message to the child. These kinds of early messages can lead to intense conflict and confusion as the child gets older.

Propaganda experts (as well as advertising people, come to think of it) understand very well the value of repetition and reinforcement. Something doesn't necessarily have to be true in order for people to believe it.

Several decades ago, many people believed that smoking cigarettes was relaxing, while at the same time invigorating and healthful. Why? Because that's what cigarette advertisements told them.

### Notes and Quotes

An advertisement for Camel cigarettes that appeared in the January 1935 issue of *Fortune* magazine includes testimony from Ray Baker of the former International News Service. Baker says, "Whenever I feel 'all in' Camels bring back my pep ..." He also notes that he can "... smoke Camels continually without jangled nerves." The ad concludes by telling consumers "You can smoke them freely since Camel's matchless blend of costlier tobaccos never upsets the nerves!"

Cigarette ads are a bit more subtle today, but they still convey the image of beautiful, happy people enjoying life as they puff away on one brand of cigarettes or another.

The point is that if you hear something often enough, you'll more likely come to believe it.

People believe that they're pretty or smart or funny because that belief has been established and reinforced. On the flip side, other people believe that they're worthless or stupid or ugly for the same reasons.

Repetition of our early messages is extremely powerful. It's not irreversible, however. If the repetition stops, the belief or condition can change.

If children are moved from abusive homes into loving foster homes, for example, they often hold on to their early beliefs for a period of time. Initially mistrustful, scared, and wary, eventually these children may become less fearful and begin to trust their environment.

They may still harbor a belief typical among abused children: that there's something wrong with them that caused their early caregivers to want to hurt them.

The beliefs might remain, but they often become less intense, allowing the children to react more positively to their environment.

# Getting to the Core of the Matter

We interpret our early environments, and the messages we receive when very young, to shape our early beliefs. As we hear these messages over and over again, they become reinforced in our minds and form our core beliefs.

Our core beliefs are a very significant part of who we believe we are and how we deal with life. They affect how we see and perceive the world, how we expect others to treat us, and how we treat others.

The meaning we attach to early messages and statements, become our core beliefs.

## *How Core Beliefs Affect Personality*

The way people think and act—their personality, in other words—is directly related to their core beliefs. Let's look at some different personality types and how core beliefs might factor in:

➤ **Upbeat and outgoing.** People who are upbeat and outgoing may truly enjoy their lives and relationships, have a positive outlook for the future, and try to make the most of what life gives them. Their core beliefs are that they're valuable and worthwhile, and have the potential to be happy and make others happy.

Or, people who act upbeat and outgoing could be compensating for a core belief that they won't be treated well by others. They might be afraid that they'll be put down or shunned, so they act very outgoing to hide their fears.

➤ **Shy and withdrawn.** Shy, withdrawn people may be that way by nature. Research shows that shyness may be a genetic condition and that some people are born with a tendency to be shy. These people may feel very good about themselves; they're just shy. To them, shy is a normal condition.

Or, shy and withdrawn people might be that way because they believe that people won't like them, so they try to draw as little attention to themselves as possible. If that's the case, their core beliefs may be that they're worthless, no good, fat, ugly, or whatever. Their beliefs make them expect that they won't be liked or accepted.

➤ **Surly and mean.** People who act surly and mean could be that way as the result of an organic personality disorder, meaning that their brains have been damaged due to trauma. Organic Personality Disorder is not in the same category as other kinds of personality problems and disorders that we discuss in this book. People who have suffered brain damage sometimes act in a very unacceptable manner and are unable to control their emotions.

Or, people who are mean and surly could have grown up in a terribly abusive environment and have a core belief of worthlessness. They may believe that everyone is "out to get them" and that they need to let everyone know they're mean so that they won't be bothered.

These are just a few examples of how core beliefs can affect personality. Everyone has core beliefs that largely shape who they are and how they act.

## A Case Study

We know someone who, by all appearances, had it made. He had a good marriage; three healthy children; a high-level position in a successful company; and was intelligent, poised, and good looking.

But, "Larry" as we'll call him, also had a deep-seated disorder that was threatening his happiness and the stability of his life.

Larry was already suffering from an obsessive-compulsive disorder that caused him to repeatedly recite a ritualistic prayer, and his problems were compounded when he was asked to give a presentation at work. Although he'd done this many times before, he was always terrified.

Larry was absolutely sure that he would fail. He couldn't give the presentation, he reasoned, because he wasn't good enough. Deep down, he believed that he was defective.

Larry's condition became so acute that he couldn't go to work. He worried about his family, fearing that he might not be able to care for them.

Treatment eventually revealed that Larry's core belief that he was somehow defective resulted from the fact that he had a mentally ill relative. As a child, Larry used to visit the relative, who required close supervision. As Larry got older, he grew to feel defective because of his genetic link with the mentally ill relative.

His obsessive-compulsive behavior disorder continued to develop, reinforcing his core belief that there was something basically and inherently wrong with him.

Treatment gradually was effective, and Larry very rarely engages in the ritualistic behavior.

## Your Brain on Cruise Control

Just as you can put your vehicle on cruise control, or an airline captain can put the plane on automatic pilot, your brain tends to generate automatic thoughts.

*Automatic thoughts* are those first thoughts that pop into your head when you're confronted with an experience or a problem. You're aware that they're there, and you might even understand where they come from, but, initially, you have little control over them while they're occurring.

Automatic thoughts don't pop into your head randomly. There's good reason why each person has his or her own set of automatic thoughts. These thoughts are the results of your core beliefs—those beliefs that are formed early in life and are enduring.

Robert's boss asks him to complete an important report by the following week. Even though it's a reasonable request and it would be quite possible for Robert to complete the report on time, Robert's automatic thought is that he can't do it.

That automatic thought doesn't happen because Robert is having a bad day. It's most likely caused by Robert's core belief, based on what he was told throughout his childhood, that he's inadequate and not likely to ever be successful.

Fortunately, Robert may be able to come to understand why he feels like he does and to modify his thoughts and behaviors. If he can recognize his automatic thoughts and allow himself to consider the evidence and re-evaluate the thoughts, he may be able to change them.

**Personality Parlance**

**Automatic thoughts** are the very first thoughts you have in response to a situation. They occur as a result of your core beliefs.

Automatic thoughts work both ways. We've probably all known "can-do" people—those who think they can do almost anything, or at least are willing to give it their best try.

Their automatic thoughts, which probably are something like, "Sure, I can do that," are the result of core beliefs that tell them they're competent people.

**Don't Go There!**

A real danger with automatic thoughts is that they tend to be self-fulfilling prophecies. If you believe you can't do something, chances are that you won't be able to. If your automatic thoughts normally are negative and pessimistic, you might want to consider getting some treatment to help you change those thoughts. At a minimum, read the last section of this book. If you don't change your negative automatic thoughts, you could be limiting what you're able to do.

Automatic thoughts are very powerful, and they often determine the outcome of a situation. In extreme circumstances, automatic thoughts could mean the difference between life and death.

Suppose that a child is trapped in an upstairs room in a burning house. Fortunately, there is a window in the room and a ladder leaning against the side of the house.

Mike, the child's neighbor, sees the child at the window and realizes how desperate the situation is. Fortunately, Mike's automatic thoughts tell him that he can save the child, not that he'll be unable to. As a result, Mike believes that he can help. He grabs the ladder, climbs to the window, and rescues the child.

Automatic thoughts occur all the time. They're extremely significant and well worth your consideration.

# What's *That* Supposed to Mean?

People often say things that have much different, deeper meanings than are at first apparent.

Let's say, for instance, that Mary tells us she can't possibly participate in her church's talent show. We ask why she thinks she couldn't be in the show. Mary tells us that it's because she never, in a thousand years, could get up on a stage in front of other people. When we ask her why, Mary hesitates, then tells us it's because she doesn't like the way she looks, and she's afraid people would laugh at her. When we take it a step further and ask Mary what she means when she says she doesn't like the way she looks, she tells us that she's ugly.

In reality, Mary's not ugly at all. But when we ask again what she means when she says she's ugly, she says that she must be ugly, because nobody likes her. When we ask how she came to believe that nobody likes her, Mary replies that it's because there's something wrong with her—that she's somehow defective or unlovable.

Mary's automatic thought is that she can't be in the talent show. The meaning that she attaches to the automatic thought leads back to her core belief that she's defective and unworthy of love.

As you can see, the concepts of early beliefs, core beliefs, automatic thoughts, and the meanings we attach to our thoughts are closely related. We are the products of what we learn and experience from the minute of our births.

# Check Yourself Out

Here are several questions to help you reflect on what you've read in this chapter, and perhaps to take the information a step or two farther in your own mind:

➤ In your own words, explain what the phrase "you are what you believe" means to you.

➤ Think of a recent situation in which your automatic thoughts affected your emotions and behavior.

➤ Can you cite any early experiences in your life that affect the way you think about things today?

➤ How has modeling affected your life?

You might benefit from discussing these questions with another person or just thinking about them on your own.

---

### The Least You Need to Know

➤ The cognitive/constructivist theory has its roots in ancient Greece. It states that people's interpretations of experiences significantly affect how they view the world, and their beliefs affect their emotions and behaviors.

➤ The messages we receive when we're babies and small children shape our beliefs about ourselves and the world.

➤ Reinforcement of early messages makes our beliefs and their influences on shaping our lives even stronger.

➤ Our core beliefs are the results of the early messages we receive, how we interpret them, and how they're reinforced. These beliefs have a profound effect on our personalities and how we live.

➤ Automatic thoughts are the results of core beliefs. They often can be recognized, re-evaluated, and changed.

➤ Core beliefs are behind the meaning of many things we say or otherwise express.

---

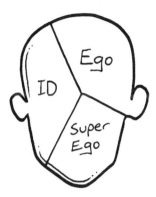

# Chapter 3

# The Psychodynamic (Huh?) Theory of Personality

---

### In This Chapter

➤ Understanding the role of the unconscious mind

➤ Learning about the origins of the psychodynamic movement

➤ How psychodynamic theory connects self and others

➤ Exploring the five stages of development

➤ Getting to know Freud and his followers

---

If you looked at the title of this chapter and drew a blank, don't get discouraged. If you've ever heard of a guy named Sigmund Freud, you've got a head start on the psychodynamic theory of personality since he was its originator.

Just like any theory, the psychodynamic theory of personality is not without faults. Although some psychologists still believe that the theory has merit, many have found serious flaws with its original formulation.

This theory was highly regarded when it was first developed in the late 1800s, however, and it is still considered to be significant.

As you read this and the other chapters on personality theories, it's important to remember one thing: Although theories are supported by facts and data, none are indisputable.

Remember that most psychologists don't depend solely on one theory or another; instead, they rely of parts of theories that are useful in their work.

Having said that, let's take a closer look at the psychodynamic theory, which is indeed interesting.

# What Is This Theory, and What Does It Mean?

The *psychodynamic theory* is based on the idea of the unconscious mind. While Freud wasn't the first person to talk about the unconscious mind, he certainly brought it into the limelight.

According to Freud, the mind has three parts.

➤ **The conscious mind.** This part of the mind contains all the things we're aware of.

➤ **The preconscious mind.** This part of the mind holds all the things we can easily retrieve, such as what we had for dinner last night or the name of our first true love.

➤ **The unconscious mind.** This houses all the things that are not easily accessible, such as vague memories; biological instincts; and our motivations for physical needs, such as food and sex.

**Personality Parlance**

With the unconscious mind as its cornerstone, the **psychodynamic theory** asserts that people are born with strong instincts and drives. The "id" is that part of personality that motivates people to seek gratification for their instincts and drives as quickly as possible, in whatever manner possible.

The psychodynamic theory states that we're born with instincts and drives, and that we operate under the *pleasure principle,* which motivates us to try to gratify all of our needs as quickly as possible. Freud believed that the sex drive is the primary motivator in everything someone does.

The pleasure principle contrasts with the *reality principle,* which assumes that, while we try to gratify our needs, we normally do so in a manner that's socially acceptable.

The psychodynamic theory also identifies three parts of the personality: the id, ego, and superego. We discuss these at length later in the chapter.

# The Importance of the Unconscious Mind

Since the unconscious mind is so vital to the psychodynamic theory, we'll need to spend some time discussing exactly what it is and why psychotherapists think it's so important.

We already learned that the unconscious mind is the area that stores all those things that aren't easily accessible.

It holds our vaguest memories, our biological instincts, and our motivations for physical needs, such as food and sex.

Freud thought that a person's physical needs, housed in the unconscious mind, tell us everything about that person.

He believed that the unconscious mind holds all sorts of interesting things, such as repressed memories of painful and traumatic events, as well as fixations acquired from a person's early stages of development and left there (you'll read more about that later in the chapter). He also thought that the unconscious mind holds symbolic representations of actual events and memories.

# Id, Ego, and Superego

Freud identified three parts of the personality: id, ego, and superego. Let's look at each of these parts:

➤ **Id.** Represents your physical needs. It is your physical drives and instincts—your life force. The id is totally centered on your needs and wants, and it drives you to satisfy those needs immediately, at whatever cost.

➤ **Ego.** Gives you a sense of yourself as a person (unlike the id, which is strictly reactive and biological). The ego causes you to meet your needs and wants in a socially acceptable manner. The ego is the beginning of the separation between yourself and others, and it recognizes the need to negotiate through the world in order to meet your needs. The ego also acts as a connector between the id and superego.

➤ **Superego.** Your conscience; describes what you come to believe as right and wrong.

**Personality Pointer**

Think of the ego as the moderator in a contract dispute. Its job is to reconcile two seemingly irreconcilable parties and to get them to agree to something.

The id and superego exist in a constant state of conflict, according to Freud and the psychodynamic theory. Fortunately, however, the ego serves as a sort of moderator between the two.

The ego spends much of its time sorting things out between the id and superego. Suppose that you see two $50 bills lying next to the cash register in the shop you're visiting. You figure the cashier left the money lying there by mistake. You're really short of cash right now, you need new shoes, there's nothing in your refrigerator, and the id part of you tells you to grab that money and run. Your superego, on the other hand, tells you that taking the money is bad—the wrong thing to do. You're in turmoil, but don't worry. The trusty ego will jump in and get things straightened out.

The ego gets tired of playing cop to the id and superego, however. Sometimes it just can't deal with it. When that happens, the ego uses defense mechanisms to block out

**33**

the conflict between the id and superego. This is why sometimes people can't remember something traumatic that happened to them, or they remember only certain parts of an event.

The ego has several defense mechanisms at its disposal:

➤ **Denial.** The ego is unable to accept the truth about something; it's too painful. So the ego pushes the wish, desire, or memory into the unconscious mind so that it doesn't have to deal with it.

➤ **Repression.** Your ego pushes something so deep into your unconscious that you can't remember it at all. You have no conscious memory of the event.

➤ **Intellectualization.** Sometimes, as a defense mechanism, you separate emotion from memory. You may remember a horrible event very dispassionately, because you've separated the feeling of the event from your memory of it.

➤ **Displacement.** When you redirect an urge, you use displacement. A child who is angry with his parents, for instance, might figure it's smarter and safer to punch his little brother instead. His brother is a substitute for the parents the angry child would really like to punch.

➤ **Projection.** We sometimes can recognize our faults and undesirable characteristics in others, but we don't see them in ourselves. You might complain about your friends who gossip too much, not realizing that you're always anxious to hear what they have to say and share your own news and opinions. That's projection.

➤ **Reaction formation.** Sometimes you modify unacceptable behavior by doing just the opposite. If you're really angry with someone who walks into the room, you may go over and offer a hug instead of a slap across the face.

➤ **Identification.** You identify with someone, or take on that person's characteristics. When faced with a moral dilemma, for example, you might ask yourself what your father would do and follow his example, rather than give in to your urges.

➤ **Regression.** This is reverting to earlier stages of development. An uncomfortable six-year-old in the early days of first grade, for instance, might seek comfort by sucking his thumb, as he did earlier in life.

➤ **Rationalization.** This is making excuses for your unacceptable thoughts or behavior.

➤ **Sublimation.** You'd like to do something, but you know it's socially unacceptable, so you do something else, instead. For example, Rob and Sharon are lovers, but Sharon is away on a temporary assignment for her job. Rob and Sharon miss each other, and their sex lives, very much. They both consider finding another partner to satisfy their sexual urges, and, in fact, Sharon does just that. Rob, on the other hand, throws all his energies into his graphic arts business, and produces some of the most creative, inspiring work he's ever done. Rob practiced sublimation, while Sharon did not.

We use defense mechanisms all the time, often without realizing it. This happens when the ego can't resolve the conflict between the id and superego.

Generally, the ego is pretty efficient at conflict resolution. When the ego becomes ineffective, the id or the superego may become dominant.

# The Five Stages of Development

According to the psychodynamic theory, people must successfully pass through five stages of development in order to become healthy, well-adjusted adults. Each stage has a goal that must be accomplished successfully. If the goal is not realized, the person becomes fixated at the uncompleted stage, which results in problems later in life.

## The Oral Stage

The oral stage lasts from birth until about 18 months of age. As you probably assumed, this stage is all centered on the mouth—primarily, eating, drinking, and sucking.

The goal of the oral stage is successful weaning. If that goal is not realized, a person becomes fixated at the oral stage and experiences oral-based issues later in life. These issues could become apparent with behavior that includes inappropriate biting, eating, drinking, and smoking.

## The Anal Stage

The anal stage lasts from about 18 months to about four years of age. Its focus is expulsion and excrement, and the goal of this stage is successful potty-training.

If the goal is not successfully met, a person can become anally fixated. This can result in anal-retentiveness: The person typically is very clean, a perfectionist, or very stingy.

**Personality Pointer**

Defense mechanisms are automatic responses. We don't plan to use them; they just happen.

**Don't Go There!**

The psychodynamic stages of development pose a danger in that they provide excuses for problems that people have and perhaps choose not to try to overcome. Someone who is extremely obese, for instance, may blame the problem on not being properly weaned in the oral stage. The stages are worth a look, but be careful not to go overboard with applications.

The flip side to being anal-retentive is to be anal-expulsive, which includes traits such as extreme sloppiness and disorganization.

## The Phallic Stage

The phallic stage extends from about four years old to about seven years old. Its focus is sexual organs, and the goal of the stage is to resolve the Oedipus complex—that means that a boy has to figure out his sexual relationship with his mother—or the Electra complex in the case of a girl who has to figure out her sexual relationship with her father. A girl also must deal with penis envy at this stage.

People who do not meet these goals could become fixated in the phallic stage and would likely suffer from esteem problems—especially regarding sex—later in life. They also would probably have trouble with sexual relationships.

## The Latency Period

The latency period lasts from about seven years old to the start of puberty. As the name indicates, this is a quiet stage, during which no real issues must be resolved.

The lesson is, if you have children in this age group, enjoy them. It won't last!

## The Genital Stage

The genital stage is the last stage of development, beginning at the onset of puberty and lasting for the rest of one's life.

The goal of this stage is for people to resolve their sexual identity. Success or failure to do so affects people's outlook and esteem.

# A Guy Named Freud and His Followers

By all standards, Sigmund Freud was one of the most influential thinkers of his time, leaving behind a legacy of ideas and theories that are still considered important and relevant by many.

Freud had a devoted group of followers, including his daughter Anna, Carl Gustav Jung, and Erik Erikson. Freud reputedly insisted that his followers share his views and rejected those who did not completely agree with him. He is known to have alienated quite a few people by this tactic.

## Sigmund Freud

Freud was born on May 6, 1856, in Freiberg, a small town in Moravia. He was recognized as being brilliant from the time he was very young. By age eight, Freud was reading Shakespeare. He was always at the top of his class, and he entered medical school at Vienna University when he was 17. While a student there, Freud also became known as a brilliant researcher.

After working with a doctor who was studying the use of hypnosis to treat disorders such as hysteria, Freud began focusing his studies on nervous ailments. During the 1890s, he founded the psychoanalytic theory of mind.

Some of Freud's views, many of which are discussed in this chapter, became well-known, and some were quite controversial. Freud attracted a following, and they formed a group that met weekly to write papers and journal articles expressing their views and theories. The psychoanalytic movement expanded as the views became more widely known and accepted.

Freud also was known for the books he wrote. Some of his most well-known are *The Interpretation of Dreams* (1890); *The Psychopathology of Everyday Life* (1901); and *Beyond the Pleasure Principle,* Freud's theory of the death drive, which he wrote soon after World War I when one of his daughters died of influenza. Freud and his wife, Martha, had six children. The youngest, Anna, was reputedly Freud's favorite and worked closely with her father. Freud's three sons all served in World War I.

Although Freud developed cancer and was ill for the last years of his life, he kept working practically until his death. He wrote *Civilization and Its Discontents* in 1930, a cynical book about modern civilization being on the verge of catastrophe. His last book was *Moses and Monotheism.* Freud died on September 23, 1939. He was 83 years old.

## Anna Freud

Anna Freud was born on December 3, 1895, the youngest of Sigmund and Martha Freud's six children. She became a schoolteacher but was deeply influenced by her father and eventually gave up teaching to study psychoanalysis.

**Notes and Quotes**

After a long bout with cancer, Freud reportedly decided to end his life by asking his doctor to give him a fatal dose of morphine.

When Anna was 27, she was accepted as a member of the Vienna Psychoanalytic Society; the following year, she started her own psychoanalytical practice with children. She also taught a seminar at the Vienna Psychoanalytic Training Institute.

When Sigmund Freud became ill with cancer, his daughter nursed him, along with running her practice, organizing conferences, and serving as general secretary of the International Psychoanalytical Association. She also attended all public occasions as her father's representative.

Anna continued to work with children and became well-known and respected. Her views mirrored those of her father.

When World War II broke out in Austria, the Freuds fled to England, and Sigmund died shortly thereafter. Anna remained committed to working with children. She also traveled—often to the United States—to lecture, teach, and visit friends. She died in 1982.

**Notes and Quotes**

Anna Freud once said while talking about her life, "I don't think I'd be a good subject for biography, there's not enough action. You would say all there is to say in a few sentences—she spent her life with children!"

## Carl Gustav Jung

Carl Jung was born in Switzerland on July 26, 1875. He attended boarding school, and although he was interested in architecture, he enrolled at the University of Basel in Switzerland to study medicine.

Jung met Sigmund Freud in Vienna in 1907, and the two struck up a fast and deep friendship. Jung was certainly very influenced by Freud, who considered him to be like a son until Jung's views and theories began to diverge somewhat from his own.

Jung also acknowledged three parts of the mind, but he saw them somewhat differently:

➤ **Conscious.** This contains the things we're aware of.

➤ **Personal unconscious.** The part of the mind that remembers things from the past.

➤ **Collective unconscious.** A reservoir of everything human that has been passed down from generations. It includes biology, knowledge, instincts, and so forth. Jung said that all humans are born with a full set of knowledge, but it's stored in the collective unconscious and not fully used.

Jung also thought humans possess something called *archetypes.*

Archetypes resemble instincts, but they're more specific. Archetypes are unlearned tendencies to experience things in a certain manner.

For instance, a person with a mother archetype has a built-in tendency to form relationships with motherlike people.

Jung said all humans have a self archetype, which is a drive to become perfect. To achieve perfection, Jung thought, you have to resolve and integrate all parts of your personality. Unfortunately, he believed, you can only accomplish this at death.

Jung also established personality typologies, which are very important. The best known of Jung's typologies are introversion and extroversion.

An *introvert,* according to Jung, is one who prefers his inner world of thoughts and fantasies to the external world. An *extrovert* prefers the external world.

Jung's theory also states that people use four functions to make themselves more comfortable with the world:

> ➤ **Sensing.** Getting information through the senses.

> ➤ **Thinking.** Logical, rational thought.

> ➤ **Intuiting.** Using intuition to organize complex information. Intuiting is based on feeling, as opposed to thinking, which is based on logical, rational thought.

> ➤ **Feeling.** An emotional response to events and situations.

As you've probably noticed, Jung is far more spiritual than Freud, and he downplayed the importance of sex in the human psyche. Jung was very interested in and sympathetic toward issues such as reincarnation, near-death experiences, channeling, and so forth.

Jung traveled extensively in the later years of his life, then retired in 1946. He died on June 6, 1961, in Zurich. He was 86 years old.

**Personality Parlance**

An **archetype** is like an instinct, but it points toward a more specific goal than an instinct does.

**Notes and Quotes**

The well-known and popular Myers-Briggs personality tests are based on the theories of Carl Jung.

## Erik Erikson

Erik Erikson was born in Frankfurt, Germany, on June 15, 1902. His mother was Karla Abrahamsen, and his father was an unnamed Danish man who abandoned Erik's mother before Erik was born. When Erik was three, his mother married Theodor Homberger, a pediatrician, and Erik became known as Erik Homberger.

Erik was tall and blonde—very Nordic-looking—with a Jewish name. This resulted in much teasing from fellow students.

Some people speculate that Erikson's later work dealing with the development of human identity may be a reflection of his own childhood search for his identity.

After graduating from high school, Erikson, who wanted to be an artist, wandered throughout Europe and eventually got a job teaching art at an experimental school run by Anna Freud's friend, Dorothy Burlingham.

While teaching at the school, Erikson earned a certificate in Montessori education, a method of education (based on the observations and discoveries of Dr. Maria Montessori) designed to help every child reach his or her fullest potential; as well as one from the Vienna Psychoanalytic Society. He was psychoanalyzed and influenced by Anna Freud.

### Notes and Quotes

Erikson was known as Erik Homberger until he moved to the United States and became a U.S. citizen. Why he abandoned his last name and chose the name Erikson is not entirely clear.

As the Nazis were coming into power, Erikson and his wife, Joan Serson Erikson, a dance teacher at Burlingham's school, fled Vienna. They went first to Copenhagen, and then to Boston, where Erikson had a private practice in child psychoanalysis. He also taught at the Harvard Medical School.

He later taught at Yale and the University of California at Berkeley. He left Berkeley in 1950, when professors there were asked to sign "loyalty oaths" in the wake of unleashed McCarthyism. Erikson went back to Boston, where he worked and taught at a clinic until 1960. He then returned to Harvard, where he taught for 10 more years.

Erikson accepted Freud's ideas as being basically correct, but he was much more focused on society and culture than Freud and the strict Freudians were.

Erikson's theory of the stages of development and personality is so important that we discuss it in detail in Chapter 6, "Other Personality Theories." Basically, it sets down eight stages that extend throughout life, not stopping at puberty, as Freud's five stages did.

Erikson retired in 1970 and spent the last years of his life writing and researching with his wife. He died in 1994 at the age of 92.

As you can see, while Freud's followers embraced many of his ideas, they were not afraid to step outside of his influence to develop their own theories. This may have alienated them from Freud, but it also made the psychodynamic field richer and more diverse.

# Check Yourself Out

Here are several questions to help you reflect on what you've read in this chapter, and perhaps to take the information a step or two farther in your own mind:

➤ How high do you rate the significance of the unconscious mind? Do you feel it's important to your personality?

➤ To what degree do you agree with Freud's concept that sexual instinct is extremely significant?

➤ Do you agree with the theorists who assert that there are stages of development you must pass through in order to become a healthy person?

➤ Which theorist's focus seems to make the most sense to you: Freud's focus on sex? Jung's on spirituality? or Erikson's on social influences?

➤ If you were experiencing personal problems, would you want to see a psychoanalyst?

➤ You might benefit from discussing these questions with another person, or just thinking about them on your own.

---

### The Least You Need to Know

➤ The psychodynamic theory is influential and important.

➤ Freud considered the unconscious mind to be extremely important and the source of most of a person's personality.

➤ The ego serves as a moderator between the id and superego; it is the connection between self and others.

➤ When the ego can't resolve a conflict between the id and superego, defense mechanisms kick in.

➤ Freud had a dedicated group of followers, but their beliefs sometimes strayed from his.

# Chapter 4

# The Learning Theory of Personality

## In This Chapter

➤ Moving from the unconscious to the conscious mind

➤ How the learning theory got its start

➤ Putting the theory into action today

➤ Pioneers of the learning theory

➤ Looking at the reasons for behavior

➤ The science behind the theory

The psychodynamic theory, as discussed in Chapter 3, "The Psychodynamic (Huh?) Theory of Personality," is certainly an interesting one. It may not be all that convincing, but it's fun to consider.

Once you've finished digesting all that information about the unconscious mind and the id, ego, and superego, however, you'll need to prepare yourself to learn about something that's very, very different.

The psychodynamic theory and the learning theory we discuss in this chapter are just about at opposite ends of the spectrum.

While Freud and his followers wallowed in the past, searching for buried clues about why people do the things they do, John B. Watson and other behaviorists said "nonsense."

The learning theory of personality focuses on what's going on now. It's almost completely up front, in the conscious mind, and in our opinion, it's refreshingly scientific when compared to the psychodynamic theory.

So, clear your mind (your conscious mind, that is) of the psychodynamic theory, and let's have a look at the learning theory of personality.

# What It Is and How It Works

The learning theory focuses entirely on what's going on in a person's conscious mind.

The theory doesn't accept—and in some cases, doesn't even *acknowledge*—that there's such a thing as the unconscious mind. The unconscious simply isn't considered to be important or relevant to the learning theory.

**Personality Parlance**

**Behaviorists** are those who believe in and practice the learning theory of personality.

**Personality Pointer**

While psychoanalysts delve into a person's past to uncover the source of a current problem, behaviorists focus on the present and what can be done to correct a problem behavior.

The learning theory describes behavior in terms of cause and effect relationships. *Behaviorists*—those who subscribe to and work with the learning theory—believe in close temporal proximity. That means that they describe things as "A causes B."

Let's look at an example.

Consider a person with a public speaking phobia. This person, Melissa, let's call her, is absolutely terrified at the thought of having to stand (or even sit) in front of a group of people and say something.

Melissa sometimes dreams that she's in front of a group and can't think of a thing to say. She's deathly afraid of even the thought of having to speak.

Think back to Chapter 3 for a minute, and try to predict how psychoanalysts would explain Melissa's public speaking phobia.

Those psychoanalysts, no doubt, would be very interested in Melissa's early life experiences. They would say that Melissa has repressed issues from an earlier experience, and that she will never be able to overcome her fear of public speaking until she discovers what those issues are and resolves them.

Behaviorists, on the other hand, say enough already of what happened when Melissa was three months old. Get over it.

Behaviorists are interested in Melissa's current behaviors and the feelings of extreme anxiety she experiences when faced with the possibility of public speaking.

They'd say that Melissa needs relaxation training to become more assertive and should get social skills training. The last thing Melissa needs, behaviorists believe, is to go back into her past and dredge up a lot of issues.

This viewpoint is very appealing to many people, who prefer to move forward rather than go back to a time in their lives of which they have little, if any, memory. Why waste time in the past, the sentiment is, when we can move ahead and fix the problem?

Behaviorists have great regard for and interest in action—that is, what a person does. Behaviorists look at what they can see, not at what may have happened much earlier in a person's life.

While behaviorists will consider what a person is *feeling*, they pretty much disregard the person's thoughts and the meanings of those thoughts. They assert that, while the action is important, the thoughts and meanings behind the action are not.

So if Melissa throws a fit every time she's faced with the prospect of public speaking, behaviorists will focus on what she does, not what she's thinking about while she does it. They'll want to know how Melissa feels, but they won't try to dredge up some childhood trauma that may have resulted in her phobia. So instead of asking Melissa what she thinks, a behaviorist would want to know what she does.

**Personality Parlance**

The **scientific method** is a formal testing process used to study behavior and other observable, concrete things.

The learning theory of personality is based on scientific study, or the *scientific method*. Behaviorists contend that it's much easier to study something that can be observed and measured—such as behavior—than it is to observe and measure meaning.

While it's quite feasible and practical to observe the behavior of someone who has, let's say, obsessive-compulsive disorder, it's far more difficult to observe and measure the connection between an event long ago and the disorder the person suffers from. If you can observe it, behaviorists assert, it can be measured and studied.

The learning theory is based on the belief that a person's behavior, that which can be observed and measured, is learned behavior. It's not genetic, or a result of having lived 14 previous lives, or instinctive, or from some sort of collective unconscious.

All behavior, the learning theory states, is learned after birth. People act and feel the way they do in response to their environments.

If you're having a flashback right about now to Chapter 2, "You Are What You Believe," where we discussed early messages and how those messages form our core beliefs and affect how we perceive ourselves and the world, you're right on track. Strict behaviorists, however, do not accept the concept of core beliefs.

The learning theory, while incompatible with the psychodynamic theory, can complement the concepts of early messages and core beliefs.

Let's take a look at the history of the learning theory and how these popular views came to be.

# The Learning Theory's Beginnings

Russian physiologist Ivan Petrovich Pavlov was the first person to document a basic concept of learning. This learning concept became known as the *conditioned response* and is instrumental to the learning theory of personality.

Through his work, Pavlov was able to recognize and create a conditioned response in dogs to what had previously been a neutral stimulus.

When a dog sees or smells food, it begins to salivate. The food is an unconditioned stimulus; nobody taught the dog to salivate when it sees food, it's just something a dog does. The dog's reaction to seeing food—that is, the salivation—is an unconditioned response.

A dog does not, however, automatically begin salivating when it hears the tone of a bell.

To get the dogs to salivate when they heard the bell, Pavlov paired the sound of the bell with the presentation of the dogs' food.

After a while, the dogs would start to salivate when they heard the bell, because they had learned that their food was coming. Soon, the dogs would salivate at the sound of the bell even when there was no food to be had.

The dogs' salivation to the tone of the bell was a conditioned response. It was learned behavior.

Pavlov caused the dogs to have a conditioned response (salivation) to a conditioned stimulus (the sound of the bell). This is called *classical conditioning.*

**Personality Parlance**

**Classical conditioning** is a conditioned response to a conditioned stimulus. It's the process of learning behavior.

The most important thing about classical conditioning is that it pairs, or links, two things so that either of those things will produce the same result.

Pavlov linked the presentation of food with the tone of the bell. There are many examples of pairings in our daily lives. Some of them, just as with Pavlov's dogs, are food related.

Have you ever been looking at a magazine and come across a photo of a great-looking chocolate cake? If you have, and you're like many people, that picture will be enough to induce some classical conditioning. You'll start to feel hungry for a piece of that cake.

## *Is the Learning Theory Relevant Today?*

The learning theory is without question relevant and widely employed today. It's important in terms of how children are assimilated into society—how they learn to deal with everyday life.

It's important in our schools, it's important to our society's standards of discipline and punishment, and it's important in how we learn to fear certain things.

While the learning theory is important, it's not without its shortcomings.

The theory is limited just by the fact that it's so focused on behavior, with little regard for what goes on in the mind. While very few people dispute that observable behavior is extremely relevant and important, there's an awful lot of evidence that there's stuff going on in our heads that's not observable.

And the evidence points in the direction of that nonobservable stuff being very relevant to, and closely linked with, observable behavior.

Another problem with the learning theory is that, while its assertions hold true much of the time, they don't always work. The learning theory states that children develop new behaviors for which they've received reinforcement (you'll learn more about this later in the chapter). That's perfectly true. Children, however, also sometimes learn new behaviors without reinforcement.

**Don't Go There!**

A problem with subscribing solely to one theory is that it limits your flexibility and sometimes traps you. Don't make the mistake of limiting yourself and considering only one theory to be correct. Most psychologists use pieces of several theories in their work.

# Learning Theory Big Shots: John B. Watson and His Followers

In addition to Ivan Pavlov, there are several names that stand out in the field of behaviorism.

John B. Watson, Edward Lee Thorndike, and B.F. Skinner are closely associated with the behavior theory and deserve some mention in this chapter. Each man is recognized for his accomplishments in the area of behaviorism.

## *John B. Watson*

Sometimes referred to as "the founder of behaviorism," John B. Watson believed that psychology was as much of a pure science as biology, chemistry, or physics, and that the study of behavior could be conducted as scientifically as the study of any of those disciplines.

Watson was the first to use the word "behaviorism." He believed that behavior could be measured objectively, instead of through the use of subjective judgments and symbolism, such as dream interpretations.

Watson also believed that he could, through classical conditioning, control the emotions of a human subject. His well-known study became known as the Little Albert experiment.

In the experiment, Watson conditioned Albert, an 11-month-old boy, to fear a rat.

Albert didn't have a natural fear of rats. Before the experiment, in fact, he liked to play with them.

At the beginning of Watson's experiment, when Albert would reach out to get a rat to play with, Watson would generate a very loud noise.

While Albert had no fear of rats, he *was* very afraid of loud noises. Every time he reached for a rat, Watson created in him a startle response.

Eventually, Albert, who was upset by the noise, cried and moved away from the rats.

### Don't Go There!

If you're feeling really sorry for Little Albert about now, you probably wouldn't make the best behaviorist. Behaviorists must be able to view behavior objectively.

### Personality Pointer

Watson's techniques are still used today to help people overcome fears and phobias.

Notice that Watson, a true behaviorist, focused almost exclusively on Albert's observable behavior. The little boy heard the noise, he cried, and he moved away from the rats. While behaviorists do ask about feelings and the intensity of feelings (on a scale of 1 to 10, how anxious do you feel at this moment?), they are primarily concerned with the behaviors they can see.

Albert was a tenacious little boy and eager to get back to playing with the rats. He returned to the rats seven times, and each time he reached for one to play with, the loud noise scared him.

After Albert paired the noise with the rats seven times, he was scared of a rat that was placed before him, even though no loud noise accompanied the rat.

In the Little Albert experiment, the unconditioned stimulus was the loud noise. Nobody taught Albert to be afraid of the noise; he just was. The conditioned stimulus was the rat, and the conditioned response was fear of the rat.

Watson believed that many fears people have are the result of conditioning.

Before you get to feeling too bad for little Albert, we'll tell you the rest of the story. Not content to have taught the boy to fear rats, Watson set out to teach Albert to lose his fear.

In this unlearning process, Watson gave Albert food to make him feel good. The food was the unconditioned stimulus—nobody told Albert to like the food, he just did.

While Albert was enjoying the food Watson gave him, Watson reintroduced a rat to Albert. The rat was the conditioned stimulus. At first, Albert was afraid of the rat—food or no food. After having the food and rat paired together for a while, however, Albert relearned how to feel good about the rat. Learning to like the rats again was a conditioned response from Albert.

Just as Watson had thought he could, he was able to control Albert's emotions by using classical conditioning. He taught Albert certain fears and responses, and then undid them.

## Edward Lee Thorndike

Edward Thorndike, who was born in 1874 in Williamsburg, Massachusetts, was the first psychologist to study the effect that a positive or negative stimulus has when presented *following* a response.

Thorndike called this type of conditioning *operant conditioning*. It differs from classical conditioning, which uses the pairing of unconditioned and conditioned stimuli.

Operant conditioning is a method of reinforcing behavior by presenting a stimulus after a response. B.F. Skinner, who you'll read about a bit later in this chapter, did a lot of work with pigeons and operant conditioning.

Thorndike theorized that if you reinforce a certain response with something either positive or negative, the reinforcement will increase the likelihood of the person responding in the same manner again.

For instance, let's say you're trying to potty-train your child. This is something many of us can relate to, so it makes a good example.

If, after the child uses the potty, you give him an M&M, he is more likely to use the potty again the next time. And the sooner he gets the M&M after producing the desired behavior, the more likely he will be to repeat the behavior.

Nobody had to tell you that, right? Well, Thorndike's experiments were a little more sophisticated,

**Personality Pointer**

**Operant conditioning** is a method of reinforcing behavior by presenting a stimulus after a response.

**Don't Go There!**

Be careful if you're using M&Ms or other positive reinforcement to encourage certain responses in children—they catch on very quickly. Within a short time, one of the author's daughters was asking for M&Ms before she would use the potty.

but the theory is the same. The M&M is a reward, or a positive reinforcement, for the child's response (using the potty).

Thorndike asserted that the act of the child learning that if he used the potty an M&M would follow is the connection between the stimulus and the response. He called that theory *connectionism.*

Operant conditioning and the connectionism theory became widely known and influential, and Thorndike was widely recognized for his work.

He was most recognized for his *law of effect:* the idea that reinforcement increases the occurrence of a desired behavior.

## B.F. Skinner

Burrhus Frederic (now you see why he's called B.F.; his friends called him Fred) Skinner, who was born in 1904 in Susquehanna, Pennsylvania, continued with Thorndike's ideas concerning the reinforcement of behavior.

Skinner, in fact, believed that reinforcement is the primary factor that shapes behavior, and that behavior is based exclusively on external consequences.

Behavior does not result from anything that goes on inside people, Skinner said, only from what happens around them.

Based on his findings, Skinner concluded that behavior could be controlled by applying external consequences or reinforcers.

If you give your daughter an M&M when she uses the potty, for instance, you're using a reinforcer. Because of that, you should be able to predict that she'll also use the potty the next time. You're gaining a measure of control over her behavior.

# The Role of Reinforcing Behavior

The learning theory asserts that different types of reinforcement affect whether or not a particular behavior will be repeated. While we generally tend to use the word "reinforcement" in a positive way, behaviorists use it negatively, as well.

There are different kinds of reinforcement:

➤ **Positive reinforcement** is a reward given for a particular response, such as giving an M&M to a child who uses the potty. By rewarding the desirable behavior, you increase the likelihood that the behavior will be repeated.

Another sort of positive reinforcement that sometimes occurs with children is when parents react to a temper tantrum by yelling and screaming. On the surface, this doesn't sound like positive reinforcement, because the parents are giving the child negative attention. To a child, though, any attention is a reward.

➤ **Negative reinforcement** is often confused with punishment, but it's much different. Negative reinforcement occurs when you take away a reinforcer, and in doing so, you increase the likelihood of a particular response. We know, it's confusing. Let's try to explain by using an example.

It's winter, and Jack lives in a cabin in the woods that has no heat except for the area directly around the fireplace. He does, however, have a shower. The shower is far away from the fireplace, and when Jack steps out of the shower, it's an *extremely* uncomfortable situation. This is not a problem for Jack during the warmer months.

Jack has pretty much stopped taking showers because of this temperature situation—the freezing conditions are a real deterrent. His boss and co-workers, however, are getting fed up with his lack of hygiene.

Hank, Jack's best friend, doesn't want to see Jack lose his job over the shower situation, so being the smart behaviorist that he is, Hank puts a space heater in Jack's bathroom. By removing the extreme cold from the bathroom, Hank is greatly increasing the chance that Jack will go back to taking showers, which is the desired behavior. It seems like Hank gave something to Jack, but actually, in this case, he removed the impediment (the cold room) to achieve the desired behavior on Jack's part.

➤ **Extinction** is the theory that if you stop providing reinforcement, the response will eventually disappear. If you stop giving M&Ms, too soon, to reinforce potty use, the likelihood that potty-training will continue successfully, at that point, is lessened.

On the other hand, if you stop yelling and screaming at your two-year-old throwing a tantrum in the Safeway, the likelihood of these tantrums occurring in the future also is lessened.

➤ **Punishment** is inducing pain with the expectation that it will suppress a behavior. Spanking is often used for this purpose, but research has shown that punishment doesn't work nearly as well as other types of reinforcement.

## Focus on Research

Behaviorists rely greatly on research. They use the scientific theory and have developed extremely respectable methods of gathering information.

The learning theory, unlike some of the other theories regarding personality, lends itself nicely to scientific research. That's because it focuses on behavior, which is easily observed and monitored.

# Check Yourself Out

Here are several questions to help you reflect on what you've read in this chapter, and perhaps to take the information a step or two farther in your own mind:

➤ What are your thoughts about the tendency of learning theorists to focus totally on behavior and ignore the unconscious mind?

➤ What degree of importance do you place on the scientific method used by behaviorists?

➤ How ethical do you feel it was for J.B. Watson to condition "Little Albert" to be afraid of rats?

➤ Why do you think some people continue to practice punishment when it's been proven that it isn't as effective as positive reinforcement?

➤ How does the learning theory fit into your views of personality development?

You might benefit from discussing these questions with another person or just thinking about them on your own.

---

### The Least You Need to Know

➤ The learning theory of personality asserts that behavior is not genetic or due to anything in our unconscious mind, but that it's all learned.

➤ The learning theory deals with what's in the conscious mind, not with things that happened early in a person's life.

➤ The learning theory is very relevant and widely used today.

➤ Ivan Pavlov, John B. Watson, Edward Thorndike, and B.F. Skinner are important names in the behaviorist field.

➤ Behaviorists assert that we do the things we do because of conditioning.

➤ There are various types of reinforcement—not all of them positive.

# Chapter 5

# The Humanistic Theory of Personality

**In This Chapter**

➤ The ideas behind the humanistic theory

➤ Examining the history and relevance of the theory

➤ Recognizing the importance of each person

➤ On the road to self-actualization

➤ Understanding the limits of the theory

Although some of the thoughts and ideas associated with the humanistic theory of personality date back to the ancient Greeks, it's thought of primarily as a modern, or contemporary theory.

The humanistic theory, which emphasizes the uniqueness and value of every individual, is widely recognized and influential. Parts of it (which we discuss later in the chapter) are controversial, however.

It's an important theory, especially as a segment of our society appears to be moving away from accepting and valuing each person for his or her unique qualities. We've read stories and heard newscasts about a black man being dragged to death behind a truck; a homosexual being tied to a fence, tortured, and left to die; and a newborn being thrown into a dumpster by the young, affluent parents who didn't want their lives interrupted by a baby.

Incidents such as these aren't just abhorrent to the great majority of the people who hear of them. These incidents are abruptly and directly in opposition to the humanistic theory of personality.

# What It Is and How It Works

The humanistic theory of personality emphasizes the uniqueness of the individual. It recognizes people as being self-directed toward personal growth, which eventually results in self-actualization.

The theory claims that all people, regardless of who they are or what they do, have a desire to grow and to realize their potential to the best of their ability. People will do what they need to do to attain that goal, the theory states.

Also, the humanistic theory contains the idea that if someone commits a deplorable act, such as murder, we should not hate that person for doing so. This concept is extremely difficult for many people to accept. Humanists, however, feel that, although we might hate what the person has *done,* we should not judge or hate the *person.*

## *The Humanistic Theory's Beginnings*

Researchers claim that the humanistic theory has been around for a very long time, dating back centuries and centuries.

The early humanism movement began in fifteenth-century Europe as a protest against closed-minded church leaders and philosophers. The theory emerged again in the United States in the 1960s as a backlash to a learning system that was considered by many at that time to be mechanistic and not geared toward individuals.

**Notes and Quotes**

Abraham Maslow, a leader in the humanistic movement, believed that actualization was the driving force of human personality. Maslow wrote in his 1954 book, *Motivation and Personality,* that "a musician must make music, an artist must paint, a poet must write, if he is to be ultimately at peace with himself. What a man can be, he must be."

Three major figures are associated with contemporary humanistic theory:

➤ Abraham Maslow

➤ Carl Rogers

➤ Victor Frankl

Rogers and Maslow were instrumental in establishing the psychological foundations of the humanistic movement in education, and many schools were changed as a result of their efforts.

The open-education concept, probably best exemplified in the United States by the Montessori program schools, became popular and flourished. Public schools also made changes in response to Rogers and Maslow.

## *Is the Humanistic Theory Relevant Today?*

The humanistic theory still exerts a strong influence.

Even learning theorists who seem like they would oppose the humanistic theory recognize the importance of individual preferences and have acknowledged the wisdom of a collaborative approach to changing behavior.

Many humanistic values and ideas cross over into other disciplines of psychology and are embraced by psychologists of all types. Our society struggles constantly with issues that are closely related to humanism. A few of those issues include the death penalty, treatment for prisoners, educational methods, and personal fulfillment.

# Recognizing the Value and Dignity of Every Person

Indeed, the idea that each person is valuable and should be treated with dignity is the cornerstone of the humanistic theory.

We are all thought to possess free will and a sense of self-direction. As we noted in the preceding section, these ideas aren't new. They came back into play in a big way, however, as people tired of the psychodynamic and learning theories.

The humanistic theory contends that each person has value and worth based solely on his or her existence. If someone *is*, then he or she is valuable.

Every person, the theory states, should be treated equally, regardless of age, sex, race, religion, or social standing. There's no room for bigotry or prejudice in thought in the humanistic theory. Everyone is considered important as a single entity.

The theory also claims that it's unfair and meaningless to compare people, or to lump them together in classes or categories. Even people who do horrible things should be respected for who they are, not for what they've done.

As mentioned earlier, this is where the humanistic theory gets difficult for many people: where it states that if somebody commits a violent act, we should deplore the act but not the person.

It could be, humanists point out, that people who commit violent acts have unmet needs or feel misunderstood. Humanists acknowledge that committing violent acts is an inappropriate way for people to express their needs or to try to have those needs met. It doesn't mean, however, that they are bad people.

### Notes and Quotes

We don't believe it was coincidental that the re-emergence of this theory in America occurred about the same time as the civil rights movement. There's probably no hard evidence to back that assertion, but we think the movement was one of the things going on during that time that brought many people to the humanistic theory.

While many people have difficulty with the idea that someone who kills another person should be accepted as a valuable and worthwhile person, others have trouble being accepting of themselves.

**Don't Go There!**

It's common for victims of abuse to somehow blame themselves for what happened to them. This is because they've been given the message that they're bad, and they believe that's why the abuse occurred. This can be a very serious problem for abuse victims and something for which treatment might be necessary.

People who have very low self-esteem tend to use a double standard. They can be accepting and humanistic toward other people, but they're harder on themselves and less accepting.

Many times, people with low self-esteem judge themselves poorly because they blame themselves for bad things that have happened to them. Victims of sexual abuse, for instance, might blame themselves for what occurred in their lives. They may think they're bad people because they didn't stop the bad thing from happening.

Many victims of abuse may blame and hate themselves but be very accepting of other people who have been abused.

Humanists accept every person, including themselves, as unique with special gifts to share with the world. And because people are unique, special, and in pursuit of personal fulfillment, humanists say that all people should be free to go after what they want to do.

# Emphasizing Individual Freedoms

Humanists emphasize individual freedoms, that's for certain. That doesn't mean, however, that we all should feel free to run roughshod over others in order to meet our goals. Nor does it imply that we shouldn't be held accountable for our actions.

Humanistic theorists—those who subscribe to the humanistic theory—say that freedom is the pursuit of personal fulfillment. This pursuit is a natural process, they say, and the process itself is a positive one.

Humanists believe that people seeking personal fulfillment do indeed make mistakes along the way. Sometimes these mistakes are very serious ones, and sometimes they cause harm to others. When someone makes a mistake, however, it should be viewed as a mistake, not as an intentional effort to cause harm to another person.

True humanists believe that every person is good at the core. Because of that innate and fundamental goodness, humanists assert, people do things for good and honorable reasons.

Humanists acknowledge, however, that people sometimes use unacceptable methods in their efforts to attain personal fulfillment. If Sam murders John, for instance, humanists may believe that Sam committed the act because he needs recognition and love. Perhaps Sam feels emptiness—a great void—because someone who's very important to him has rejected him.

In killing John, the humanistic theory sets forth, Sam may have been trying to deal with his emptiness and pain. While it appears that Sam acted to cause harm to John, he really was trying to find a way to deal with his own intense emotional pain.

While the humanistic theory encourages those with emotional pain to try to learn how to deal with that pain, it certainly doesn't condone murder or other violent or hurtful acts. It does, however, sympathize with those who are so misdirected and wounded that they commit violent acts as a way to cope with their pain.

According to the humanistic theory, all people have an internal map that provides direction for their lives. The trick, then, is learning to read our maps. In our attempts to discover our direction, as provided on our internal map, we make decisions and express personal preferences. Sometimes the preferences and decisions people express bring them into conflict with society.

According to the humanistic theory, society must decide how much latitude to allow for individuals while still being able to fit them into the social system. Everyone should be encouraged to try to discover his or her own direction. At the same time, we must all live under societal rules in order to make our environments safe and comfortable.

Humanists believe that most of the problems people encounter are caused by their family and society. Humanists believe that all people have good intentions, and that the process of self-fulfillment is healthy and good, regardless of where it may lead.

# The "Here and Now" Factor

Unlike the psychodynamic theory, which focuses on past events, and the learning theory, which focuses on the present but considers past learning, the humanistic theory is based only on the present.

It considers what a person may be thinking and feeling at the moment, rather than what unresolved issues may have occurred in the past.

While setting a course for self-fulfillment or resolving issues of maladjustment, humanists focus on the thoughts, feelings, and actions that are occurring at the present time. They accept that there may be instinctual and unconscious influences in our lives, but they feel that it's not necessary to deal with them to address current problems.

**Personality Pointer**

Humanists acknowledge human instincts such as the need for food and safety, but they believe that there is so much more to personal fulfillment.

Humanists use techniques designed to help people become fully aware of their present position or situation. It's extremely important, humanists feel, to be in touch with your emotional state and to experience to the fullest what's going on around you.

It's also important that people are aware of how their emotional state affects their physiological condition. Humanists early on acknowledged physical-emotional connections, such as headaches caused by stress or tension.

# Self-Actualization: Where It's At

A major concept of the humanistic theory is self-actualization. Abraham Maslow, who was one of a group of influential psychologists and sociologists in the Chicago area, developed the concept of the *hierarchy of needs,* which describes the motivations people encounter on their journey toward self-actualization. Self-actualization is the highest goal, but other, lower motivations must be realized along the way.

Maslow said that these lower goals, which include motivations such as hunger and safety, must be met in a sequential, hierarchical manner. There are five levels to Maslow's hierarchy:

1. **Physiological.** Our need for food, water, air, bodily functioning, maintaining a constant body temperature, and so on.

2. **Safety and security.** At a basic level, this includes housing or shelter. It's expanded sometimes to include military forces necessary to protect us, job security, financial security, emotional security, and so on.

3. **Love and belonging.** The need to be accepted by others for who you are and to have the opportunity to express love for your family, friends, and so forth.

4. **Esteem.** We seek esteem on two levels. The first level occurs when others acknowledge our skills and personal characteristics. The second level occurs when we learn to appreciate *ourselves* for those skills and characteristics.

5. **Self-actualization.** This is the most difficult step to define and to achieve. All the other needs must be satisfied before self-actualization can occur, and that's not an easy task. If you're able to realize the first four steps, your final need will be to become yourself and to fulfill your inner drives.

The hierarchy works in the order in which it's presented for practical reasons.

If you're hungry, for instance, it's difficult to focus on doing something noble like finding a cure for cancer or writing a beautiful piece of music. You have to satisfy your hunger and other needs before you can start thinking about fulfilling who you are.

It may help to visualize Maslow's hierarchy to think of it as a pyramid. The lower goals—physiological, and safety and security—form the base of the pyramid, love and belonging are in the middle of it, and esteem and self-actualization are the top layers.

Be aware, however, that there are many different motivations for our actions. Not everyone who writes a beautiful piece of music is looking for self-fulfillment. Some songwriters may compose music in order to have enough money for food and clothing. Others may write poetry, not because they feel a deep need to do so, but in the hopes of getting the poems published to satisfy their egos.

While Maslow's hierarchy of motivation is widely recognized, it's not without its shortcomings.

It's important to realize that Maslow developed this theory by studying a rather small and elite group that he thought exemplified self-actualization, such as Abraham Lincoln and Albert Einstein. He then studied their lives to figure out what steps they'd gone through.

The fact that Maslow's concept of self-actualization wasn't something that he defined through studies of large groups of people is sometimes noted as a weakness of his theory of hierarchy.

Maslow's contemporary, Carl Rogers, also concentrated on the self-actualization part of the humanistic theory. Like Freud, but unlike Maslow, Rogers developed his theories based on a lifetime of clinical work.

Rogers believed that all people have an *actualizing* tendency—that is, an inherent drive to develop to their fullest potential. Rogers, in fact, took his theory a few steps further to include animals and other living things. Even mushrooms, Rogers believed, want to be the best mushrooms possible!

While Rogers believed that all living things are constantly working to be the very best of whatever they are, he did acknowledge that not every person and thing accomplishes that goal.

Many factors can interfere with a person's, an animal's, or even a mushroom's struggle for self-actualization.

**Personality Pointer**

People sometimes think they're striving for self-actualization when they're really just trying to meet some of their lower needs. The need for esteem often is confused with the quest for self-actualization.

**Personality Parlance**

The tendency toward **actualization** is the inherent desire and drive that all living things have to develop to their fullest potential.

## The Ideal Self

A person who is successful in achieving self-actualization experiences the revealing of his or her *real self*. The real self, which is discovered only through self-actualization, differs from the *ideal self*.

The ideal self is the concept each of us has of what we should be. You might think you should be a good student, or a successful businessman like your dad, or a stay-at-home mom, or whatever. Your ideal self is based on the expectations that surround you from society and family. We all get ideas of what we think we should be, and those ideas are based on what we're told throughout our lives. They're the expectations placed on us from the time we're very small children.

**Personality Parlance**

Your **ideal self** is the person you think you should be, based on the expectations of society, family, and peers. It may be very different from your **real self,** who only emerges at the end of the process of actualization.

Think about how your parents talked to you as you were growing up and, maybe, how you talk to your own children. How many times did you hear something like, "I expect you to get good grades in school," or "I expect you to try harder when you're on the football field?"

## *The Real Self*

While your ideal self is based on what you're told, your real self is internal. You can only discover your real self by following through with the actualizing tendency within you.

Humanists are adamant that we all should be looking to get past our ideal selves and find our real selves. People who have only realized their ideal selves and are still far from finding their real selves will experience problems, humanists say.

**Personality Parlance**

**Existentialism** states that each person exists as an individual and must make his or her own purpose in a purposeless world. It focuses on the importance of free will.

Many things get in the way of finding our real selves. Society—including family, government, schools, religion, and so forth—does a good job of telling us how we should be and reinforcing our ideal selves. Societal demands and expectations often get in the way of our actualizing tendency, which is internal. As a result, we're often unable to develop and discover our real selves.

# The Role of Meaning in Personal Development

Victor Frankl, the third of the important humanists mentioned earlier in the chapter, was concerned with the existential theory.

As with other existentialists, Frankl's central concern was the role of meaning in our lives.

Frankl was a student of Freud, but unlike Freud, who escaped the concentration camps of World War II, Frankl was imprisoned with all his family members. Everyone else in Frankl's family was killed or died in the camps.

During his imprisonment, Frankl studied the survival techniques used by other prisoners. He saw that those who were psychologically strong also were spiritually strong. He concluded that the reason some people were able to survive while so many others were not was due to the ability of the survivors to make some kind of sense out of what was happening to them. They were able to assign some reason to the chaos that was going on around them.

Our goal, Frankl asserted, is to find reason for our human struggles and our finite existence. We're to try to understand why we're on this earth, with all its problems, struggles, disease, and pain and suffering. Our job is to make sense out of why all those things occur. Only when we can find some meaning in our existence and the hardships that we encounter will we be able to make sense out of our lives.

Frankl said that the way to find meaning in our lives is through values, and that values are acquired through our work, in our relationships, and by confronting our pain. As we work, participate in relationships, and experience pain, we get a sense of what's important to us and our lives. Once we understand what's important, we're able to assign meaning to our lives.

Once you've assigned meaning to your life, you're able to rise above the earthly struggles that you'll experience.

# Current Views of the Humanistic Theory

Much of the humanistic theory is broadly accepted by psychologists of all schools of thought; all psychologists endorse the concept of respect for all people and acknowledge the worth and value of each individual. Psychologists other than humanists, however, don't always accept the methods that humanists employ.

While behavioral, psychodynamic, or other types of psychologists may use treatments that are in some ways similar to those used by humanists, there are many differences in their techniques. And every type of psychologist may have a different understanding or explanation for why they do what they do during treatment.

It's ironic that a big problem with the humanistic theory is that it only allows the study of one person at a time. The very nature of the theory—the qualities that make it the humanistic theory—therefore cause problems with research.

While individual case studies are fascinating, they normally don't have the same authority as controlled studies. It's difficult to use some of the more powerful research designs when conducting individual studies, and that affects or determines the kinds of conclusions that can be drawn from the research.

Still, the humanistic theory is alive and well, and overlaps frequently into other areas of psychology.

# Check Yourself Out

Here are several questions to help you reflect on what you've read in this chapter, and perhaps to take the information a step or two farther in your own mind:

➤ What are your feelings about the theory that all people should be unconditionally accepted, regardless of what they've done?

➤ Do you agree that the way you feel—right here and now—is what's most important?

➤ Where do you see yourself as belonging on the self-actualization hierarchy?

➤ How close are you to reaching your real self?

➤ How do you go about creating purpose in your world?

You might benefit from discussing these questions with another person or just thinking about them on your own.

---

### The Least You Need to Know

➤ The humanistic theory is based on the value and uniqueness of every person.

➤ The humanistic theory has roots that are centuries old, but it began to flourish in the United States in the 1960s.

➤ While the deeds committed by individuals may be deplorable, humanists believe that the people who commit them are not to be judged or hated.

➤ The humanistic theory is based on the present and considers what a person may be thinking and feeling at the moment.

➤ Humanists believe that all people go through a series of stages during their journey toward self-actualization.

➤ The humanistic theory states that the job of all people is to try to find meaning in their lives and daily struggles.

➤ The very nature of the humanistic theory limits the types of studies researchers can conduct.

---

# Chapter 6

# Other Personality Theories

---

## In This Chapter

➤ Looking at Neo-Freudian, or social theories

➤ Understanding the human quest for perfection

➤ Considering the issue of birth order

➤ Separating neurotic needs from normal needs

➤ Looking at developmentalists and their theories

➤ Understanding biological influences

---

If you've read the last four chapters, you know more than a little about some of the major theories of personality. You've learned about the cognitive and constructivist theories, the psychodynamic theory, the learning theory, and the humanistic theory, all of which have been—and remain—extremely important to the study of personality and the broad area of psychology.

Those major theories, however, are not the only ones that pertain to the subject of personality. In Chapter 1, "The Personality Puzzle," we touched on some lesser-known theories concerning personality. Remember the one called *phrenology*, which says the shape and size of your head are responsible for your mental abilities and personal characteristics?

How about the Japanese theory that asserts that it's blood type that determines the type of personality a person has? And then there's the astrology theory, which assigns personality traits to people depending on celestial conditions at the time of their birth. Hmmmm ... while all these theories are interesting and might be fun to consider, they don't warrant the degree of attention and respect that the major psychological theories do.

In this chapter, you'll learn about some other psychological theories of personality. While they're not considered to be as major as the theories presented in the last four chapters, they're certainly important and worth a look.

Here we focus primarily on some of the theories developed by Neo-Freudians. These theories are known collectively as the *Neo-Freudian theory,* but they actually are a group of theories related to different topics.

Now let's get started by looking at some other theories of personality.

# Neo-Freudian, or Social Theories

As you might expect, the Neo-Freudian theories contain some, but not all, of the important elements of Freud's psychodynamic theory of personality.

Neo-Freudian psychoanalysts (how's that for a mouthful?) fully accept Freud's fundamental idea of the unconscious mind and the importance that Freud asserted it has in determining one's personality. They reject other aspects of Freud's theories, however, such as sex drive being a person's primary motivator throughout life.

Important Neo-Freudians, who sometimes are called *social theorists,* include Alfred Adler, Karen Horney, and Harry Stack Sullivan. Some of the notable ideas and concepts that resulted from the Neo-Freudian movement include birth order, inferiority complex, and neurosis.

### Notes and Quotes

Who knows why, but many of the theorists mentioned in this book lived to quite an old age. Erik Erikson was 92 when he died, and his contemporary, Jean Piaget, was 84. B.F. Skinner was 86, Carl Rogers was 85, Sigmund Freud was 83, and Carl Jung was 86. Considering that the life expectancy at the time these men lived was significantly less than it is today, their life spans were quite extraordinary.

It's important to keep in mind that in some cases, theories containing very different ideas have names that are very similar. While Neo-Freudian theorists are sometimes called *social theorists,* this doesn't mean that they subscribe to the social learning the-ory, or social psychology, even though the name implies so.

You're right. It is confusing, and if we had it to do all over again, perhaps we'd come up with clearer names to describe various theories and the people who work with them. For now, however, we have to deal with the names we have. So just be aware that the terms *social theorist* and *Neo-Freudian* are used interchangeably. Now let's look at some of the major Neo-Freudians—or should we say *social theorists?*

# Alfred Adler

One of the most notable Neo-Freudians is Alfred Adler (1870-1937), who developed the theory of individual psychology. Of all the Neo-Freudian theories of overall per-sonality, Adler's is considered one of the most comprehensive.

Adler, born to Jewish parents in Vienna, Austria, was a sickly child and decided early on that he would be a doctor. He started as an eye doctor but soon switched to gen-eral practice. Adler's interest in psychology began as he treated circus performers in a lower-class section of Vienna. He was intrigued by the unusual strengths and weak-nesses of the performers, and what they did to utilize, overcome, and compensate for them.

He shifted from medicine to psychiatry and became associated with Sigmund Freud; he was even invited to join Freud's discussion group.

While the early papers that Adler wrote concurred with Freud's theories, some of his later ones did not. This caused a rift between the two, and Adler eventually dropped out of Freud's Vienna Psychoanalytic Society to form his own group.

## *Individual Psychology*

The key element to Adler's work in *individual psychology* is the idea that people tend to strive for perfection. He noted that most people work hard—some endlessly—to develop their potential and abilities, and to overcome their difficulties.

Adler asserted that people strive for perfection in these ways:

➤ **They're drawn toward an ideal.** After people establish an ideal of who they want to be, they work toward that ideal by choosing a particular career, certain hobbies, and so forth.

➤ **People are drawn toward others who can help them achieve an ideal.** People seeking

**Personality Parlance**

**Individual psychology** stresses the idea that each individual should be viewed as a whole person, rather than as a compila-tion of parts. The word "individ-ual" literally means "not divided."

their ideal tend to look to others for help in achieving it. A woman, for instance, might marry a man who can help her achieve her ideal, or she might network with co-workers who can help her advance in her career.

What people do to move toward their ideal depends on what their ideal is. Obviously, different people have very different ideals.

While Robert believes that the only worthwhile ideal is to be extremely successful in business, Jack's ideal is to be a loving father and husband, and to have a close family to care for and rely on.

Some people—remember Mother Teresa?—live to serve the human race, while others live to become famous and ensure themselves a place in history. Some (think Donald Trump) consider great wealth to be the ideal; others (consider those who climb Mt. Everest) look for excitement and adventure.

Ironically, these varying ideals create an inherent problem with Adler's theory of individual psychology: It's extremely difficult to measure perfection if everyone has a different idea of what it is, difficult for the individuals themselves as well as for the psychologists who treat them.

How do people striving for perfection ever know if they've reached their goal? The terms "perfectionism" and "striving for perfectionism" aren't well defined, and this creates difficulties with Adler's theory. These difficulties don't make the theory invalid or unworthy of consideration, but they are worth keeping in mind.

Adler was very concerned about people who fail to achieve their ideals. If you don't achieve your ideal, Adler said, you suffer from a feeling of inferiority. As long as you feel that you're moving toward perfection or toward your ideal, you're not likely to experience feelings of inferiority, according to Adler.

If you're unable to continue moving toward your ideal, however, look out. You've probably got an inferiority complex knocking at your door.

Just about everybody, Adler thought, suffers from some level of inferiority. There's probably a point in everyone's life when they don't feel they're making progress toward their ideal.

These inferiority complexes that result from being stymied in our quest for perfection are at the root of all of life's problems, Adler said. Because we find the complexes to be so bothersome, we've come up with some standard methods of dealing with them:

### Notes and Quotes

Freud considered men superior to women and thought nothing about saying so publicly. Adler, on the other hand, recognized that men were *treated* as though they were superior in the society in which he lived, but were not innately so. Men become superior to women, Adler said, only because they're told that they are.

➤ **Compensate for our weaknesses.** If we feel inferior in one area, we may try to compensate by excelling in another area. For instance, if a man feels he's unattractive, he may try to compensate by getting better grades than anyone else in his class. Or a man who's not good at sports may compensate by becoming an accomplished musician.

➤ **Assume superiority in order to fool people.** If Joe feels inferior during a business meeting, he may act very assertive and self-confident in order to hide his feelings from his peers. If Mary feels inferior in a social situation, she may act very vivacious and outgoing in order to fool others.

## Birth Order

Adler was the first theorist to address the matter of birth order and how children are affected by their siblings. His concepts regarding birth order are widely recognized and applicable today.

Basically, Adler said that an only child is likely to be a pampered child, a first child will be treated like an only child until a second child arrives, a second child will compete with the first child, and the youngest child will be subject to pampering. Let's take a closer look:

➤ **Only child.** An only child receives the parents' full measure of attention. If the parents are concerned and loving, the child is likely to be pampered, which can backfire later in life. Pampered children may never learn to do things for themselves, and realize later that they are inferior because of it. Pampered children also may have trouble dealing with people later in life because they have always been given whatever they wanted and haven't learned to negotiate and compromise.

On the other hand, an only child of abusive parents would be forced to bear any abuse alone instead of having it distributed among all the siblings.

**Don't Go There!**

Avoid the temptation to stereotype others or to blame your own problems on birth order. There may be some validity to Adler's points, but it's dangerous to use birth order to rationalize your shortcomings or to evade addressing problem areas you might have.

➤ **First child.** A first child generally is treated like an only child until the next one comes along. You can guess what happens .... The older child may resent the baby and the parental attention it requires. The older child feels dethroned and may become disobedient, rebellious, sullen, or withdrawn. Adler believed that first children were more likely than their siblings to be troubled.

➤ **Second child.** The second child, on the other hand, often becomes competitive with the firstborn, trying to keep up or surpass that sibling's achievements. This can result in sibling rivalry and feelings of inferiority on the part of the child whose accomplishments are lesser.

➤ **Youngest child.** Youngest children are likely to be pampered or spoiled and assume a "special" place in the family because they never get dethroned. This pampering can cause the same problems it does in only children. Some youngest children develop an inferiority complex because they feel that everyone else must be better, because they are older.

While birth order is widely recognized as a factor in personality, it's by no means definitive. If there's a long period of time between the birth of two children, for instance, the first-child versus second-child relationship may be very different than if the births were closer.

An only child could be neglected, rendering the pampered theory invalid. A lone boy in a family of six children may feel more like an only child than a sibling, and so forth.

Adler's theory of birth order is not clearly defined, and it doesn't hold true in all cases. Still, it's interesting and has been shown to have some merit.

# Harry Stack Sullivan

Another Neo-Freudian/social theorist worth mentioning is Harry Stack Sullivan (1892-1949), who focused on relationships as they affect personality.

**Personality Pointer**

All interpersonal relationships are influenced by one of three things, or possibly a combination of the three, Sullivan said. These factors are security (which is influenced by and affects self-worth), intimacy (meaning friendships and closer relationships), and lust.

Sullivan's primary theory is called the *interpersonal theory*. It basically says that healthy relationships contribute to a healthy personality, while unhealthy relationships don't.

Sullivan believed that it's impossible to understand an individual without first understanding the social context within which the person lives, and that interpersonal relationships are the basis of a person's social sphere.

When we experience problems with interpersonal relationships, Sullivan said, it results in anxiety. Sullivan considered anxiety to be the greatest problem of most people.

Fortunately, according to Sullivan, anxieties caused by interpersonal problems can be resolved by later positive social relationships. If your father beat you regularly when you were a child, for instance, it's likely to cause you some problems down the road. You may be able to resolve those problems later on, however, by experiencing positive relationships with your father or other males.

Sullivan thought that personality develops according to your perception of how people view you. For instance, if you perceive that you're treated with respect, then you're more likely to develop self-respect and like who you are. If, on the other hand, you think people are constantly putting you down and making fun of you, you're likely to feel inferior or worthless.

Sullivan's theory makes sense and is easy to understand. These factors probably contribute to a renewed interest in the interpersonal theory within the past 10 or 15 years.

**Notes and Quotes**

Sullivan's idea that your personality develops according to your perception of how others view you coincides with some of the theories discussed earlier in the book. The messages we get from others are an important factor in the cognitive theory of personality, discussed in Chapter 2.

# Karen Horney

The third Neo-Freudian/social theorist we look at is Karen Danielson Horney (1885-1952), who developed a theory concerning neurosis.

Karen Horney didn't originate the idea of neurosis, but she presented a different way of looking at it, which became widely accepted.

While other theorists had viewed neurosis as something very abnormal, Horney thought of it as being more common and mainstream. She said that all people—not only neurotic ones—struggle to cope with problems of living. The only difference, Horney said, is that most of us manage to stay on top of our struggles, while neurotic people fail to keep up. This is due to excessive neediness on the part of neurotic people. We all have needs, but neurotic people expect their needs to be fulfilled to an extreme and unrealistic degree.

Horney pinpointed 10 neurotic needs. The needs are not limited to those who are neurotic; in fact, they're basic needs most people have. Neurotic people, however, are excessively needy and want their needs met in an unrealistic way.

Here are the needs Horney identified in neurotic people:

1. **Affection and approval.** While we all want these things, neurotics may expect or demand affection from everyone they meet in all circumstances. They may become anxious and fearful if they think someone doesn't like them.

2. **Desire for a partner.** While this is not an uncommon desire, neurotic people might look for a partner to take over their life or to solve all their problems.

### Personality Pointer

It's important to remember that not all neurotic needs are different from the needs of most people. Neurotic people tend to need compulsively and irrationally. They may demand that all their needs be met immediately, or they may put their needs ahead of others' needs. It's not that the needs of neurotics are so different from others' needs; it's that there are differences in how neurotics expect their needs to be met.

3. **Restricting life to narrow borders.** Neurotics may feel unable to cope with the complexities of life and attempt to grossly oversimplify matters. They may be extremely undemanding or seek to become inconspicuous and unnoticed.

4. **Desire for power or control over others.** While most of us like to be in control on occasion, neurotics have an excessive need to be in control. They may disdain weaknesses in others and try to establish dominance for its own sake.

5. **Exploitation of others.** Some neurotic people might believe that others are meant to be manipulated and used, and that exploiting them is their right.

6. **Social recognition.** Everyone likes to be appreciated and recognized, but neurotics can be extreme in their desire for it. They may be panicky at the thought of not being considered popular or part of the "in-crowd."

7. **Personal admiration from others.** Again, we all like to be admired, but this desire in neurotics is irrational. Neurotics may constantly remind people that they're worthy of admiration by pointing out their good qualities, whether they're real or imagined.

8. **Personal achievement.** Seeking achievement is positive, but it can become excessive in neurotics, who may feel the need to be the best at everything they do. Never content to be second-best, neurotics may try to diminish the accomplishments of others in an effort to make themselves look better.

9. **Self-sufficiency and independence.** Neurotic people may find it difficult to accept any sort of help, thinking they should be able to do everything themselves. They may avoid close relationships because they see depending on another person as a weakness.

10. **Perfection.** Many people have some perfectionist tendencies, but neurotics may be unable to admit that they are ever wrong and may try to cover up mistakes or shortcomings.

In addition to identifying 10 neurotic needs, Horney grouped the needs into three categories in order to identify how people might try to cope with them.

Here is Horney's coping strategy breakdown:

➤ **Compliance.** Includes numbers 1 through 3 on the preceding list. A person might reason that *If I can make you love me, then you won't hurt me.*

➤ **Aggression.** Includes numbers 4 through 8. The coping strategy here is *If I have power, nobody can hurt me.*

➤ **Withdrawal.** Includes numbers 3, 9, and 10 (3 overlaps two coping strategies). The strategy is *If I withdraw, then nothing can hurt me.*

Horney's theory of neurosis contains similarities and overlaps the theories of Alfred Adler and Carl Rogers, who we discussed in Chapter 5, "The Humanistic Theory of Personality." It's very common in psychology for theories to overlap. It's rare, in fact, that a theory can be neatly placed into just one category.

**Notes and Quotes**

Karen Horney's understanding of psychological problems was enhanced by her own experiences with depression and stress. At one point of her life, she was so depressed that she contemplated suicide and sought help through psychoanalysis.

## Development Theorists and Theories

While Neo-Freudians are an important group in developing personality theories, another important group of theorists is the developmentalists.

Developmentalists, those responsible for the development theory, propose stages of growth and change as they relate to cognitive and maturation issues.

Two prominent developmentalists whose theories we'll discuss are Jean Piaget and Erik Erikson. Both include stages of development through which humans pass on their way to becoming fulfilled adults.

### Jean Piaget

Jean Piaget was born in Switzerland in 1896 and was trained in natural sciences. He had a keen interest in children and how they learn, and he based his theory of intellectual development on his observations of children, some of whom were his own.

Piaget's theory describes the course of intellectual development from birth through adulthood. Here are the stages he outlined:

➤ **The sensorimotor stage.** *Ages birth to 2.* Children are in an early perceptual mode. They see, hear, feel, and begin to attach meaning to some symbols. If they see a car, for instance, they may know that they're going for a ride.

➤ **The preoperational stage.** *Ages 2 to 7.* Children begin to use words and are able to make very specific references as opposed to generalizations. They'll tell you, for instance, that they want a bologna sandwich, not merely that they're hungry and want something to eat. They learn to interact with other people during this stage and go through an intuitive stage, in which they develop vague impressions and judgments. Children during this stage make broad statements without having facts to back them up. They rely on what feels right to them instead of using facts or logic.

➤ **The concrete operational stage.** *Ages 7 to 12.* Children learn to follow logical reasoning, but only with the help of real, concrete examples. They remain extremely literal, finding it difficult to grasp symbolism or abstraction. While Piaget thought that everyone moved out of this stage at about age 12, more recent thinking indicates that some people (one estimate says between 30 and 60 percent) remain in this stage for the rest of their lives.

➤ **The formal operations stage.** *Ages 12 and up.* People can use abstract thinking and plan ahead. They can test theories and formulate explanations.

Piaget was convinced that learning did not occur passively, but required the participation of the student. Students, he said, are not vessels to be filled with facts, but must be active and involved in their learning.

He also felt that students could not learn something until they had matured to a sufficient level.

**Notes and Quotes**

Piaget was recognized early on for his superior mental capacity and ability to express himself. When he was 11, he wrote a short piece about an albino sparrow. The piece became well-known and is considered to be the premier work in Piaget's scientific career, which included his authorship of more than 60 books along with several hundred articles.

## Erik Erikson

This name should sound familiar, as you already learned a little bit about Erik Erikson in Chapter 3, "The Psychodynamic Theory of Personality." Erikson was a follower of Freud to a point, but he focused much more on society and culture than Freud did.

While Freud's five stages of development stopped at puberty, Erikson set down eight stages that extend throughout life. Each stage contains a task that must be achieved before a person can move successfully to the next stage.

1. **Trust versus distrust.** *The first year of life.* The children's task is to learn to trust their caretakers. It is the trustworthiness of the caretakers that determines whether or not children develop trust or become distrustful.

2. **Autonomy versus doubt.** *Ages 2 and 3.* This stage has to do with children being able to do things on their own. The task is to develop a sense of ability, rather than doubting that they can handle things themselves.

3. **Initiative versus guilt.** *Ages 4 and 5.* The task of this stage is to initiate action. Children should be comfortable being the force behind an action, rather than feeling guilty about asserting their agenda.

4. **Industry versus inferiority.** *Ages 6 through 11.* This stage builds on the preceding stage of willingness to take the initiative. Children during this stage are challenged with learning to keep themselves busy and involved, as opposed to feeling alienated and wondering if they're able to do something.

5. **Identity versus role confusion.** *Ages 12 through 18.* For children to complete this stage successfully, they must develop a sense of identity. They should have a good idea of their particular characteristics, abilities, and skills, and of how they are defined by these elements as individuals. They are challenged to recognize the things that set them apart from others and make them unique. If they're not successful at completing this task, they'll suffer from role confusion and have a very difficult time separating their role from the roles of others.

6. **Intimacy versus isolation.** *Young adulthood.* Once people have established who they are, their task is to learn to develop long-term, lasting relationships that go beyond friendship. If they are still confused about who they are, they'll find it very difficult to form mature relationships with others. If they're unable to do so, they may isolate themselves.

7. **Generativity versus stagnation.** *Adulthood.* This stage challenges people to go out and be productive. They develop multiple relationships and continue moving forward in growth and maturity. If this doesn't occur, they'll have a difficult time achieving maturity.

8. **Ego-integrity versus despair.** *Maturity.* It is during this stage that people develop a much deeper sense of who they are. They develop wisdom and get closer to understanding what life is all about. If this doesn't occur, they may become despairing because life makes no sense.

**Personality Pointer**

Societal circumstances have caused the age category for the intimacy versus isolation stage to be raised from early adulthood into adulthood. This is because people tend not to marry as early as they used to.

Erikson's stages of development, while not set in stone, provide a useful framework. Erikson's development theory is well-respected and remains important in education and child development.

# Understanding Biological Influences

The assertion that biological influences affect personality isn't in itself a theory, but several theories either are based on or include the assumption that our behaviors are influenced by instincts or genetics.

Instinctive behavior includes things like sucking, as well as the biological functions of temperature, elimination, and so forth.

Freudian theories, of course, are based on these ideas of instinctive and biological urges; and some mental illnesses, including schizophrenia and alcoholism, have been linked to genetic factors.

### Notes and Quotes

The January 2000 issue of the journal called *The Sciences* includes an article proposing that men rape women because it's a natural, biological phenomenon. Rape, the article asserts, is an instinctual behavior, not unlike attraction, courtship, and other factors that relate to the generation of offspring.

Theorists with medical backgrounds tend to place emphasis on biological behavior, while those with psychological backgrounds tend to lean toward learned behavior.

You can learn more about genetics and biological factors in Part 4, "Personality Disorders," which looks at gene theory in regard to certain illnesses, chemical imbalances, and so forth.

In Chapter 10, "Personality Traits," we also look at the trait theory, which explores characteristics such as introversion and extroversion.

As you can see, there are many, many theories related to personality and the issues in which it is a factor. As explained earlier, many of the theories overlap, and it can be confusing to try to pigeonhole them into categories. As we said in the very first chapter, no theory is considered absolute. All have varying strengths and weaknesses and should be looked at objectively.

# Check Yourself Out

Here are several questions to help you reflect on what you've read in this chapter, and perhaps to take the information a step or two farther in your own mind:

➤ After you encountered the idea of the unconscious mind again in this chapter, does it seem any more relevant in understanding personality than it did before?

➤ What do you think about the theory that emphasizes the influence of social factors, rather than sexual issues, on personality?

➤ After reading about cognitive, behavioral, humanistic, and social theories, which appeal to you the most?

➤ Developmental theorists take a different approach to personality. How do the developmentalist ideas fit into your understanding of personality?

➤ How does all this information about theories fit into your understanding of your own personality?

➤ You might benefit from discussing these questions with another person, or just thinking about them on your own.

---

### The Least You Need to Know

➤ Neo-Freudian theories, also known as *social theories,* deal with topics such as the human tendency to strive for perfection, birth order, and neurosis.

➤ Prominent social theorists, also called *Neo-Freudians,* were Alfred Adler, Harry Stack Sullivan, and Karen Horney.

➤ Many theories overlap, making it difficult to place them into workable categories.

➤ Developmental theories establish stages through which people must progress if they are to fulfill their potential.

➤ Biological influences are important to personality and come into play in various categories of theories.

# Part 2

# Tests, Tests, and More Tests

*A wide variety of tests is available to help us learn more about personality, to help in the diagnosis of personality disorders, and to measure personality traits.*

*Psychological tests can be used to assess whether Jack has the right stuff to be an astronaut, whether John and Mary are suited for marriage, and whether Jane is clinically depressed or suffering from "the blues."*

*There's a huge difference in the quality of tests that are out there, and before using any kind of psychological test, you should get an idea of its reliability and validity. Some tests are developed by professionals over a long period of time, carefully designed and tested to ensure their validity. Others are thrown together in a very short period of time, with little thought to their quality.*

*In this part, you'll learn more about all kinds of tests and in what circumstances they're most useful. You'll also find out why some psychological tests should definitely not be taken too seriously.*

# Chapter 7

# The Development of Psychological Tests

## In This Chapter

➤ Why psychological tests were needed and who developed them

➤ Standardizing tests for fair assessments of individuals

➤ Understanding the criteria for successful and useful tests

➤ Taking tests the old-fashioned way

➤ Understanding inkblots and other projective testing methods

Psychological tests have been used for more than a century to measure various aspects of personality, intelligence, and so forth. These tests historically have been used in the judicial system, schools, employment situations, and medical and clinical settings as well.

If the thought of taking a psychological test makes you decidedly uncomfortable, you may do well to rethink your position concerning these tests. The use of psychological tests is widespread, and there's no stigma attached to it. In fact, you're likely to have taken some form of psychological test without even realizing it.

Have you ever sat around with a couple of friends and tried to figure out from a questionnaire in a magazine the degree to which you're compatible? Maybe you and your significant other have used similar questionnaires to determine whether you're well-suited as lovers. Or maybe you've taken some sort of quiz on your own to figure out your level of resourcefulness, inner strength, or how you measure up as a friend. If so, you've taken a form of psychological test.

In this chapter, we explore the development of psychological tests and testing, the types of things tests measure, and how test results are processed. We look at some different kinds of psychological tests and how tests have changed because of technology.

Let's begin by exploring the origins of psychological tests and the people who pioneered their use.

# Whose Idea Was This, Anyway?

Not surprisingly, psychological tests first started being developed in the late 1800s by psychologists who saw a need to assess various human traits and characteristics in a unified and controlled manner.

These early test developers wanted to improve the accuracy with which problematic characteristics or behaviors were identified. Before psychological tests were developed, people with peculiar or problematic behaviors or characteristics were rather subjectively diagnosed and assessed.

It's very difficult to assess human behavior solely by observing a person, even if the observations are informed and well-meaning. Think of the times you've judged someone based on your personal observations, only to find out later that your judgment was way off-base.

Regardless of how well someone is trained to observe and assess an individual, there is always the potential for error in the process. Everyone—even skilled observers who have no reason to be anything but objective about a person—has certain biases and beliefs that may affect their perceptions. These personal biases and beliefs may lie under the surface and be unrecognized by the observer—but they're there.

### Notes and Quotes

The first test to measure intelligence was designed as a tool to identify students who need remedial teaching, not as a test to measure innate ability, as it's most widely used today. Developed in Paris by Alfred Binet and Thèodore Simon, the Simon-Binet test of intelligence first appeared in French schools in 1905 and was translated into English and first used in America in 1908.

Psychologists who saw the need for standardized testing recognized that personal observations were subjective and often incorrect, and sought to find a way to make assessment more objective and reliable. Psychological testing, which is based on standardization, reliability, and validity, gives psychologists a more unified, objective means of assessing and identifying the problems of their patients.

These tests ensured that those being tested would be asked the proper questions and would *not* be asked those that were irrelevant or unnecessary.

For many years, psychological tests were tools used only by professionals. As the public became more familiar with and interested in the idea of psychological testing, however, that changed. Today nearly everyone has easy access to tests available in magazines, on the Internet, and elsewhere.

# What Are Psychological Tests For?

As explained in Chapter 1, "The Personality Puzzle," psychological tests commonly are used to determine job aptitude, assess the suitability of a partner, and measure problems of personality. It's safe to say that psychological tests are important, because we rely on their results when making extremely important decisions. For that reason, the original normative samples for many tests—white, middle class people—were revised to more accurately reflect the increasing diversity of our society. Tests frequently are used for legal purposes, such as custody cases. They also may be used to determine whether someone has the potential to be violent or is likely to relapse, or repeat inappropriate actions or behavior. Psychological tests also often are used to measure aptitude and achievement in students.

A judge, for instance, may order psychological tests for both parents involved in a custody battle. The results would be used to evaluate their mental and emotional health, and to identify any possible abnormal psychological conditions. The judge would use the results of the test to help the court determine which parent is better suited to have custody of the child.

### Notes and Quotes

Many older tests have been re-standardized to include a broader range of people by age, ethnicity, and so forth. This ensures that they're relevant to today's society.

In business, test results may be used as the basis for deciding whether to hire or promote an employee. Again, in this instance, a test is likely to provide a more objective assessment of a person than a personal interview would.

Anyone who's ever been involved in an interview situation—whether on the giving or the getting end—probably understands the potential weaknesses of the interview system.

## Personality Pointer

In some instances, not only the parents but also the children involved in custody disputes may be required by the court to take a psychological test. Certain tests, such as the Bricklin Perceptual Scales (BPS) or the Perception-of-Relationships Test (PORT), are used to measure a child's perceptions of each parent in areas such as competency and supportiveness, or to assess how close a child feels to each parent.

Those conducting an interview may be impressed by a candidate because she bears a strong resemblance to Cindy Crawford, for example, despite the fact that her resumè indicates that it took her six-and-a-half years to complete a four-year college program. On the flip side, there's a chance that a guy who whizzed through the Harvard Business School might lose the job to another applicant because interviewers couldn't get past his unkempt appearance.

### Don't Go There!

Test results provide accurate and useful information but should never be the sole basis for making a decision about an individual. Test results are only part of the total package, which includes the individual's current circumstances, past experiences, and so forth. While they can be extremely useful, test results should never be the only factor in making important decisions about a person.

Tests used in business also can help identify the strengths and weaknesses of employees so that their abilities can be matched to the right jobs. In addition, psychological tests sometimes are used by teams to identify people who will work well together.

In clinical and medical settings, tests help professionals diagnose conditions that otherwise could possibly remain latent (and untreated) for a long time. Early detection of psychological problems, just as with physiological problems, means that treatment can begin sooner and have a better chance of being effective. Also, additional tests administered during the course of treatment can help clinical practitioners evaluate patients' progress.

Regardless of the circumstances in which they are used, it is important that psychological tests be administered in a standardized manner. Everyone taking the test must get the same questions, presented in the same way. Only when that occurs can professionals measure test results against a normative sample and determine if an individual's results fall into the normal or abnormal range.

Regardless of the setting in which it is used, it is important to administer a psychological test in a standardized manner. Only when that occurs can professionals measure test results against a normative sample, and determine if the individual's results fall into the normal or abnormal range.

Psychological tests aren't perfect, but developed and used properly, they give us accurate information that can be used in a variety of ways to help individuals, schools, businesses, and society in general.

# Consistent, Reliable Results—Are They Possible?

Some basic issues related to the development and use of psychological tests are standardization, reliability, and validity. Without these things, the tests don't work. Not only are the tests not valuable, they could actually be harmful if given and applied.

We discussed the importance of standardization in the last section; now we'll talk about consistency and *reliability*.

It's important to understand that psychological tests developed and administered by professionals are very different from some of those you can see in books and magazines, or on the Internet. (See Chapter 8, "For Professional Use Only," for a full discussion of the differences.) The psychological tests we refer to in this chapter are those used by psychologists. You can learn more about how tests are developed in the next chapter, but suffice it to say for now that creating a comprehensive test for professional use—whether it be to measure achievement, aptitude, intelligence, or personality— can take years. It also is done at great cost—often millions of dollars.

**Personality Parlance**

**Reliability** is the statistical measure of the degree of probability that, if a person who already took a test took it again, he or she would get the same score.

If someone doesn't score the same after taking a test a second time, the test developers have a problem, because they can't know whether the difference is due to something going on with the person taking the test or with the test itself. Without test reliability, it's impossible to know what the results mean—or even if they mean anything at all.

Consistent and reliable results are not only possible from a properly developed and administered test—they're absolutely required.

**Personality Pointer**

One way to check the reliability of a test is to conduct a *test retest*. Janie takes the test today and again a week later. If the test is reliable, we expect to get the same results each time Janie takes it. Another way to check is to compare *split-halves,* that is, to select every other question to create two categories (odd & even numbered questions), then do a statistical analysis to determine how similar/different the responses are in the two categories. The more similar the two halves, the greater the reliability.

# Do Tests Measure What They're Supposed To?

Now that you've heard about standardization and reliability in psychological tests, there's one more important area: validity.

Test validity is what makes us confident that we can use the results to make assessments, diagnoses, and recommendations for treatment. Validity assures us that tests measure the things they're supposed to measure.

Without validity, tests are useless.

Professionals look for three kinds of validity in psychological tests:

➤ **Content validity.** The need for a test to measure a specific characteristic, such as self-esteem.

➤ **Criterion-related validity.** The results of a test can be related to some external reality. A person whose test score indicates poor self-esteem, for instance, must in fact suffer from low self-esteem in order for the test to be considered valid. If the person is very self-confident and assured, the test cannot be considered valid.

➤ **Construct validity.** Relates the test results to other measures of the same characteristics. We would look at how the person who scored poorly for self-esteem performs at work or in school, for instance.

In discussions of psychological tests, you'll often encounter the term *face validity.* Face validity is a part of content validity and can be both an advantage and a disadvantage when it occurs in a test.

If a test has face validity, the questions are directly related to the characteristic or problem you're trying to evaluate. For instance, if we're trying to determine the presence of a substance-abuse problem, and we ask on a test, "On the average, how many drinks a day do you have?", that's a question with a high face value. It's directly related to the problem we're trying to evaluate.

An advantage of high face validity is that the questions can be simple and straightforward for the test taker. That, however, also can be a disadvantage. If we ask people how many drinks they have each day, it's easy for them to connect the question with the purpose of the test and to lie if they want to.

If a question has low face validity, on the other hand, it may appear to have little to do with anything, and the test taker may become confused.

While validity is determined in several ways, it's crucial to the value of a psychological test.

Without standardization, reliability, and validity, tests become unpredictable and of little value.

**Personality Parlance**

High **face validity** means that a test question can be directly and easily related to the characteristic or problem the test is intended to evaluate.

# Low-Tech Tests, High-Tech World

Astronauts first walked on the moon in 1969—more than 30 years ago. We conduct business by phone, fax, and computer, transferring messages across the country or to the other side of the world in seconds instead of days, weeks, or months.

**Don't Go There!**

In our fast-paced, high-tech society, we sometimes tend to downplay the importance of anything that doesn't have high-tech bells and whistles. There's a real danger in ignoring simple tools that have endured for centuries: Don't wait for your state-of-the-art food processor to break down or the electricity to go out to remember that a regular old kitchen knife, for example, can still chop up your vegetables.

We regularly zip off e-mails to friends across the United States and in other countries. Records and audiocassettes have given way to compact discs, which soon will be obsolete as well; VCRs are being replaced by DVDs; tiny computers keep track of everything from our daily schedules to our favorite recipes.

There's no doubt about it: It's a high-tech world and getting increasingly so all the time.

So why are kids still sitting at their desks in schools, their sharpened No. 2 pencils at the ready, coloring in the dots on their standardized achievement tests?

Or why are test takers given a blank sheet of paper and some pencils, and asked to draw a picture of a house or a person?

Although many test publishers are using computerized tests these days, low-tech psychological tests are still very much alive and well, and there are some good reasons for this. Let's take a look.

## Why Go Low-Tech?

The use of low-tech tests may be more a matter of practicality than anything else.

There certainly are advantages to tests that are taken on a computer and scored by a computer. The computer can read and analyze the responses, score the test, and kick back the results in a flash. It's fast, and it's easy for the person who gives the test.

The only problem is, what if the person taking the test is unfamiliar with or not comfortable with computers? Might that not skew the test results? Lots of people, especially older ones, have little experience with computers and are terribly intimidated by them. It's possible that they'd spend more time during a test worrying about what happens if they press the wrong key than they would answering the test questions.

As for young people, to our knowledge, there are very few schools in the United States that have computers for every child. Kids work on computers in shifts, they sneak in a few minutes early to get some keyboard time, or they stay after school. It's impractical and unrealistic to think that, at this point, standardized tests in schools could be given and taken on computers.

Sometimes, low-tech is still the way to go.

## Why They're Valuable

Paper-and-pencil tests (which, of course, refers to how the tests are taken) are generally in true-or-false or multiple-choice format.

A multiple-choice format may give a statement and then ask the person taking the test to mark one of the following:

➤ Never describes me

➤ Describes me sometimes

➤ Describes me most of the time

➤ Describes me all of the time

They're easy to take, they're easy to sort, and minimal training is required to administer them, with the same results.

When giving directions to someone on how to take a paper-and-pencil test, testers only need to explain how to mark either true or false, or one of the multiple-choice spaces. They don't have to explain how to use a computer, a computer mouse, or even a fancy pen. It's simple, it's comfortable, and it's worked for more than a century.

# Inkblots and Other Projective Tests

Tests that don't rely on a true-or-false or multiple-choice format are called *projective tests*. These are tests that ask, "Tell me what you see." They ask the person taking the test to add structure or provide answers to unstructured stimuli.

Projective testing includes the use of inkblots and pictures. The person is asked to tell a story, participate in word association tests, respond to sentence completion tests, or perform drawing exercises. Of all projective testing, inkblots may be the most fascinating.

Inkblots, which are nothing more than what they're called, have been used in psychological testing since the 1920s.

Probably the most popular and widely used inkblot test is the *Rorschach test,* which was developed in 1921.

In the Rorschach test, those being tested are asked to look at a series of blots and to tell the person giving the test what they see within the markings. The theory behind this type of testing is that what people see in the inkblot reflects their conscious and unconscious thoughts, needs, fears, conflicts, desires, and so forth.

People looking at the inkblots merely tell the tester what they see and may not be aware of any meaning attached to it. The person giving the test is responsible for interpreting the answers.

Projective tests aren't administered in the same way, nor are they scored or interpreted the same way as objective tests. They're not as cut and dried as objective tests.

**Personality Parlance**

The **Rorschach test,** a widely used series of inkblots, was developed by psychiatrist Hermann Rorschach in 1921 while working with mental patients in Switzerland. The first edition of the Rorschach test appeared under the name *Psychodiagnostik.*

**Don't Go There!**

All kinds of strange Internet sites offer inkblots and interpretations of what your responses to them may mean. Don't get too caught up in these nonprofessional tests. It's okay to have fun with them, but remember that they may not be reliable or valid.

Generally, projective tests—which, by the way, are sometimes also called *subjective tests*—aren't considered to be as reliable as objective tests.

One reason is that the interpretation of inkblots and other sorts of projective tests can vary greatly from interpreter to interpreter. Another is that a person looking at an inkblot may see something one day and see something different in the same blot a few weeks later. It's a little like lying on the grass and watching the clouds roll by. Some days, when you're relaxed and happy, you may see bunnies and flowers … whatever. If you're angry and upset, those clouds might look like dragons or monsters. On yet another day, they might look like nothing but clouds.

The same variations can occur with inkblot testing, which makes it less reliable than objective testing. That's not to say, however, that inkblots aren't valuable in psychological testing. People's views of inkblots certainly can provide valuable insights into their state of mind and can be useful in treatment.

## The Thematic Apperception Test

Psychologist Henry A. Murray is credited with the basis for the *Thematic Apperception Test (TAT)*, which was first introduced in 1935.

The TAT consists of a series of 31 cards; 30 contain black-and-white images, and one is blank. The person looking at the cards is asked to describe what the picture represents or what is occurring.

In normal conditions, the professional administering the test specifically chooses 10 to 15 cards for each particular test taker. The people taking the test tell stories about what they see on the cards, and the professional interprets the stories.

Often, the stories the person tells contain a common theme. An interpreter can gain valuable information by examining this theme.

## Other Kinds of Projective Tests

Other types of projective tests include word association tests, sentence completion tests, and drawing exercises.

The theory behind word association tests is that, as we progress through life, we learn what sorts of things go together. If a tester discovers that a person doesn't have a good sense of what goes together, the tester assumes that there's a reason why that's the case.

The most widely used word association tests are the Kent-Rosanoff test, which contains 100 words; and the Rapaport, Gill & Schafer test, which contains 60 words.

Word association tests have been used for a long time but have declined in popularity during the past couple of decades.

Sentence completion tests ask people to finish a sentence that has been started—for example, "I would be happier if _____."

The results of sentence completion tests normally are fairly easy to interpret, which may be one reason why they have remained popular.

Drawing exercises ask people to draw pictures and sometimes to describe what it is they've drawn.

As you can imagine, the results are sometimes difficult to interpret, and some people are put off by this type of test because they don't like to draw or feel they're not capable of doing so.

Drawing exercises and other projective tests serve a purpose, but there are some downsides to them, as well.

All in all, objective tests probably are more reliable and valid, and that's why they're more widely used.

**Personality Pointer**

Sentence completion tests tend to have significant face validity, which means that if the person taking the test isn't cooperative, the test can produce unreliable results. Can you imagine the answers you might get if you asked an uncooperative test taker to complete the sentence, "I would be happier if _____?"

# Check Yourself Out

Here are several questions to help you reflect on what you've read in this chapter, and perhaps to take the information a step or two farther in your own mind:

➤ What was your opinion about psychological tests before you read this chapter?

➤ How much reliability and validity do you think the tests you see at the newsstand have?

➤ What do you think is the most appropriate use for psychological tests?

➤ Which is more appealing to you, objective or projective tests?

➤ Has reading this chapter affected your opinion of psychological tests?

➤ You might benefit from discussing these questions with another person, or just thinking about them on your own.

## The Least You Need to Know

➤ Psychological tests were developed by psychologists who recognized the need to test everyone in the same manner in order to obtain valid, usable results.

➤ Psychological tests are used in medical and clinical settings, for business purposes, in schools, for judicial purposes, and elsewhere.

➤ In order to be useful, psychological tests must have standardization, reliability, and validity.

➤ Some test developers are moving toward high-tech methods of testing, but many psychological tests are still given the old-fashioned way.

➤ Inkblots and other projective tests are more subjective than those that use true or false or multiple-choice questions, but are still considered useful in some situations.

➤ Projective tests include sentence completion, word association, and drawing exercises, as well as inkblots.

# Chapter 8

# For Professional Use Only

## In This Chapter

➤ Understanding how psychological tests are given

➤ Differences between professional and nonprofessional tests

➤ Using psychological tests to evaluate and diagnose

➤ What tests can—and can't—tell us

➤ A look at some widely used psychological tests

Go into a large bookstore, or check out one of the big online book providers, and you'll find hundreds of books to guide you in almost any imaginable area of self-improvement.

You'll find an amazing number of books that tell you how to lose weight—each method promising to be easier and more successful than the others. You'll find books that advise you on how to avoid getting cancer and what to do if you get it. Others tell you how to cure varicose veins, improve your immune system, make your skin appear younger, reduce cellulite … the list goes on and on.

It used to be that we'd rely primarily on professionals for advice on these sorts of topics. Today, however, with the vast amount of information available to all of us, it's tempting sometimes to assume the role of a professional and make our own decisions concerning health and other matters.

While that's healthy to a degree (there's a lot to be said for trying to help yourself), there's also danger attached to it. Reading a book about skin cancer doesn't mean that you're able to diagnose and treat it yourself. For some things, we've got to rely on professional advice and expertise.

The same is true with psychological tests. Sure, you can find dozens of tests to take on your own, claiming to tell you everything from the kind of person you should marry to how intelligent you are. And while they're fun, they're not substitutes for the hundreds of tests to which only professionals have access. Some of them are used to screen for a wide variety of problem areas while others focus on one specific kind of behavior, mood, or skill.

In this chapter, we discuss the tests designed for professional use only. You'll learn a little bit about how tests are developed, what they're designed to measure, and which of them are the most widely used.

# Professional Tests—A Notch Above the Rest

Like Rome, good, professional psychological tests are not built in a day. Unlike many of the informal quizzes you'll find in magazines and on the Internet, developing professional tests requires a great investment of time, expertise, and money.

A psychological test starts out as a set of questions that experts come up with to assess a certain characteristic or ability. The types of questions depends on what the experts are trying to evaluate.

A test to determine certain personality characteristics, for instance, contains questions much different from those in a test that measures intelligence. Test construction requires item determination, and reliability and validity studies (see Chapter 1, "The Personality Puzzle"). Reliability and validity studies "try out" the tests on people of all age groups, cultural backgrounds, and socioeconomic groups to ensure that they'll be valid for everyone using them. When tests were originally developed, they were based upon the white, middle-class American experience, and many provided skewed results for test takers who were not in that group. Today, especially given the greater diversity in our society, many tests have been updated to include people with more diverse personal and cultural experiences.

As you can see, test development is neither a simple nor a fast process. tests that are carefully developed, field tested, and distributed for use by professionals also require professional administration, scoring, and interpretation guidelines. The end user (the psychologist who administers the tests) must be trained to understand and do a variety of things. Psychologists must understand the psychometrics involved in test development, be well-practiced in test administration techniques, and know how to score and interpret each individual test.

They also must be able to integrate contradictory information that shows up on tests with an individual's reported personal history and experiences.

Scoring objective tests normally is not a difficult process, and has been made even easier and more error free by computer scoring programs. Scoring projective tests, however, can be tricky. Interpreting tests probably is the most difficult aspect of testing, and it requires training and expertise to do it properly.

Also, it's important to remember that what people report about themselves may be very different from what the test scores indicate. Test results don't always give a true indication of a person's condition. This can be explained by the fact that tests are not infallible. People taking tests sometimes have reasons to try to distort the test results, and the problems they're having can make it difficult for them to be fully compliant with standardized processes. Interpretation of psychological test profiles can be a very complex task and requires advanced training.

Consider this scenario. Marsha takes a psychological test, and the results indicate that she's experiencing depressed moods. Ray—who's taken some courses in counseling but was never trained to interpret test results or schooled in other areas of psychology—looks at Marsha's test and assumes that she has major depression.

Cathy, on the other hand, is a professional who has been highly trained in interpreting test results and diagnosing patients. She looks at Marsha's test results and sees that they do, indeed, indicate that Marsha experiences depressed moods. Cathy's training and knowledge allow her to understand that Marsha's behavior and actions don't necessarily indicate major depression.

Cathy gets busy and starts looking at other factors in Marsha's life to determine what's going on. It's important for Cathy to work as quickly as possible to determine Marsha's primary diagnosis. This may or may not result in a diagnosis of major depression. There could be other things going on with Marsha—medical issues, great amounts of stress, other problems—that are affecting her and causing her to have symptoms similar to those of depression.

Ray, who only looks at her test results and is not qualified to fully diagnose Martha's condition, would simply assume that she has major depression.

### Notes and Quotes

The purchase and use of all professionally developed tests is regulated by the developers and publishers of those tests. Also, the American Psychological Association established Standards for Educational and Psycho-gical Testing that apply to the users of tests.

# How Professionals Give Psychological Tests

How a psychological test is administered depends on various factors. Each test has very specific instructions about how it is to be given. Instructions can vary greatly, depending on the particular type of test.

An intelligence test, for example, requires much greater interaction between the psychologist and the test taker than a personality test. For intelligence and neuro-psychological tests, almost every word the psychologist speaks is scripted by the test devel- oper, and the instructions must be adhered to in order to maintain standardized conditions. Standardization is essential in order to accurately score, interpret, and compare test scores.

In addition, the location of the testing, the questions to be answered by the psychological evaluation, and who the test takers are factor into how tests are administered.

To adhere to the standardization for a test, psychologists must follow instructions on administering it to the letter, providing a conducive setting, keeping track of the time on certain tests, and helping the people taking the tests feel as comfortable as possible.

The person administering the test should always be careful to use the exact words written in the test manual when relating instructions to the test takers. Anything left out of or added to the instructions could alter the manner in which the test is taken, and therefore the results.

Whenever possible, tests should be taken in quiet surroundings that will remain undisturbed throughout the testing period.

Quiet surroundings are sometimes difficult to achieve, as you might imagine. Giving a psychological test to a prisoner is a particular challenge, for instance, because prison conditions are usually anything but quiet.

Testing requirements vary, and they affect how the test is given. If a test must be closely timed, for example, it requires more attention from the administrator than a test that has no time limit.

### Notes and Quotes

Remember when you took standardized tests in school? Chances are the teacher had you and the other kids move your desks apart, or to areas where you were looking away from each other. Sure, one reason was to keep you from taking a peek at the test across the aisle, but another reason was to reduce noise and increase concentration.

If the questions or statements of a test are presented orally, the person giving the test must pay special attention to tone of voice. As you know, *how* something is said often gets your attention more than *what* is said.

The tone of a voice can actually influence the answer a person gives. It is important that the psychologist avoids giving the impression that there are right and wrong answers and doesn't lead a person to answer in a certain way. Also important are the locations of the test giver and the test taker. Normally, they'll sit across from one another. It's important for test givers to leave enough room for the test takers and to make sure they don't feel imposed upon or crowded. Some people are uncomfortable in close situations, and that could impact the test results. The more uncomfortable the test situation itself makes a person, the more difficult it will be to get reliable results from the tests.

Although these guidelines for administering tests may seem obvious, it takes a lot of practice to do everything correctly at the same time in a perfectly coordinated manner. However, as we have said, adherence to the standardization will ensure reliable test results.

# Why Only Pros Have Access to Some Tests

Think about this: If you could jump on the Internet and download a professional test used to determine admission to graduate school, what good would the test be to those who depend on it for information? The school admissions staff would have no way of knowing that you'd had access to it, giving you an unfair advantage over those who had not seen it previously.

Or if a parent about to undergo a psychological test as part of a custody dispute has prior access to the test and scoring information, wouldn't the results be completely invalid?

You've learned that not just anyone can step forward and administer professional psychological tests. A high level of expertise is required to properly administer and score such tests, as well as to interpret their results.

The validity of certain tests professionals use in clinical, educational, or business settings would be badly damaged—perhaps beyond repair—if those tests became public.

Access to psychological tests must be restricted only to qualified psychologists and other professionals who understand the tests and use them in their practice. Otherwise, the tests become unreliable and invalid.

# What the Pros Can— And Can't—Learn from Psychological Testing

Professionals can gain many insights by carefully examining and interpreting psychological tests. They can identify personality characteristics, gauge mental ability, assess job aptitude, and even get an idea of any personality disorders.

### Notes and Quotes

College and university libraries that sometimes store psychological test materials must pay special attention to the security of the tests. Access to these materials should be limited to qualified students under the supervision of a faculty member. If proper security isn't in place, the validity of the tests could be severely compromised.

### Personality Pointer

Although intelligence tests are objective and thought to be reliable, much controversy surrounds them. Some people claim that IQ tests, which are meant to test inherent intelligence, are biased because they actually test the environmental bases of intelligence. This bias, critics say, gives people of higher classes an advantage over those of lower socioeconomic status.

95

In certain situations, however, even the best tests—carefully administered, scored, and interpreted—may not result in definitive answers. Objective tests, which include neuropsychological tests, some personality tests, IQ tests, and achievement tests are typically easier to score than projective tests.

To illustrate the importance of the test taker's attitude, let's say that John and Jane are taking the same test—the Graduate Record Exam (GRE). The results will help determine whether they're admitted to attend an esteemed graduate school.

John is entirely motivated to get into this grad school. He has huge plans for his future, and he needs admittance to the school to stay on track. He knows the test is coming up, and he does his homework. Through research, he finds out what types of questions might be on the test, as well as the kinds of skills and abilities the test measures.

He can't get a copy of the test, but he's able to gain an idea of what it might be like. He psychs himself up for taking the test, makes sure he gets plenty of sleep the night before, and shows up 15 minutes early on test day.

Jane, on the other hand, isn't all that excited about going to graduate school. She's just completed four years of undergraduate work, and she feels like she could use a break. She's been offered a decent-paying job that sounds like it would be interesting, and she's tempted to take a few years off before thinking about any more school.

Jane makes no effort to learn anything about the type of test she'll be taking. In fact, she barely thinks about it at all until the day before it's scheduled. She means to get in early the night before the test, but she's having such fun with her friends that the time gets away from her.

### Don't Go There!

Don't ever assume that older people have Alzheimer's disease or other age-related ailments. They could be suffering from depression or another treatable disorder. Professional diagnosis is the best way to be sure of what's going on.

Jane shows up for the test just as the person administering it is getting ready to start the instructions. She's rushed, flustered, and feeling a little fuzzy from a few too many margaritas the night before.

John and Jane may have equal abilities, but who do you suppose is going to do better on this test? From the test giver's perspective, how accurate are the test results in measuring what he or she hopes to measure?

Another example of a difficult-to-diagnose test—even if the diagnosis is based on the results of sound, reliable tests—involves elderly test subjects. It's often difficult to tell the difference between, say, depression and dementia in an older person.

When we move from objective to projective tests, other variables and factors come into play.

Professionals with different backgrounds and orientations may interpret the results of projective tests in very different ways. A psychologist with a Freudian background, for instance, might attach a more sexual interpretation to a set of test results. Someone with a Jungian background, on the other hand, may interpret the same results as being more spiritual.

And, because different people attach different meanings to symbols and objects, it's difficult to be sure that an interpretation is correct.

Suppose that Ann looks at an inkblot and sees a man with a hammer. Barbara looks at the same inkblot, and she also sees a man with a hammer.

The difference is that, to Ann, the image she sees in the inkblot is threatening. It signifies destruction and aggression.

To Barbara, however, the image is a positive one. A person with a hammer is someone who's building something—he's constructing … working.

Both women see the same image in the inkblot, but it means different things to each of them. Just as each person taking a test may see different things, the test givers interpret things differently. This was more of a problem in the past. Today, scoring guidelines for the projective tests have greatly improved scoring consistency, but the problem has not been completely resolved.

As you can see, certain drawbacks and weaknesses are associated with psychological testing. Still, tests are valuable tools for professionals trained to recognize these weaknesses and to compensate for them whenever possible.

### Personality Pointer

You can learn more about psychological tests at the Association of Test Publishers' Web site. Go to http://www.testpublishers.org and start with the "Questions About Tests" section.

# Widely Used Psychological Tests

You've heard an awful lot about professional tests in this chapter. Perhaps by now you're wondering just what some of these tests are like.

A wide variety of professional psychological tests are designed to assess everything from how well you pay attention to whether you have the potential to be a company president.

In this section, you'll learn a bit about some of the better-known tests. Three basic types of tests exist: neuropsychological tests, personality tests, and intelligence tests. There also are projective tests, which are used to gain insight into a patient's thoughts and feelings.

## Neuropsychological Tests

The most widely used neuropsychological test is the Halstead Reitan Battery. It's used to assess brain-behavior relationships. If people are acting in a manner that indicates a problem, this set of tests can help find out if brain injury or disease is affecting their behavior.

The tests, which take about five hours to complete, measure things like the ability to pay attention, to do abstract thinking, verbal skills, cognitive skills, and motor abilities.

A brain that functions in a normal manner doesn't cause a person's behavior to change, but if the brain is injured or sick, it might affect a person's ability to concentrate or to reason. It also could affect a person's motor skills, personality, or other factors. The Halstead Reitan Battery can provide an idea of whether brain function is normal. It's given along with an IQ test and a personality test.

## Personality Tests

The oldest and most-researched personality test is the *Minnesota Multiphasic Personality Inventory,* or the MMPI.

Used in hospitals, clinics, counseling programs, and private practices, the MMPI helps diagnose the possible presence of mental disorders.

### Notes and Quotes

The original version of the MMPI test was written by Starke R. Hathaway, Ph.D., and J.C. McKinley, M.D. Both were working at the University of Minnesota hospitals when the test was first published in 1943.

The test was originally published in 1943 and was re-standardized in 1989. The new version of the test is called the MMPI-2. The test is in a true-or-false format, with 567 questions. The restandardization was done to update the language and to make it appropriate for a more diverse population.

To make an assessment, a professional looks at the answers to all the questions and applies the answers to templates that indicate conditions such as depression or anxiety. Computer scoring and interpretation of test responses is often used today to reduce errors and quickly screen for many different kinds of psychological problems.

The MMPI-2 often is used for employment purposes. Potential police officers, nuclear power plant operators, and others often are required to take the test to determine the possible presence of any personal instability. An adolescent version of the MMPI-2 also exists.

Another widely used psychological test is the *Millon Clinical Multiaxial Inventory,* known as the MCMI. The MCMI also has been updated and is now the MCMI-III. It was written by Dr. Theodore Millon, founding editor of the *Journal of Personality Disorders.* Millon has been a professor at Harvard Medical School and the University of Miami.

The MCMI-III is different from the MMPI-2 because it's designed specifically to assess personality disorders. While the MMPI test screens for a broad range of psychological problems the MCMI tests specifically for personality patterns such as schizoid, antisocial, compulsive, narcissistic, depressive, dependent, and avoidant.

The MCMI-III, which consists of 175 true-or-false questions, is primarily used for clinical purposes. An adolescent version of the MCMI-III also exists.

The *Sixteen Primary Factor Inventory,* known as the 16PF or the Cattell 16PF, is another widely used personality test. A more positive sort of test than the ones mentioned previously, it evaluates personality traits and identifies the test taker's strengths.

The 16PF, developed by Raymond Cattell, is used for employment purposes and in clinical settings. It also can be used to assess relationship strengths and weaknesses.

## Intelligence Tests

Intelligence tests are widely used and are no strangers to controversy. Many people feel that intelligence tests are biased against certain groups or classes of people.

A widely used intelligence test is the Wechsler Adult Intelligence Scale, which also comes in an adolescent version. First introduced in 1939, it was written by David Wechsler. It, too, has been updated to reduce bias in the testing and scoring process.

Another popular test is the Stanford-Binet Intelligence test, first developed in 1910. It measures verbal and nonverbal areas of development, mathematical reasoning, and short-term memory.

The Stanford-Binet test and the children's version of the Wechsler test are the most widely used intelligence assessments in schools. There are many other tests used to assess overall intelligence, academic achievement, and specific learning disabilities. Typically, a battery of tests will be administered to assess intelligence, personality, and brain-behavior relationships.

**Notes and Quotes**

Intelligence tests are frequently updated and revised in attempts to make them more inclusive and less discriminatory.

## *Projective Tests*

You got a lot of information about projective tests in Chapter 7, "The Development of Psychological Tests," so we won't spend much time talking about them here.

The two most widely used are the Rorschach test and the *Thematic Apperception Test* (*TAT*). The Rorschach, if you'll recall, is a series of inkblots; test takers are asked to describe what they see in these blots. The images that those being tested see provide psychologists with insights to their state of mind, and are useful in treatment.

**Personality Pointer**

For a complete listing of all available psychological tests and reviews about them, see the *Buros Mental Measurement Yearbook.* It's available in most libraries.

The TAT is a series of pictures; test takers are asked to form stories based on these pictures. Often, the stories an individual tells contain a common theme, from which an interpreter can gain valuable information. Some of the large publishers of psychological tests include National Computer Systems, the Psychological Corporation, and Psychological Assessment Resources.

As you can see, many different psychological tests are designed for specific purposes. Psychological testing is extremely important to professionals and has helped them assess, diagnose, and treat many patients.

## Check Yourself Out

Here are several questions to help you reflect on what you've read in this chapter, and perhaps to take the information a step or two farther in your own mind:

➤ If you were to take a psychological test right now, what would your attitude about doing so be?

➤ Do you think psychological tests serve a legitimate purpose?

➤ Would you prefer to take an objective test or a projective test?

➤ In what situations do you think the use of psychological tests is appropriate?

➤ What questions do you still have about the psychological tests used by professionals?

You might find it helpful to talk about the questions with another person, or simply to think about them on your own.

## The Least You Need to Know

➤ There's more involved in administering a psychological test than most people realize, and professional training is necessary in order to give a test properly.

➤ Professional tests are carefully researched and developed, making them a notch above many of the nonprofessional tests located in magazines and on the Internet.

➤ Access to professional psychological tests must be restricted in order to preserve the reliability and validity of the tests.

➤ Professional tests can reveal many aspects of personality characteristics and problems, but they should be used along with other assessment methods.

➤ Three types of psychological tests are those that measure neuropsychological factors, personality, and Intelligence.

# Chapter 9

# Tests for Everyone to Take

## In This Chapter

➤ Hunting down tests in magazines, books, and on the Internet

➤ Web sites that offer psychological tests

➤ Understanding the difference between professional and nonprofessional tests

➤ The benefits of nonprofessional tests

➤ Tips for making tests more useful and worthwhile

➤ Knowing when not to take test results too seriously

Tests that measure—or claim to measure—personality characteristics are readily available. You can hardly get through the grocery store checkout line without spotting a magazine that includes some sort of personality quiz or survey.

The Internet, as you might imagine, is loaded with sites containing personality profiles and tests. You can—at least according to the information on the sites—determine your IQ, test yourself for a substance-abuse problem, check out what types of jobs you're best suited for, screen yourself for an eating disorder, find out if you rate as desirable ... and the list goes on and on. We look at some of these tests a little later in the chapter.

Be aware, however, that the tests out there waiting to be taken are very different from professional psychological tests. We talk more about that later in this chapter as well. For now, take a look at two of the most common sources of personality tests: the Internet and magazines.

# Where to Find Psychological Tests

**Personality Pointer**

While magazines and the Internet are loaded with personality tests, don't overlook other sources, such as self–help books. Your local library or bookstore probably offers a variety of books containing such tests.

You may encounter psychological tests in many places. They may get passed around your workplace, with co-workers comparing notes on how they scored and what the scores mean.

Many of us receive all kinds of quizzes and surveys along with our daily e-mails. Or maybe you've purchased books that include personality tests and quizzes.

Two of the most popular sources of psychological tests are magazines and the Internet. If you can't find these tests in one of those places, it's only because you're not looking hard enough. Let's have a little fun and find out what appears where.

## Magazines

Unless you're too occupied with the candy selection in the grocery checkout line, or with your three-year-old who's occupied with the candy selection, chances are you look now and then at those teasers on the covers of the magazines next to the checkout.

If so, chances are you've seen various teasers for different kinds of personality tests inside.

*Cosmopolitan* magazine has a monthly quiz that's meant to assess various components of its readers' personalities. The quiz in the March 2000 issue is called "Are Your Guy Standards Too High" and addresses how readers deal with relationships.

A few of the questions, along with possible answers, follow:

1. Your guy falls asleep halfway through a video viewing of *Thelma & Louise,* your all-time favorite. You …

    a. Consider dumping him. If he doesn't get the movie, how could he ever understand the real you?

    b. Tell him it's no big deal but add that you secretly think his fave flick, *Citizen Kane,* is a big snooze.

    c. Apologize and run back to the video store for *Enemy of the State.*

2. A cool guy you've been chatting with and gave your number to at a bar gets up to leave, and you discover he's really short. You …

    **a.** Tell yourself it's just the way the floor slopes and pray that he calls.

    **b.** Decide not to date him—no Mini-Mes for you.

    **c.** Grit your teeth, think of Tom and Nicole, and wear flats on your first date.

After answering all the questions, readers use a scoring guide to determine whether their guy standards are, indeed, too high.

The August 1999 issue of *Beauty* magazine features a quiz called "How Stressed Do You Get?" Aimed at teen-aged girls, the quiz includes the following questions and possible answers:

1. You're finishing a major history term paper when your computer crashes. You hadn't saved for a while, so the whole last part is lost. You …

    **a.** Turn off the computer and go watch TV. Since you obviously can't get the whole thing done on time, why even bother?

    **b.** Turn white as a sheet, curl up on the floor, and stay there for two hours.

    **c.** Make an outline of everything you can remember writing, then go to the kitchen and pour yourself some soda. Ugh. Looks like the night's gonna be even longer than you thought.

2. Your mom's in an uproar because your grams is coming to visit. As she's running around the house frantically, snapping at you about the single hair on the bathroom sink, you …

    **a.** Scream at her to take a chill pill. It's not like your grandmother has never seen a dirty room!

    **b.** Sweep your little brothers out from under your mom's feet and plant them in front of *The Lion King*. If she's having a fit, it's better if the brats don't make it worse.

    **c.** Hide in your room until Hurricane Mom blows over. Sheesh, your gram's white-glove cleaning standards aren't *your* problem!

**Personality Pointer**

Keep in mind that most of us don't fit neatly into categories listed on test score codes. It's perfectly okay to be somewhere in between what's included in the codes.

A scoring code after the tests advises readers whether they live in "stress-out city"; qualify as calm, cool, and collected; or are deep in denial.

Now let's look at some of the tests available on the Internet.

## *The Internet*

Anyone who's ever used the Internet has an idea of the vast amount of stuff that's on it. Information, entertainment, opinion, junk .... If you want it, you probably can find it on the Internet.

Personality tests seem to be very popular on the World Wide Web. The Web Crawler search engine turns up 47,435 results when you type "personality tests" in the search box. Other search engines, undoubtedly, turn up just as many.

Some of the online tests are pretty amusing. A five-question personality quiz asks the following questions and provides these possible answers:

1. If possible, where do you want to live?

    a. In the south of China

    b. In the Alps

    c. In China

    d. In a field

    e. In a desert

2. If you are going on holidays, when do you feel most happy?

    a. One day before leaving

    b. When everybody has fun together

    c. When talking

    d. When leaving and when coming back home

    e. When eating

3. You have a dream about achieving something. What does that dream mean to you?

    a. You will achieve it in reality

    b. Your effort will pay off

    c. You will fail

    d. Only success in a dream—so what?

    e. No special meaning

4. Lots of different dishes on the dining table—what do you want to eat first?

    a. Soup or curry

    b. Rice or bread

    c. Salad

    d. Vegetables

    e. Dessert and fruits

5. When seeing the light of sunset, what does it mean to you?

    **a.** Wow! How beautiful!

    **b.** Oh! How sad!

    **c.** Nice weather

    **d.** Want to shout as loud as you can

    **e.** Tomorrow you must try harder

Just for fun, I answered "b" to the first and second questions, "e" to the third question, and "a" to questions four and five.

The instant analysis of someone who responds to the questions with the particular answers I punched in is …

➤ Your ideal mate has a good figure.

➤ About your wish: You always compare with others. You set your wish too high.

➤ Your attitudes toward success: You don't care about your success.

➤ Your attitudes toward society: You are a person of principle. You respect the social rules and regulations.

➤ About your personality: You are sincere and optimistic.

Wow! All that information just from answering five questions.

Another, shall we say, interesting personality test is one located at the Quiz Box at http://www.quizbox.com.

This quiz has only two questions. Suppose that you're going to be looking at two pictures, and you have to tell what it is you'd like to see in each picture.

Here are the choices for the first picture:

➤ A tree

➤ A wall

➤ A man

➤ A cloud

➤ A car

Here are the choices for the second picture:

➤ A lion

➤ A rabbit

➤ A bear

➤ A bird

➤ A cat

If you type in that you'd like to see a tree in the first picture and a rabbit in the second, the instant personality analysis tells you that the most important thing in your life is a well-developed mind, and that the friends you want are the strong and active type.

If you prefer to see a car in the first picture and a lion in the second, the analysis tells you that the most important thing in your life is money, and that the friends you want are the charming type.

If you say you'd like to see a cloud in the first picture and a bird in the second, the analysis informs you that the most important thing in your life is a special person, and you prefer friends who are talkative.

**Don't Go There!**

While some of these brief Internet tests may be able to give you insight into one particular part of your personality, a two-, or four-, or six-question test can't begin to give you a comprehensive picture.

See what you can find out about yourself just by spending a few minutes online? Amazing!

There's a huge variety of these Internet tests and quizzes. Tests are available to determine the type of mother you are, your working style, your level of self-esteem, what career you should have, and how well you'd hold up if your lover walked out on you.

Other tests determine your level of social anxiety, whether you're a Type A or Type B personality, how your sun sign affects your personality, how assertive you are, whether you drink too much, and the list goes on and on.

Many online IQ tests are also there for the taking. One at http://www.iqtest.com measures your intelligence with a series of true and false questions. Here's a sampling of the questions:

➤ An upside-down clock's minute hand points to the right when it is 12:45.

➤ The second vowel that appears in this sentence is the letter "e."

➤ If you turn a left-handed glove inside out, it will fit on a right hand.

➤ Jim weighs 150 pounds. Jack is 130 pounds. Joe is 200 pounds. Two of them standing together on the same scale could weigh 350 pounds.

➤ If John looks in the mirror and touches his left ear, the image of John touches its right ear.

➤ Using exactly three colors of paint, it is possible to color the sides of a cube in such a way that two sides having the same color never touch.

You need to answer all the questions in a certain amount of time, or you lose points. If you finish in less than the average time, you gain points. After grading the test and telling you what your IQ is, the program offers you a "complete personality intelligence profile." That, however, has to be ordered, and it'll cost you $19.99. Isn't the Internet great?

Here's a short list of some sites where you'll find personality tests. For a more comprehensive listing, just go to any search engine and type in "personality tests."

### Don't Go There!

Watch out for online tests that actually are ploys to get you to buy something. They're sometimes tied in with items for sale, such as psychological profiles or self-help materials.

➤ www.2h.com   Provides more than 50 IQ, personality, and entrepreneurial tests.

➤ http://keirsey.com   The Keirsey Temperament and Character Web site.

➤ www.scientology.org/oca.htm   A personality test from the Church of Scientology International.

➤ www.looksmart.com   Provides a guide to online personality tests, plus tests to determine your career and love paths.

➤ www.queendom.com   Offers tests and puzzles, free psychological counseling (look out!), and articles for women from Body-Mind QueenDom.

➤ www.colorquiz.com   A five-minute test using color psychology to determine your personality.

➤ www.quincyweb.net   Test categories include Humor and Fun, Serious, IQ, Love and Purity, Substance Abuse, and Vocational.

This is just a very small sampling of a very large arena of tests. Some of the tests were written by Ph.D.s, claim to be reliable and valid, and are copyrighted. Others are just, well, out there.

If you want to use personality tests you find in magazines or on the Internet, go ahead. Have fun with them, and keep your mind open to what you might learn. Don't think that they're overly important or significant, however.

Now let's look at how the tests you'll find on the Internet or in your favorite magazine are different from professional tests.

## Popular Versus Professional Tests

Chapter 8, "For Professional Use Only," is full of information about how professional tests are designed, administered, scored, and interpreted. We hope you learned that developing a good psychological test is an extremely time-consuming, difficult, expensive venture.

**Personality Pointer**

You can find clues to help you determine how sophisticated or valid an online test is. If the questions are worded awkwardly or incorrectly, or there are misspelled words, consider that as you contemplate the validity of the test.

**Notes and Quotes**

The psychology departments of some colleges and universities have Web sites filled with all sorts of interesting and usable information. Don't overlook these in your Web travels.

Tests that show up on the Internet or in magazines may also be carefully designed and developed. Many are written by doctors or other professionals.

Some tests, however, are not developed appropriately. This is the problem especially with Internet tests. Realistically, anybody can put together a couple of questions, call it a personality test, and get it onto a Web site.

That's why, unless the Web site provides information about how the test was developed and how it's scored, you should use the test with a grain of salt.

Here are some questions you should think about when checking out Web sites that contain personality tests:

➤ How was the test developed, and what information does the publisher make available about its reliability and validity?

➤ Are the tests applicable to you, or were they developed for other groups of people and irrelevant to your situation?

➤ How reliable and valid is the test?

➤ How clear are the instructions?

➤ Are there standard scores to use for interpretation and comparison?

➤ If there are cutoff scores, how was the cutoff established?

Some of the better sites give you this information, but most do not. It's important to get the answers to these questions, though, so that you can decide how effective the test may be for you.

While tests are fun for everyone to take, and the results can be informative, you probably shouldn't take them too seriously. And remember that they're not substitutes for well-designed and reliably administered professional tests.

## Some Benefits of Nonprofessional Tests

Although you shouldn't consider nonprofessional tests on the same level as professional tests, they do serve a purpose and offer some benefits.

A questionnaire you see in a magazine while waiting at the doctor's office might heighten your awareness of a particular condition or habit, such as depression or smoking. Maybe you or someone you know has symptoms of depression but didn't realize what they meant. These types of quizzes can be valuable for early intervention.

Many popular tests can be educational. If it's a test to determine whether you're depressed, for instance, it may provide good information about depression along with the questions.

Or maybe you're concerned that you've been drinking too much lately and may have a drinking problem. A quiz on drinking probably will include information about alcoholism, getting help for the problem, and so forth.

Sometimes a quiz that you can look at and take in private serves as a good wake-up call. It can help you face up to a problem or accept reality without feeling shameful or defensive.

Another benefit of readily available psychological tests is that they tend to stimulate discussion.

Let's say that you're concerned about your relationship with your spouse. It just doesn't seem that the warmth you used to feel for each other is evident anymore. You rarely laugh together, and you don't seem to enjoy each other's company the way you used to. Your sex life is suffering, and there's a feeling of tension between the two of you most of the time.

You feel like you'd like to talk with your spouse about what's going on, but you don't know how to start the conversation or how your spouse might respond. A questionnaire in a magazine might be just the tool you need to initiate a conversation about your own situation.

These nonprofessional tests are usually short, quick, and easy to take. You're not investing a lot of time in them, and they don't cost you anything—except maybe the price of the magazine.

Sometimes, taking a personality test can be a source of feedback and positive reinforcement. Maybe you take a test in a magazine, and you find out that you're compassionate, helpful, and sincere. Those are pretty nice things to know about yourself, wouldn't you say?

You also could use a personality test to reach out to another person. If you're concerned about your best friend because he's been acting sad and withdrawn, for instance, you could hand him a test to take that determines whether he might be suffering from depression.

**Don't Go There!**

Many of us are so busy and so rushed that we don't take time for meaningful discussions with the people who are important to us. That's a dangerous thing to do, because neglecting important discussions can get to be a habit. Don't put an important relationship at risk by being too busy to talk out significant issues.

Of course, your friend would want to get a professional opinion if the test indicates that he is suffering from depression. Tests you take yourself can be good indicators but should not be considered definitive.

# Tips for Taking Psychological Tests

Keeping certain tips in mind will enhance the benefits you can get from taking a nonprofessional psychological test. If you're going to spend the time to take a test, you might as well get as much out of the experience as you can.

➤ Remember to read the directions. Yes, that sounds terribly obvious, but many people just don't bother to. Many of these tests have very specific directions, and you won't get valid results if you don't follow them.

➤ Many—probably most—of the tests you'll find online or in magazines are true-or-false tests. While these are easy, a problem with them is that some statements might not be true or false all of the time.

If a test asks, for instance, if you feel angry when your spouse criticizes the way you do the dishes, you might find it difficult to answer definitively. Maybe sometimes you feel very angry when your spouse criticizes your dishwashing technique, but other times it doesn't bother you at all.

If you find yourself in that situation, consider whether true or false applies to you most of the time. If you get angry 51 percent of the time, you should give a "true" answer to the question.

➤ Psychological tests in magazines or on the Internet should be written at no more than about a sixth-grade level. If you find that the test is written on a very technical level with lots of jargon, you might be setting yourself up for frustration if you take it.

Check out the language and make sure you understand it before you begin testing.

➤ A psychological test can't give you a true assessment of yourself if you don't answer the questions honestly. Be sure to base your answers on the truth, not on what you wish were true.

We sometimes tend to filter out things we don't want to believe about ourselves. Maybe we don't want to believe that we get angry over insignificant matters, or that we don't handle stress well, or that we drink too much. Regardless of what you'd like to believe, you've got to be honest in order for the test you're taking to work.

These tips may seem obvious, but they're something to keep in mind when you consider taking a personality or IQ or other type of test. Remember to ...

➤ Read the directions.

➤ Give the answer that applies *most* of the time.

➤ Make sure you understand the language of the test before you begin.

➤ Answer the questions honestly.

By following this advice, you'll be more certain that the tests you take will be beneficial and helpful.

### Personality Pointer

If a popular magazine runs a quiz to determine whether readers are suffering from depression, how they're handling stress, or whether their self-esteem is okay, you can be sure these are areas many people are concerned about. Magazines want to sell copies, so they address issues of widespread concern. If your self-esteem could use a boost, you can be sure you have plenty of company in other readers.

# Some Warnings About Nonprofessional Tests

The psychological tests you find on the Internet and in magazines can be useful, but they have some downsides to them you should know about.

Probably the biggest risk associated with these kinds of tests is that of attaching greater meaning to them than is warranted.

Keep in mind that some of the tests you'll come across may have no legitimate means of substantiating the claims they make. Regardless of what they may claim, these tests might not be able to tell you whether you're desirable, have inner strength, or handle stress well.

Even if the tests are valid, you should consider the results carefully before jumping to conclusions about your personality or intelligence.

In the worst-case scenario, people who are lacking in confidence or have been anxious about a particular issue or behavior may look at the results of one of these tests and conclude that they have a gigantic problem, when in reality, that's not the case.

Self-diagnosis can be a dangerous endeavor. While nonprofessional tests can sometimes help us recognize a problem or a potential problem, being overly concerned about the results can be destructive.

## Personality Pointer

We just can't stress enough how important it is to seek professional help if you think you have a problem after taking one of these tests. A professional can confirm whether a problem really exists and recommend treatment. If the cost of professional help is beyond your means, call a human services agency in your area to see what clinics or other low-cost services are available.

If you take a test, for instance, and the results indicate that you worry too much, don't let those results make you worry even more. Keep the results of these tests in perspective. If the results show that you're not a great organizer, so what? Plenty of people get through life just fine without being models of efficiency and organization.

Similarly, if test results indicate that you're doing something really well, you can be pleased, but don't get too full of yourself.

If test results indicate a problem, and you acknowledge such a problem, remember that nearly everyone has something about their personality they'd like to change.

A personality flaw—such as being a poor organizer or not having vast quantities of inner strength—doesn't make you a bad person.

When professionals diagnose problems in their patients, they don't make value judgments. They maintain a nonjudgmental opinion of the people they've diagnosed. Many times, patients are harder on themselves than a doctor ever would be. If you suspect you have a problem, try not to put a judgment on it. If you're sure you have a problem, there is most likely a way to solve it or at least treat it.

So, if you want to take nonprofessional psychological tests, go ahead. Have a good time with them. Just remember that the tests aren't always reliable, and the results are not always valid. Use the tests for what they're worth, but don't take them too seriously, and don't rely too heavily on what they tell you about yourself.

## Check Yourself Out

Here are several questions to help you reflect on what you've read in this chapter, and perhaps to take the information a step or two farther in your own mind:

➤ How much credibility have you given to psychological tests you've taken in the past?

➤ If you were to look for a psychological test to take, what area would it be in?

➤ How well have you handled the results of psychological tests you've taken?

➤ How easy, or difficult, is it for you to be truly honest when you take psychological tests?

➤ After reading these chapters, what recommendations about using psychological tests would you make to a friend?

➤ You might benefit from discussing these questions with another person, or just thinking about them on your own.

---

### The Least You Need to Know

➤ Thousands of nonprofessional psychological tests are available; you can find nearly every kind imaginable in magazines or on the Internet.

➤ Nonprofessional tests are likely to be less valid and less reliable than those developed by people who are highly trained in that area.

➤ Tests you find in magazines, books, or on the Internet can be useful and have some real benefits.

➤ When taking any kind of psychological test, be sure to read and understand the directions and the language in the test. Also, answer the questions as accurately and honestly as possible.

➤ If test results indicate you have a problem, don't automatically assume the worst.

➤ Never use nonprofessional tests as a substitute for professional advice and help.

# Part 3
# Personality Characteristics

*You've no doubt noticed that people think about things differently, view the world differently, and react differently to various situations.*

*We all have distinct personality characteristics that affect our views and beliefs. Jim is extremely impulsive, while Roger is very deliberate. Jim jumps at the chance to move up the company ladder by packing up his family and moving to Nevada, while Roger agonizes over the decision for weeks on end, repeatedly going over the pros and cons of every related aspect.*

*Our different traits and our schemas—or the way we process beliefs and information—affect how we think about ourselves and expect others to treat us. They affect our level of self-esteem, which is our own measure of what we think of ourselves.*

*In the chapters in Part 3, we look at personality traits, schemas, and the important issue of self-esteem. We also explore the concept of temporary states, or moods.*

*Part 3 also looks at how psychological states can affect physical health.*

# Personality Traits

When we talk about personality traits, we generally are referring to certain characteristics of a person's overall makeup. We say, for instance, that Joey is a very outgoing child, while little Beth is very shy and subdued. Ellen might be described as very relaxed and carefree, while John seems to worry constantly about everything.

Janet whines and complains much of the time, and seems to be fundamentally grouchy. Her friend, Debbie, on the other hand, is always cheerful and optimistic.

These kinds of characteristics are referred to as *traits* or *personality traits*. They help make each of us the sort of person we are.

In this chapter, we discuss various traits, theories on the origin of traits, and how to identify traits and use them to compile personality profiles. You'll also learn about some of the used personality to identify personality traits.

# What Personality Traits Say About Who We Are

People have long been fascinated with the idea of personality traits and types.

Hippocrates, the Greek physician regarded as "the Father of Medicine," claimed that there are four types of personalities. Hippocrates called these the four *humors* of the Greeks (humors being personalities) and listed them as *choleric, phlegmatic, melancholic,* and *sanguine.*

Keep in mind that Hippocrates lived somewhere between 300 and 400 B.C.E., so as you can see, this interest in personality and personality traits is nothing new.

A brief look at the four humors of the Greeks reveals that the Greeks Hippocrates considered choleric had a tendency to be easily irritated or angry. We probably all know a few people who could fit into that category.

Phlegmatic Greeks were sluggish or apathetic—calm to the point of being dull.

Greeks who were melancholic, as you might suspect, were subject to excessive gloom or depression. Sanguine Greeks were cheerful, confident, and optimistic. Every person, Hippocrates thought, can be classified as one of these types of personalities.

While hardly anybody still thinks that black bile is responsible for depression, we still tend to categorize personality according to traits.

Today many psychologists recognize traits as having a biological basis.

*Temperament,* in the days of Hippocrates, referred specifically to the four humors of the Greeks, but today the term is used more generally to describe a person's overall disposition. Some people consider temperament to be biological at the genetic level.

That means that we inherit our tendencies toward certain temperaments. How many times have you heard somebody say something like "Jack's miserable, isn't he—just like his old man." Or "Those Smith kids are all really outgoing—just like their parents."

If we do subscribe to the commonly held thought that personality traits are caused by biological factors (that

### Notes and Quotes

Hippocrates thought each of the four humors of the Greeks was based on a type of body fluid. A person whose dominant body fluid is phlegm is, of course, phlegmatic. One whose dominant fluid is yellow bile is choleric, black bile is melancholic, and blood is sanguine. Pretty interesting, huh?

### Personality Parlance

**Temperament** refers to the biologically determined part of one's personality or disposition. In medieval physiology, the word referred specifically to the four humors of the Greeks, but the meaning has been altered.

is, inherited), then we accept that we have no say in what we get. We don't get to custom order our personalities to be optimistic or outgoing. It might be nice if we were able to do that, but that's not the way it works. We pretty much just get what we get.

Our temperaments, or general dispositions, are largely determined by these inherited traits. Regardless of which traits you inherit, they describe your general disposition and demeanor. That disposition most likely will remain with you throughout your life.

If you have a tendency to be shy, for instance, you're likely to be on the quiet side when you're around other people. This doesn't mean that you feel uncomfortable with people, or that you'll never be able to participate in a play or on an athletic team. It may mean, however, that you're not inclined to walk into a large cocktail party and work the room.

Our personality traits are relatively fixed, but they're not completely inflexible. As is the case with many of the topics we discuss in this book, our environment influences our development of traits and interacts with biological factors. Note: If something is learned from the environment, it can be unlearned.

**Personality Pointer**

It's important to recognize that there's a big difference between shyness and social anxiety. Shyness is a normal tendency; it's simply a trait, whereas social anxiety is a defined problem.

While the biological/genetic view of personality traits is widely held, it's not accepted by everyone. In the next section, we look at some of the differ-ent explanations for personality traits and the peo-ple who came up with them.

## Explanations of Personality Traits

Just to keep things interesting, some groups of psychologists reject the idea that per-sonality traits are caused by biological influences.

Behaviorists—you know, those guys from Chapter 4, "The Learning Theory of Personality," like Ivan Pavlov, John B. Watson, Edward Thorndike, and B.F. Skinner—don't acknowledge biological influences. Everything, they say—is attributed to what we learn through our environments. If you're basically happy, it's because of how you were rewarded in the environment you were raised in, not some inherited tendency.

This difference in opinion is hardly surprising. You've probably gotten the idea by now that psychology and personality are areas of frequent debate.

# Personality Trait Theories

Just as there are differences in opinion regarding the origins of personality traits, there are different theories that analyze and categorize traits.

Here are three of the best-known theories:

➤ The Cattell Trait Theory

➤ The Eysenck Trait Theory

➤ The Five Factor Theory

Let's look at the similarities and differences in each of these theories.

## *The Cattell Trait Model*

Raymond B. Cattell, a prominent psychologist who was born and educated in England, developed a 16-trait inventory through factor analysis, known as the Sixteen Primary Factor Inventory, or the 16PF. This is the essence of the Cattell Trait Theory.

Cattell used a complex statistical method called *factor analysis* to come up with the categories, or scales, of the 16PF.

Factor analysis is a statistical procedure whereby traits—or anything—with similar characteristics are lumped into the same category. For instance, the characteristics of being shy and being quiet are so much alike that both may be placed into one category called *shyness*.

**Personality Parlance**

**Factor analysis** is a complex statistical procedure in which large numbers of objects, traits, or whatever are classified and put into larger categories. The process is not complete until everything has been separated into the smallest number of categories.

You keep putting whatever elements you're working with—traits, in this instance—into fewer numbers of large categories.

Within Cattell's model, there are 16 traits. These 16 traits are called *first-order traits*.

The 16 primary scales used as the basis for the 16PF and for describing personality follow:

➤ **Reserved** (more detached) vs. **Warmhearted** (interested in others)

➤ **Less intelligent** vs. **More Intelligent**

➤ **Affected by feeling** (easily upset) vs. Emotionally **Stable** (calm and patient)

➤ **Mild** (accommodating) vs. **Assertive** (competitive)

➤ **Sober** (serious) vs. **Happy-Go-Lucky** (impulsive)

➤ **Expedient** (disregards rules) vs. **Conscientious** (persevering)

➤ **Shy** (timid) vs. **Venturesome** (socially bold)

➤ **Tough-minded** (self-reliant; realistic) vs. **Tender-Minded** (unrealistic; sensitive)

➤ **Trusting** (adaptable) vs. **Suspicious** (skeptical)

➤ **Practical** (conventional) vs. **Imaginative** (unconventional)

➤ **Forthright** (unpretentious) vs. **Shrewd** (calculating)

➤ **Unperturbed** (confident) vs. **Apprehensive** (worrisome)

➤ **Conservative** (tolerant of tradition) vs. **Experimenting** (liberal)

➤ **Group-oriented** (joiner) vs. **Self-Sufficient** (makes own decisions)

➤ **Undisciplined self-conduct** (careless of protocol) vs. **Controlled** (compulsive)

➤ **Relaxed** (tranquil) vs. **Tense** (driven)

Take this example of how the scales of the 16PF are set up. If you picture a continuum, you'd have "happy-go-lucky" at one end and "sober" at the other.

People who are more on the happy-go-lucky side are flexible, or able to go with the flow. People who are at the extreme end of happy-go-lucky may be impulsive, irresponsible, or antisocial (breaking laws). This extreme behavior can be a warning signal for addictive behavior—as in *If it feels good, do it.*

People on the sober side of the continuum are serious and deliberate. Their reasoning is that *If it's worth doing, it's worth doing right.* In the mild form, "sober" people take responsibility and plan ahead. In extreme cases, they are compulsive. Some examples of compulsive behavior are when people can't help doing things over and over, are workaholics, check again and again to make sure the door is locked, or wash their hands repeatedly.

The categories on the 16PF scale raise the question of whether one side of the category is better than the other. Is it better to be happy-go-lucky or to be sober? Is it better to be practical or to be imaginative, trusting or suspicious?

Generally speaking, healthy behavior occurs in the mild form of any of the categories, or when there's a combination of both sides of a category. When you get into the extreme form of any of the behaviors, it's likely to be disruptive to your lifestyle, cause problems, and affect your normal level of functioning.

## *The Eysenck Trait Theory*

While Cattell used a statistical method to reduce all personality traits to 16 categories, Hans J. Eysenck, a German-born psychologist, reduced all traits to three categories.

The personality test based on Eysenck's theory has become known as the *P.E.N. test,* named for the categories:

➤ Psychoticism

➤ Extroversion

➤ Neuroticism

Each of these three factors, Eysenck asserted, has a biological basis. Let's look at each factor and see what Eysenck thought about them:

➤ **Psychoticism.** Someone who scores high on the psychoticism scale, Eysenck said, is high in aggression or psychotic features. The biological basis for this is an increased level of testosterone.

*Psychosis* refers loosely to a kind of breaking with reality. The break could be as mild as disorganized thinking, such as when a person "goes off on a tangent," or as severe as having hallucinations and delusions. When a person sees or hears things that are not really there it is called a hallucination. Delusions are false beliefs. Aggressive tendencies are also considered to be measured by this scale.

Keep in mind that there are different ways to manifest aggression. A person could be violent or simply an aggressive salesperson. Someone who's a very aggressive salesperson may score high on the psychoticism scale, just as someone who's truly psychotic would. This reinforces the importance of having well-trained psychologists to interpret test results, as referred to in Chapter 8, "For Professional Use Only."

People who are paranoid—another example of being out of touch with reality—think there is a conspiracy against them or that somebody is out to get them, when there's no evidence to support that belief. That's called a *delusional belief.* If people design their lifestyle around a delusional belief, this belief can be severely disruptive and destructive.

Delusional beliefs are much different than fact-based beliefs. If someone has made threats to harm you, you have reason to be afraid. The fears of paranoid people, on the other hand, are not based on any factual evidence.

**Personality Parlance**

**Delusional beliefs** are beliefs based on suspicion and distrust, not on any evidence of conspiracy. These beliefs come from the person who holds them, not from any exterior sources.

➤ **Extroversion.** According to Eysenck, those who rate high on the extroversion scale, which refers to social interests, probably are experiencing cortical arousal, or stimulation of the brain cells.

On Eysenck's scale, everyone rates as either an extrovert or an introvert. The brain cells of introverts are overly aroused, so they tend to stay within themselves because they have all the internal stimulation they need.

Extroverts, on the other hand, don't get enough cortical arousal. This causes them to get bored and seek excitement.

A person with the trait of extroversion has social interests and a positive disposition. Extroverts are characterized by their motivation and tendencies toward such things as achievement, success, action, novelty seeking, mania, and impulsiveness.

Our society tends to reward extroverts, but Carl Jung and others say that introversion is better, because people who are introverted tend to be more thoughtful and insightful than extroverts. Extroverts like to be around other people, while introverts tend to prefer to be with smaller groups or to be alone.

Both extroversion and introversion have good points. They are, however, very different, and they make the people who possess them different from one another.

Ideally, people will not be so reclusive (extreme introversion) or so extroverted that it interferes with their work or prevents them from having a social life.

➤ **Neuroticism.** People who score high on the neuroticism scale most likely are anxious, worried sorts, even when things are going well. They often experience the "flight or fight" syndrome, which is accompanied by increased heart rate, muscle tension, and so forth.

The biological cause for this, Eysenck claimed, is the activity level of the sympathetic nervous system. People who are neurotic have a low threshold for activity within their sympathetic nervous system and are easily upset. People who are stable have a high threshold for activity within the sympathetic nervous system, so they remain calm, even under pressure.

Neuroticism is characterized by anxiety, avoidance, inhibition, fear of failure, and negative attitude. All of these traits sound fairly negative. People who score high on this scale are likely to be emotionally unstable, to not feel good about themselves, to anticipate negative experiences, and to avoid situations that would provoke negative feelings.

Eysenck's P.E.N. test is frequently used by professionals to assess personality traits.

## The Five Factor Theory

The Five Factor theory was presented by R.R. McCrae and P.T. Casta, Jr. in 1990. It was based somewhat on the Big Five Theory introduced in 1963. Written by Warren Norman, the Big Five Theory covered much of the same material as Cattell's original 16PF research but the number of categories has been reduced to five.

Here are the elements of the Five Factor Theory:

➤ Extroversion

➤ Agreeableness

➤ Conscientiousness

➤ Neuroticism

➤ Openness

As you can see, theories concerning personality traits have certain areas where they overlap, but they measure similar traits in different ways. And these are by no means all the existing theories; they just happen to be the best-known and most widely referenced.

Now that you've learned a bit about trait origins and trait theories, let's look at how personality traits fit into personality profiles.

# Personality Profiles

Personality profiles are fascinating pieces of information that can give you insight into all sorts of vital and interesting aspects of a person.

One thing to remember, though, is that although tests can be used to develop a personality profile, a personality profile is not a personality test.

A personality profile obtained by using personality tests and personal interviews includes three kinds of information:

➤ Personality traits

➤ Habits

➤ Specific behaviors

**Personality Pointer**

Traits indicate that we have a tendency to go in a particular direction, but they don't determine how far in that direction we'll go.

For instance, a personality profile would tell you that Barbara carries the personality trait of extroversion.

In addition, the profile will include information about Barbara's habits. Maybe she likes to go to parties and other social events, but she never goes to bars. She participates in a choral group and jogs with a friend every other morning.

A profile also tells you about specific behaviors. For instance, what exactly does Barbara do when she's at a party or when she's with the other singers at the choral group?

Looking at each of these three areas of information—traits, habits, and specific behaviors—helps us to obtain an understanding of a person's complete personality. It's like peeling away the layers of an onion to find out what makes a person an individual. Let's look at each area and what it tells us about a person.

## Personality Traits

Barbara has the genetic trait of extroversion, and she behaves in an outgoing, gregarious manner. Not everyone who's genetically inclined toward extroversion, however, acts the same way.

That's why personality profiles tell us about habits and behaviors as well as traits. People who share common traits don't always act the same.

Sean also has a genetic tendency toward extroversion, but he was raised in an environment that espoused that children should be seen and not heard. Sean, despite his trait of extroversion, probably won't be as outgoing as Barbara is. That doesn't mean that he doesn't have the genetic tendency toward extroversion. His upbringing, however, affects how far in the direction of extroversion he'll go.

In the same light, someone who has a genetic tendency toward psychoticism but was raised in a very warm, supportive environment, probably will have far less of a tendency toward aggression or psychosis than someone raised in an abusive, hostile environment.

The next step when formulating a personality profile is to look at habits.

**Personality Pointer**

It's important to remember that, although different people have common personality traits, that doesn't mean they'll act in the same manner. Think of personality traits as a car chassis. The chassis of a 2000-model Jaguar S is exactly the same as the chassis of a 2000 Lincoln. They're different kinds of cars; they run differently and look different, but they have identical chassis.

## Habits

If you know that your cousin Joe has a neuroticism trait, the next step is to look at his habits.

Does he have the habit of acting a certain way, thinking a certain way, or feeling a certain way in specific situations?

Just because people have the trait of neuroticism doesn't mean they'll have a specific mental disorder. If they have a high score on neuroticism they could still be normal or, they could have social anxiety, obsessive-compulsive disorder, or a specific phobia.

## Specific Behaviors

If our extrovert, Barbara, tends to go to parties, we'll want to know what she actually does while she's there. Knowing this allows us to peel off another layer of the onion to find out what she's really like.

Some extroverts can be *aggressive* toward others, while others are more *assertive*. The difference between being aggressive and assertive is that aggressive people railroad over others without regard for their needs and rights, while assertive people express their needs while also considering the needs of others.

**Personality Parlance**

Psychologists can use **self-rating** or **self-report** by asking those being evaluated to rate themselves on a scale of 0 to 10. This often gives evaluators a good idea of their subjects' state of mind and view of themselves.

Some introverts, on the other hand, might not go to parties. They may stay home and read a book instead. This is one specific behavior of an introvert that would be factored into a personality profile.

Certain tests, such as the Beck Depression scale, can measure depression. Sometimes, however, a therapist simply asks a patient "On scale of 0 to 10, how depressed do you feel?" It's possible to get a quantitative measure of a person's thoughts, feelings, and behaviors by using a 0-to-10 rating scale. This is called *self-report* or *self-rating*.

All of these factors—traits, habits, and specific behaviors—are important to a personality profile. You can get an idea of a person from any one area, but you can get a more complete picture when you consider all three factors.

## Tests Used in Profiling

Different kinds of tests measure different things. Some measure personality traits, while others gauge habits and behaviors.

A comprehensive personality profile may use a battery of tests to determine traits, habits, and behaviors.

Some personality tests are useful to assess moods and temperaments, while others focus on specific behaviors, such as assertiveness.

Let's look at some of the tests experts use when compiling a personality profile, and how personality traits fit into the overall profile.

You now know that a personality profile includes the three categories of traits, habits, and specific behaviors. You also know that different tests are used to assess these factors. Several of the professional personality tests discussed in Chapter 8 are included in the following list of tests used to assess overall disposition or traits:

➤ The Eysenck Personality Inventory

➤ The *Minnesota Multiphasic Personality Inventory* (*MMPI*)

➤ The *Millon Clinical Multiaxial Inventory* (*MCMI*)

➤ The Sixteen Primary Factor Inventory, also known as the 16PF or the Cattell 16PF

➤ The Myers-Briggs Personality Profile Test

Some scales on the tests assess moods and temperaments, and some scales focus on specific behaviors, such as assertiveness, introversion, extroversion, and so forth.

Professionals involved in personality profiling normally learn about people's habits from their experience with the people themselves or from others who know those people well. They get this kind of information through structured interviewing and questionnaires but rarely from a test.

Information about specific moods and behaviors can reveal the extent to which a person is involved in a particular behavior, as well as the kinds of problems that person has had as a result of engaging in the behavior.

# One from Column A ...

You've probably heard a lot about Type A and Type B personalities over the years.

These personality types, which are probably the most familiar and the most discussed, were first reported in 1959 by cardiologists Meyer Friedman and Ray Rosenman.

Their report, which basically categorizes all people as one of these two personality types, summarizes decades of research. Let's look at some of the characteristics of Type A and Type B personalities, and you can try to figure out if you fall into one of these categories.

## Type A

Type A personalities frequently experience time urgency. They're always in a hurry, regardless of where they're going or what they're doing. Type A's tend to interrupt others and can be competitive, achievement-oriented, status conscious, hostile, and aggressive.

You've probably known these people. They're the ones who look at their watches frequently when they're talking to you to make sure they're not getting behind schedule.

They're the ones who cut in and out of lanes on the freeway, dangerously anxious to get to wherever it is they're going. They're the men and women who work 10- or 12-hour days and still get to the gym on their way home.

They tend to have high stress and high blood pressure, and they often experience physical problems, such as heart trouble, because of it.

# Type B

Type B personalities are easygoing, relaxed, and tend to go with the flow. Type B's cope better with daily situations. They manage stress better, and they tend to have more normal blood pressure and to avoid physical problems.

Type B's aren't the kind of people who cut you off on the expressway or rush to get ahead of you in line at the movies. Type B's know the joy of sitting along the bank of a creek with a fishing pole in their hand, whether or not they catch any fish.

Type B's don't agonize over unfinished work; they figure it will get done tomorrow. A crooked picture frame or some dust on the coffee table doesn't make Type B's nuts; they're able to look to something else and take care of the dust later.

Given all that, it's certainly no surprise that the health of Type B's tends to remain more stable than that of As.

# Looking for Middle Ground

Too much of either Type A or Type B personality can be equally debilitating. Probably the most desirable personality is one that combines some of the characteristics of A and B.

**Don't Go There!**

Although personality type is significant as it relates to health, don't think that means you can overlook lifestyle. Type B personalities who smoke two packs of cigarettes a day and down a couple of six packs every night are putting their health at risk—personality type aside.

Friedman and Rosenman found in their study that Type A men are two to three times more likely to suffer angina, heart attacks, and sudden death than Type B men.

Our fast-moving society, Friedman and Rosenman asserted, tends to look favorably on Type A's, while Type B's tend to be left behind.

To find out whether you're a Type A or Type B, go to any search engine and enter "Type A." You're bound to find a test or two you can take that will tell you instantly where you fall on the A to B scale. One Web site you might want to try is at http://www.queendom.com/typea.html.

If you take the test on this site, you answer "Disagree," "Cannot Say," or "Agree" to 17 statements. You're then informed of your personality type. Statements include the following:

➤ I think that hobbies such as fishing or bowling are just a waste of time.

➤ It doesn't bother me if I cannot finish what I planned for the day.

➤ I get no particular pleasure out of acquiring things.

➤ I find it useless and difficult to confide in someone.

Just answer all the questions, and within minutes, you'll know if you're Type A or Type B.

# Check Yourself Out

Here are several questions to help you reflect on what you've read in this chapter, and perhaps to take the information a step or two farther in your own mind:

➤ What do you see as your strongest personality traits?

➤ Which of the three trait theories make the most sense to you?

➤ Can you do a self-profile on yourself? Identify a trait, a habit, and a specific behavior that go together.

➤ Are you more like a Type A or Type B personality?

➤ How do your personality traits fit in with your beliefs?

You might benefit from discussing these questions with another person or just thinking about them on your own.

---

### The Least You Need to Know

➤ Personality traits are the biological or genetically determined parts of our personalities.

➤ Some theorists—the behaviorists—don't recognize personality traits as being an important part of our makeup.

➤ Trait theorists use a statistical procedure called factor analysis to come up with trait scales that they use to identify personality traits in individuals.

➤ Some psychological tests contain scales to identify overall personality features and some have scales for specific behaviors. Some have both.

➤ People with Type A personality are much more prone to experience stress and health problems. Type B personalities are more laid-back and take things as they come.

# Chapter 11

# Schemas and So Forth

## In This Chapter

➤ Identifying just what a schema is

➤ Learning why we use schemas

➤ Sampling the different schema flavors

➤ Understanding how schemas are formed

➤ Maintaining schemas once we have them

➤ Some problems with schema theories

We tend to take a lot for granted when it comes to our personalities. Most of us probably have a basic understanding of what our personalities are and could describe them if we were pressed to do so. Generally, however, it's not something we spend a lot of time thinking about.

We probably find it easier to describe another person's personality than to describe our own. Introspection is often a difficult—and sometimes a downright uncomfortable—chore.

Think about it. If someone asks you what kind of personality your best friend Jennifer has, you'd probably be able to say with some authority, "Oh, she's really outgoing and happy, and always optimistic about what's going to happen."

If someone asks you to describe your own personality, however, would you be able to do so as easily? Even if you were, chances are pretty good that you wouldn't be able to pinpoint just how and when you came to hold the beliefs and expectations you do. Well, you can just relax. In this chapter, you'll learn about exactly that.

The brain is a complex and fascinating piece of equipment. It has an amazing ability to sort and process information, often without us realizing that it's happening. Let's look at how it works to take information and sort it into the compartments or categories that we call *schemas*.

# What Is a Schema?

The idea of a schema originated with the work of Jean Piaget, whom you met in Chapter 6, "Other Personality Theories." A developmentalist, Piaget had a keen interest in children and how they learn. He spent much time observing children, including his own, and based his theory of intellectual development on those observations.

While observing and studying children, Piaget also noticed that children have an ability to sort things out and compartmentalize them. Piaget called the compartments *cognitive structures,* or *schemas.* We use these terms interchangeably throughout this chapter.

Piaget said that children learn by constructing a schema for each set of material they learn. These schemas, or cognitive structures, give children a place to keep the material—to store it.

**Personality Parlance**

**Schemas** are themes in our lives that are made up of memories, emotions associated with those memories, and core beliefs.

Try to think of a schema as being like a computer program. It sorts out what goes in (to the brain) and what doesn't go in. It also determines how information is stored once it's in the brain.

While constructing a schema, children rule in or rule out information or data. Children either accept it or reject it, depending on the rules they write along the way. They're sort of writing their own programs as they go along. The schemas they form are like the algorithms of a computer program.

In simple terms, schemas provide us with the structure to support memories, emotional reactions, and core beliefs. They help us sort out and process the beliefs we have.

# What Are Schemas Used For?

Schemas are the ground floor on which our core beliefs, assumptions, and automatic thoughts rest.

Schemas allow us to use our experiences to process new experiences or information.

Suppose that Johnny is a young child who's lived all his life in a happy, nurturing home with kind, loving parents. When Johnny meets new adults, he'll tend to assume that those adults, like his parents, are loving and kind.

On the other hand, suppose that Amy grows up in a house where her father beats her and her mother every night. She's likely to assume that all fathers—and all men—are hurtful and not to be trusted.

Children learn to make associations and assumptions. They reason *If this happens, then that will happen,* or *If someone does this, it means that they'll do that.*

Schemas support our *core beliefs* and the thoughts and assumptions that go along with them (refer to Chapter 2, "You Are What You Believe," for more about core beliefs). Schemas give us a framework we use to process our thoughts and beliefs. Let's look at a couple of examples.

Fred has a core belief of helplessness. Deep down, he thinks he's pretty much incapable of doing anything. By the way, Fred also never learned to fix a flat tire.

One day Fred's driving along and gets a flat tire. As he utters an expletive, he simultaneously has an automatic thought: *Oh my God, I need to find somebody to help me.* That automatic thought is based on Fred's belief that he needs help to solve a problem.

The automatic thought is based on the belief Fred has that he's unable to solve problems by himself. That belief is based on Fred's core belief that he's helpless.

Greg also has a core belief of helplessness, and like Fred, he's never learned to fix a flat tire. When Greg gets a flat, however, his automatic thought is very different than Fred's.

**Personality Parlance**

**Core beliefs,** as you learned in Chapter 2, are our most basic, fundamental beliefs. They're formed partly by our early environment and the messages we receive when very young. As we hear these messages over and over again, how we interpret them forms our core beliefs.

Greg says to himself, *Well, I've got to figure out a way to fix this myself.* That automatic thought is based on Greg's rule that you never ask anyone for help.

The rule is based on the assumption that if you don't ask for help, you can avoid dealing with your core belief of helplessness. Greg is overcompensating for his belief of helplessness. He needs to appear capable so that nobody will discover his flaw, and he won't have to face it.

Both Fred and Greg have the same core beliefs, but the way they process them is very different. They both use the same schema or process, but the contents within their schemas are different.

As another example of how the processing of core beliefs can differ, let's consider Lisa and Sue: Both have the core belief that they're unlovable.

Lisa is invited to a party, and her automatic thought is, *Oh no, I can't go.* Her automatic thought is based on the rule that she doesn't attend social functions.

The rule comes from the assumption that if she does attend a social event, nobody will talk to her and she'll have a terrible time. Her assumption stems from her core belief that she's unlovable.

Sue, on the other hand, gets invited to the party and immediately accepts. The acceptance, or her automatic thought, is based on her rule that she must attend every social event that she possibly can.

That rule is based on the assumption that if she attends many social events and is seen in social situations, she can mask, and therefore won't have to deal with, her core belief that she's unlovable.

You can see how the process that Lisa and Sue use is very different, even though their core beliefs are the same.

It's important to understand that much of this processing is done unconsciously. Schemas often are put into place at a very young age without much conscious thought at all.

## Different Schema Schemes

As you learned in the preceding section, schemas are formed in different ways, depending on a person's "hardware" and "software."

Regardless of how schemas are formed, however, cognitive theorists think that schemas function in about the same way for everyone.

The following list of six types of schemas was proposed by Jeffrey Young, Ph.D. Young is the director of the Cognitive Therapy centers of New York and Connecticut. He teaches at Columbia University and is the author of *Cognitive Therapy for Personality Disorders: A Schema-Focused Approach.* He's widely recognized for his work on schemas.

According to Dr. Young, five schema domains, or areas, exist.

➤ Disconnection and Rejection

➤ Impaired Autonomy and Performance

➤ Impaired Limits

➤ Other-Directedness

➤ Overvigilance and Inhibition

Remember that these are schemas, not stages that we pass through. As we grow up, we all deal with these

**Notes and Quotes**

While most of Dr. Young's work is scholarly, he also wrote *Reinventing Your Life*, a self-help book based on the schema approach. You can find it at your local library or bookstore, or order it on the Internet from Amazon or Barnes and Noble. You also can visit Young's Web site at www.schematherapy.com.

issues. Will our caregivers be loving or abusive? Will we grow up with good self-esteem, or will we think we're somehow defective or no good?

As we deal with these and other issues, and as we process our experiences, we're actually setting up schemas. We come out of childhood thinking that caregivers and other people are good and loving, or that others can't be trusted because they'll abandon and hurt us. Or we land somewhere in the middle of the continuum and understand that while most caregivers and others are good, there are some we need to watch out for.

Much of this processing and sorting happens unconsciously—we're not aware that it's happening. But the information is available to our conscious minds.

# How Are Schemas Formed?

The good news is, we've developed a lot of information about schemas, and we've been able to give them some practical applications in education and other areas.

We understand what schemas are, what purposes they serve, and how to use them.

The bad news is, we still don't fully understand how schemas are formed.

Again, the dilemma goes back to this question: When forming schemas, what percent is based on biological factors and what percent is based on environmental factors and what percent is based on our interpretation of the other two?

People's biological abilities, such as their memory capacity, attention span, and mental quickness, can be compared to computer hardware. Biological ability is the machinery people have to work with.

People with good memory capacity are better able to remember what's happened to them and to process those experiences differently than someone without good memory capacity. People with good memory capacity are likely to come up with different interpretations of what's happened than those with poor memory capacity. You could say that the people with good memory capacity have more data to process and to base their conclusions on.

Consider this scenario. Bob and Bill take a cross-country train trip. They see all kinds of sights and experience many things along the way.

**Personality Pointer**

It shouldn't surprise you to know that different disciplines and groups of theorists have varying ideas concerning schemas and how they're formed. It seems that no psychological theory is ever unanimously accepted.

Bob has severe mental retardation and Bill has an IQ of 160. Is it reasonable to assume that Bob and Bill will have the same impressions of the trip and the same interpretations of the experiences they had during the trip? Of course not.

Obviously, Bob will process the experience very differently from Bill. Their memories will be different, their interpretations will be different, and the rules and assumptions they draw from their experience will be very, very different.

Bill will have many more concrete memories and facts—data, if you will—on which to base his assumptions.

The difference in how Bill and Bob process their experiences also occurs between young children and mature adults, though not for the same reasons. Bob's way of processing parallels a child's, because without a fully developed brain, the child lacks the capability to fully understand or store information in the same way an adult would.

The difference in how children and adults base assumptions is twofold. It's both a developmental issue, as discussed in the preceding section, and a difference in the amount of life experience.

If biological factors are our hardware, then the assumptions and beliefs that affect our processes of building schemas are our software. And it's important to know that, just as with a computer, one can't work without the other. You need both hardware and software to get a program running.

While we don't fully understand everything about how schemas are formed, it's generally acknowledged that certain factors are necessary for their formation, and other factors are required to maintain them.

The first necessary component, temperament, is a biological factor; the second, early environment, is, of course, an environmental one.

### Don't Go There!

It's dangerous to expect the same reactions from children as you would from adults. Young children who experience the death of a parent, for instance, may react in ways that adults consider inappropriate. They may act like they don't care or want to get back to whatever they were doing before the death occurred. It's not because the child doesn't care about the parent who died, it's just that he or she is unable to fully comprehend what's happened or to deal with it in an "appropriate" way. Putting adult expectations on kids only confuses them and causes problems.

# Temperament

Temperament, a word used to describe a person's overall disposition, is considered to be biological at the genetic level. In other words, we come by our temperaments honestly, inherited along the way from our genetic gene pool.

Dr. Young, who outlined five schema domains (refer to the section "Different Schema Schemes," earlier in this chapter), also set up a continuum of five possible dimensions of temperament. Theoretically, everyone falls somewhere within these categories:

➤ Shy vs. outgoing

➤ Passive vs. aggressive

➤ Emotionally flat vs. emotionally intense

➤ Anxious vs. fearless

➤ Sensitive vs. invulnerable

Although temperament is thought to be primarily biological, it's affected by a person's environment. When biological and environmental influences interact, the results can affect the personality.

If Sam has an invulnerable temperament, for instance, but his parents are very critical of him, Sam will turn out to be more sensitive than if his parents had accepted the kind of temperament he had. He would be nudged along the sensitive vs. invulnerable continuum toward sensitive.

If Jackie has a passive temperament but is raised in a very supportive environment where she's taught that she's important and that what she thinks matters, she'll move along the continuum toward assertiveness.

# Early Environment

Another factor necessary for the formation of schemas is early environment. It's no secret that our early environment is critical to what our core beliefs are, how we think about ourselves, and how we expect to be treated by others. In *Reinventing Your Life,* which Dr. Young wrote with Janet Klosko, Ph.D., they identified nine environments that are particularly destructive to children and negatively impact the schemas they form:

➤ One parent is abusive, while the other is helpless or passive.

➤ Parents are emotionally distant, with high expectations for the child's achievement.

➤ Parents fight all the time, with the child caught in the middle.

➤ One parent is sick or depressed, and the other parent is absent, forcing the child into a caretaker role.

➤ The child is closely meshed with one parent and becomes a substitute spouse.

➤ The parents (or parent) are phobic, and the phobia is expressed in being overly protective of the child or fearful for themselves, making them cling to the child.

➤ The parents (or parent) are critical, and nothing the child does is good enough.

➤ The parents (or parent) overindulge the child and fail to set limits.

➤ The child is rejected by peers or grows up feeling different from others.

Understand that, to some extent, we all fall into one or more of these categories. The degree to which these situations occur is what's important in determining our early environments. The more serious the degree of these situations, the more maladaptive the environment will be.

Temperament and early environment are important factors in how our schemas are formed. Once we have schemas, there are several factors that maintain them.

# Maintaining Schemas After They're Formed

Once we have our schemas formed and in place, we develop methods of maintaining them to keep them intact.

Dr. Young states that we use one of the following tactics to maintain our schemas:

➤ Schema Maintenance

➤ Schema Avoidance

➤ Schema Compensation

## *Cognitive Distortions*

Judith Beck, Ph.D., author of *Cognitive Therapy: Basics and Beyond,* modified an early version of *cognitive distortions.* She asserts that cognitive distortions are nothing more than faulty thinking. They result when a person has a belief that's not based on factual evidence.

For example, Jane may hold a core belief to be true when it's not true at all (such as all men are bad) because of what happened to her in the past.

The following list of cognitive distortions is provided by Dr. J. Beck:

➤ **All-or-nothing thinking.** A person who uses cognitive distortion to maintain a schema or belief tends to think about things as occurring either totally or not at all. There's no middle road. Everything is in black or white. The

**Personality Parlance**

**Cognitive distortions**—errors in thinking—are ways of maintaining schemas. People hold on to faulty thinking because it works within their schema.

person may use words like "always" and "never" and is completely at one end of reasoning or the other.

➤ **Catastrophizing.** Some people predict that the future will be terrible. When catastrophizing, these people believe that nothing good is going to happen, and that's all there is to it.

➤ **Disregarding the positive.** People who use this method of cognitive distortion simply discount or ignore anything positive about themselves. If they have low self-esteem, they disregard anything nice that someone says about them.

➤ **Emotional reasoning.** People who feel very strongly about something simply assume that it must be true, even if facts indicate otherwise.

➤ **Labeling.** People make broad statements based on a prejudice or bias against a certain race, class, gender, or age.

**Notes and Quotes**

Dr. Judith Beck is the daughter of Aaron Beck M.D., who is recognized as having developed cognitive therapy. Such father-daughter or father-son links aren't uncommon in the field of psychology. Many prominent psychologists, including Sigmund Freud, have had a child, or even several children, follow in their footsteps.

➤ **Magnifying and minimizing.** People who do this tend to exaggerate negative thoughts and minimize positive ones.

➤ **Using a mental filter.** Some people focus an excessive amount of attention on one negative detail and do not view the overall situation, which indeed could be positive.

➤ **Mind reading.** Some people assume they can know what other people are thinking. Mind reading often is a factor in relationships and can be a major cause of communication problems.

➤ **Overgeneralizing.** Sometimes people make overall negative conclusions beyond what is supported by the actual situation—for example, "If it's bad here, then it must be bad everywhere."

➤ **Personalizing.** Sometimes people explain other people's behaviors or intentions based on what they assume those people think about them. If David is having a bad day, for instance, and he snaps at John, John assumes that David's behavior is based on the fact that David doesn't like him.

➤ **Making *should* or *must* statements.** People make demands about how things should be or must be and expect the world to conform.

➤ **Having tunnel vision.** Someone with tunnel vision sees only the negative regarding the situation, never anything positive.

**Don't Go There!**

People who constantly engage in behaviors such as taking drugs, gambling, overeating, or drinking excessively to distract them from their pain run the risk of falling into addictive behaviors. It's dangerous to rely on something—a substance or a behavior—to distract you from what's going on inside you.

By using cognitive distortions, people can maintain their schemas and core beliefs because they don't have to consider anything else. The distortions keep on fueling the fire. People protect their beliefs by refusing to acknowledge anything different.

## Schema Avoidance

Facing a negative core belief, such as the belief that we're unlovable or helpless, can be very uncomfortable. It can, in fact, be downright painful.

While some people are able to acknowledge their negative beliefs and deal with them, others go to great lengths to avoid having to think about or face beliefs that are painful.

If Sandy was abused as a child, for instance, she just may not be able to face thinking about it. She simply doesn't want to acknowledge the fact that her parents didn't value her or that she was unloved.

If Sandy can block out any thoughts about the abuse, she can avoid thinking about her parents' disregard for her; she simply doesn't have to deal with it.

Some people do this rather well. They're able to avoid the things that trigger painful memories. They simply don't think about what hurts. Others use drugs, gambling, shopping, eating, or drinking to avoid thinking about painful issues. Their behavior distracts them from what's bothering them.

People who are unable or unwilling to face painful beliefs may do these things without realizing why. They may do whatever they can, consciously or unconsciously, to avoid experiencing their pain.

## Overcompensating to Maintain Schemas or Beliefs

People who overcompensate to maintain a schema or belief may act in a way that is just the opposite of what you may have expected.

Remember earlier in the chapter when Greg immediately decided that he'd have to figure out how to fix the tire on his own? Or when Sue accepted the party invitation without hesitation, despite her core belief that she was unlovable?

Both Greg and Sue were overcompensating for their feelings of helplessness or of being unlovable. By refusing to accept any help, Greg can ignore the fact that he feels helpless. After all, how can a person who never asks for help be helpless?

And Sue, by going to every social occasion she's invited to, denies the fact that she feels unlovable. If she's always out with others, that must mean that others like her. Or she may depend on the people she sees to boost her sagging self-esteem.

Overcompensating is doing the opposite of what's expected, based on your schemas.

# Schema Shortcomings

As people interact with their environment, they use the cognitive structures—or *schemas*—they've built and have used up to that point. If a new experience is similar to a past experience, it is assimilated into an existing schema.

If a new experience occurs that doesn't fit into an existing structure, people must make a new structure in which they can process the new experience.

If they're able to assimilate all the new experiences into existing schemas, they experiences equilibrium. If new experiences occur that can't be assimilated, however, there's a loss of equilibrium.

When a loss of equilibrium occurs, people must learn the process of accommodation, which means they need to build new schemas with which to process and assimilate their experiences. If they don't learn this process of accommodation, equilibrium can't be restored.

Piaget thought this was particularly true of children as they learn and experience new things quickly. He was fascinated by their abilities to sort through and process new situations.

The difficulty with Piaget's thoughts on schemas is that it's hard to identify equilibrium and what the loss of equilibrium means. It's hard to be sure if all new experiences are being assimilated or if some are falling by the wayside.

These are very nebulous determinations and difficult to track in yourself and other people.

**Personality Parlance**

The plural for **schema,** according to Mr. Webster, is *schemata.* It's become acceptable in both academic and nonacademic writings, however, to use *schemas* instead.

Our ideas about and explanations for schemas aren't perfect. We do acknowledge that cognitive structures, or schemas, exist, however. We also recognize that, in these schemas, certain rules, assumptions, and beliefs affect how our experiences are recognized and interpreted.

# Check Yourself Out

Here are some questions to help you reflect on what you read in this chapter, and perhaps take the information a step or two farther in your own mind:

**143**

➤ How would you describe your temperament?

➤ What kind of environment did you grow up in?

➤ Which cognitive distortions do you tend to use?

➤ Do you do certain things to avoid painful feelings?

You might find it helpful to talk about the questions with another person, or simply to think about them on your own.

---

### The Least You Need to Know

➤ Schemas are the rules we make to support our assumptions and beliefs, our memories, emotions associated with memories, and core beliefs.

➤ We use schemas to organize our thoughts and beliefs, and to deal with the experiences that come our way.

➤ According to psychologist Dr. Jeffrey Young, there are five schema domains.

➤ Temperament and early environment are factors necessary for forming schemas.

➤ Schema maintenance, schema avoidance, and schema compensation are tactics used to maintain beliefs and schemas.

➤ Although schemas are widely acknowledged and accepted, it's understood that certain problems are associated with schema theories.

# Chapter 12

# The All-Important Self-Esteem Factor

## In This Chapter

➤ Defining self-esteem

➤ How self-esteem affects what we think and do

➤ Exploring how we build self-esteem

➤ Why some people have more self-esteem than others

➤ Boosting your self-esteem through assertiveness

➤ Learning that it's okay to say no

We all hear a lot about self-esteem these days. Lots of people work hard to boost it—parents in their children, coaches in their players, employers in their employees, and teachers in their students.

We often refer to a person's level of self-esteem, sometimes using it to explain, or even excuse, attitudes and behavior.

To be sure, our society is pretty focused on self-esteem. You can attend conferences and seminars dealing with it, read about it in magazines, and hear television news reports on it.

Many businesses sponsor programs designed to bolster self-esteem among employees. Children with poor self-images are identified and referred to guidance counselors for counseling designed to improve their self-esteem.

Because self-esteem is a topic of such frequent discussion and the focus of so much attention, it's important to fully understand what it is and how it affects our personalities and pretty much everything we do.

# Everybody Talks About It, but What Exactly Is It?

Self-esteem is described by different people in different ways, some dramatically different. But basically, self-esteem is your own measure of what you think of yourself. It's the way you answer the question, "How do I measure up?"

## What the Theorists Say About Self-Esteem

Several theorists you've already read about—Alfred Adler, Harry Stack Sullivan, and Albert Bandura—considered self-esteem to be a very important influence on a person's overall personality.

Sullivan maintained that all our relationships are affected by three things:

➤ Security

➤ Intimacy

➤ Lust

Self-esteem, Sullivan said, is closely tied to security. If we don't have a reasonable degree of self-esteem, we'll lack a sense of security. That lack will adversely affect our ability to have successful relationships.

Based on Sullivan's reasoning, healthy self-esteem is a vital factor in developing and maintaining good relationships.

Adler also stressed self-esteem, putting it in the middle of a continuum with inferiority at one end and superiority at the other (see the following illustration).

*Alfred Adler's self-esteem continuum.*

| Inferiority | Self-Esteem | Superiority |
|---|---|---|

The goal of personality, Adler said, is to strive for superiority over difficulties. That means that you want to be able to solve problems and deal with the everyday stuff that life hands you. If you can do that, you're on the positive side of the self-esteem continuum.

Adler believed that when a person sets an unrealistic goal of achieving superiority over all other people, mental illness occurs. Those who constantly compare themselves to others put not just their self-esteem but their mental health at risk.

Adler also said that people often recognize and try to compensate for feelings of inferiority early in life. Jack, for example, might react to how his dad made fun of him when they played catch in the back yard.

Jack's dad, who was a decent high school athlete and never forgot it, was disgusted with his son, who didn't seem to be particularly interested in sports. He belittled Jack constantly, making fun of his lack of skills and abilities, which made Jack feel extremely inferior.

As Jack grows older, he compensates for his feelings of inferiority by becoming the best baseball player his high school has ever had. He practices constantly. He begs to be able to go to baseball camps, and he learns everything he can about the sport. Jack has developed pretty good baseball skills, and even his old man has to admit Jack's come a long way since their backyard practice sessions.

But Jack's compensation for his early feelings of inferiority may or may not result in his achieving a positive sense of self-esteem, security, and success. Overcompensation can mask deep-seated feelings of inferiority but can't necessarily overcome them.

**Personality Pointer**

Unfortunately, not everybody compensates for feelings of inferiority and ultimately achieves success and self-esteem. Many people never get over those feelings of inferiority and are affected by them the rest of their lives.

If people feel inferior, Adler said, their sense of inferiority often is determined by the height of the goal they've set for themselves compared with what they've been able to achieve.

If Sarah, for example, sets a goal of singing with New York's Metropolitan Opera by the time she's 18 years old, she's probably setting herself up for a big dip in her self-esteem level. Chances are that at 18, she'll be nowhere near her goal, and she'll consider herself a failure.

If, instead, she sets a goal of getting into a good music school when she's 18, training and putting in time with local and regional operas until she's 27, and breaking into New York's Metropolitan Opera when she's 28, she's more likely to stay on track and protect her self-esteem.

If Jonathan decides early on that he'll get nothing but A's during his entire school career, and that anything less than an A is a disgrace, he puts a tremendous amount of pressure on himself. He's really setting himself up to fail. If he sets a goal of A's and B's, and understands that a C every now and then isn't the end of the world, he has a much better chance of achieving his goals and doing his self-esteem a big favor.

Meeting lofty goals and attaining a good level of self-esteem is not the sole factor in mental health, however.

**Notes and Quotes**

Remember that Adler is one of the social theorists who stresses the importance of feeling connected with other people. Feeling connected makes us feel that we're equal to others, and that's good for our self-esteem.

Adler said that the goal of mental health is threefold:

➤ To be connected with other people

➤ To develop oneself fully

➤ To contribute to others

### Personality Parlance

**Self-efficacy** is the belief that we have some control over our lives, and our actions and accomplishments will affect the direction and path of our lives.

### Notes and Quotes

Psychology has the odd habit of tending to substitute one word or phrase for another that has a similar but not identical meaning. For example, the terms *self-esteem, self-concept,* and *self-efficacy* often are used interchangeably, even though their meanings aren't identical. Close as their meanings are, there are some subtle differences between them.

Bandura, whose work and research resulted in the social learning theory, also stressed the importance of self-esteem and its effects on many areas of our lives.

Bandura concentrated on the link between self-esteem and *self-efficacy*—that is, our perception of our effectiveness or our expectations of what we'll be able to accomplish.

A good level of *self-efficacy* allows us to believe that we have some control over our lives and that what we do impacts the path of our lives.

An example of the power of self-efficacy often is displayed when a person becomes sick.

Jenny finds out she's in the early stages of multiple sclerosis. Understandably, she's devastated. The doctor advises her to begin an exercise or therapy program, but she refuses. She becomes increasingly fearful as she waits to see what course the illness will take. Jenny has a very low level of self-efficacy. She believes that nothing she does will help her to become well and that she can't help herself.

Jane also learns that she's in the early stage of MS, but because she has a high level of self-efficacy, she takes control of her situation. She reads everything she can about the disease, completely changes her diet by eliminating any sort of processed food, and begins a daily exercise program. She follows her doctor's advice while supplementing it with her own findings. Jane has a very high level of self-efficacy.

The self-esteem of these women is closely linked to their levels of self-efficacy. Jenny, whose attitude is one of helplessness and defeat, doesn't feel very good about herself. Jane, who capably puts herself in control of her illness, has a much higher self-esteem level.

Along the same line of thought, Bandura linked people's motivations to their perceptions of capability. If

Sam thinks he can give a great presentation at work, he'll be motivated to prepare for it, practice it, and present it in a positive manner.

If Sam tells himself that his presentation will be awful because he's no good at getting up in front of people, he won't be motivated to prepare and practice for it.

As you might imagine, the self-concept we have of our abilities affects a variety of achievement behaviors.

People with positive perceptions of their abilities generally approach tasks with reasonable expectations of success. As a result, they usually perform better. They expect more of themselves, and they generally live up to their expectations.

As the adage *Nothing succeeds like success* implies, the better people do, the better they are and the better they *can* do. Those with good self-esteem and positive expectations of outcomes generally perform better than those with low self-esteem and low expectations. Each success maintains and even raises their self-esteem, while that of those who fail is threatened.

**Notes and Quotes**

Albert Bandura explained the concept of achieving what we expect to achieve in this quote: "People's level of motivation, affective states, and actions are based more on what they believe than on what is objectively the case."

## What Does Self-Esteem Do for You?

Self-esteem is a pretty pervasive thing. It affects many aspects of our moods and personalities. It affects what we agree to do or not to do, how well we think we'll be able to perform a task, and how we feel after we've completed it.

Our level of self-esteem affects how we treat others and how we expect others to treat us. It affects the jobs and careers we choose, the level of education we pursue, and how we live our lives.

Self-esteem affects—and is affected by—all our beliefs and assumptions. The upward spiral of success and increased self-esteem described earlier is an example of how self-perception and individual actions can affect each other in a positive way. Good self-esteem can be viewed as an aspect of positive psychology—an area that has experienced renewed interest recently.

Martin Seligman, a guest editor of the trade journal *American Psychologist* and a former president of the American Psychological Association, has been a strong proponent of reviving positive psychology.

In a special January 2000 issue of *American Psychologist*, Seligman and Mihaly Csikszentmihalyi explain positive psychology like this:

> *The field of positive psychology at the subjective level is about valued, subjective experience, that is: well being, contentment, and satisfaction in the past, and hope and optimism for the future, and flow and happiness in the present.*
>
> *At the individual level, it is about positive, individual traits; it's the capacity for love and vocation, courage, interpersonal skills, aesthetic sensibility, perseverance, forgiveness, originality, future mindedness, spirituality, high talent, and wisdom.*

While self-esteem is not specifically mentioned in that quote, it's difficult to think that a person could possess all the characteristics the quote enumerates without a healthy level of self-esteem. Self-esteem is so important in our lives that it affects nearly everything we think and do.

# Where Does Self-Esteem Come From?

What people base their self-esteem on varies from individual to individual.

Amy, for example, may base her self-esteem on her success in business. She is the vice president of a major corporation and makes more than $1 million a year—before bonuses and stock options. That makes her feel pretty good about herself.

Carol, on the other hand, may base her self-esteem on her role as a mother. Seeing her children grow into kind, responsible people may be the primary reason she feels good about herself.

Nearly everyone asks themselves from time to time, *Am I the kind of parent/spouse/son/ daughter/sibling/employee/friend that I should be?*

The answers we give ourselves to those questions impact our self-esteem.

Everyone has self-esteem. Unfortunately, not everyone has positive self-esteem. You'll find out later in the chapter why that happens.

If we constantly question what we do and why we do it, assume that others can always complete tasks more successfully than we can, and convince ourselves that we're not the kind of person we should be, our self-esteem certainly will suffer.

If, on the other hand, we tell ourselves that we do okay, at least most of the time, and that we're good people, despite our shortcomings, we're bolstering our self-esteem.

## Different Measures of Self-Esteem

All of us use different measuring sticks to determine our self-esteem.

Becky, for example, may have very high self-esteem, even though she doesn't do anything out of the ordinary or receive any special recognition or praise. She's not particularly attractive, nor is she any sort of genius. She's just an ordinary person who feels good about herself and likes who she is and how she lives her life.

Mark, on the other hand, may have very low self-esteem, even though he's on every committee in town, is president of the school's parent-teacher association, holds down a good job, and is widely recognized and often honored for his community involvement. Mark's a great-looking guy and has more degrees than there's room on his office walls to display them.

Becky and Mark feel different about themselves because their measuring sticks are different. Why? Well, there are differences in opinion on that matter, but it's widely held that our self-esteem is influenced by biology, our environment, and how we choose to look at ourselves.

People's environments are a tremendous influence on their self-esteem—there's no question about it. Ask any teacher or counselor about the kids with low self-esteem they interact with, and they'll tell you about the kids' environments.

Children who are repeatedly told that they're no good, worthless, or stupid have an extremely difficult time establishing good self-esteem. Why wouldn't they? The people they care about the most are telling them they're no good. Of course that's very damaging to children's self-images.

On the other side of the coin, children who are doted on, pampered, and constantly getting their egos stroked sometimes suffer from a different kind of self-esteem problem. They may develop an unrealistically high level of self-esteem, only to find out later in life that they're not as great as they were told they were as children.

Regardless of our environments, however, we ultimately draw our own conclusions about who we are and what we're worth. We've all heard stories of people who overcame terrible circumstances and went on to achieve great things. Somehow those people managed to believe in themselves, and that belief allowed them to reach their goals.

Just as with many other aspects of personality, most psychologists agree that self-esteem is determined and affected by biological and environmental factors.

**Personality Pointer**

Many teachers today say that bolstering self-esteem in their students is one of the biggest challenges they face. Many students, especially those with parents who don't support and nurture them, suffer from low self-esteem. Increased attention was drawn to this problem after the April 1999 shootings at Columbine High School in Colorado.

**Notes and Quotes**

*American Psychologist* is a highly regarded monthly journal with many interesting articles pertaining to all aspects of psychology. You can see the table of contents for the most recent issues, as well as some selected articles, by accessing the journal from the American Psychological Association's Web site at http:// www. apa.org/journals/amp.html.

# Inherent or Developed?

The special January 2000 issue of *American Psychologist* also includes an article by David M. Buss called "The Evolution of Happiness."

Buss says that all humans have the capacity to experience psychological pain, depression, anxiety, fear, jealousy, and anger. That capacity, according to Buss, has been passed down through evolution; it's not something we learn. Experiencing such emotions gets in the way of our happiness. To improve the quality of our lives and achieve happiness, we need to overcome the negative effects of these emotions.

Most of us can do that to a certain extent. However, if, along with the capacity to experience pain, we also inherit the tendency to embrace it and wallow in it, we're likely to have a difficult time finding happiness and good self-esteem.

In this sense, our capacity for self-esteem is affected by evolution—that is, biology.

Our self-esteem is also affected by our environmental factors.

### Don't Go There!

Don't make the mistake of generalizing about the effects of environmental circumstances on self-esteem levels. If you know people with poor self-esteem, it's not necessarily because their environments are very bad. And don't assume that everyone with high self-esteem comes from a positive environment. This usually is the case, but not always, and it's dangerous to generalize.

Remember the discussion in Chapter 2, "You Are What You Believe," about the effects of our early environment on our core beliefs? These same early environment experiences play a big role in our self-esteem levels.

Children who are loved, supported, and encouraged to grow and try things on their own generally learn that they can succeed. They have the confidence to try new activities and tasks, and they develop the sense that they're worthwhile and valuable—good self-esteem.

Children who are abused, neglected, and told they're incapable of doing anything on their own generally grow up expecting to fail. Because they've been given the clear message that they're defective, incapable, and unlovable, they lack the confidence needed to take on new experiences and tasks. Since they don't gain the positive effects of succeeding at challenges, their self-esteem remains poor.

There are exceptions, of course. For the most part, however, these predictions of how environmental factors affect self-esteem hold pretty true.

# Making Sure We Foster Self-Esteem in Others

Another article from the same issue of *American Psychologist*, "Toward a Psychology of Positive Youth Development," addresses the issue of building self-esteem. Reed W. Larson, the author of the article, proposes that initiative is the "core quality of positive youth development."

Larson believes that initiative is related to autonomous action. He says " … initiative is the core requirement for other components of positive development, such as creativity, leadership, altruism, and civic engagement."

Larson feels that kids should regularly participate in structured activities that have links to businesses, civic organizations, and the arts.

By participating in these things, Larson says, kids will learn "an operating language for sustaining their own motivation and directing and monitoring their actions over time."

In other words, by getting involved in valuable activities and seeing how adults within these activities operate, kids tend to learn how to motivate themselves and keep themselves motivated. They learn the language of self-encouragement.

Participating in such activities both requires and builds self-esteem. Young people need a certain level of self-esteem to get started in a civic, business, or arts-related activity. Once they do, their self-esteem tends to improve.

Larson's idea for fostering self-esteem is a good one; it's no more important, however, than what parents do at home to foster self-esteem.

What we say and model to our kids greatly influences their opinions of themselves. We can foster self-esteem in adults, too, by how we treat them. Ask your child, your spouse, your parents, and your friends for their opinions on important topics. Let them know that they're important and valuable to you.

Show respect for all people and be encouraging. Help with problem-solving when possible, and listen when someone talks to you.

### Notes and Quotes

Jo Biehele, a teacher in Ashland, Kentucky, and the recipient of a widely recognized teacher achievement award, keeps a red recipe box in her fourth-grade classroom. In the box are ideas for short classroom exercises designed to help her students feel good about themselves and each other. She calls the exercises her recipes for self-esteem.

# How Some People Get Shortchanged

Did you ever know somebody who was just downright unpleasant to be around? Always grouchy, cool, sarcastic … you get the picture.

As unfair as it seems, that person may just have been born with that temperament. There's evidence that traits such as jealousy, anger, fear, and general unpleasantness are passed along genetically.

Other people are born with varying degrees of brain damage. Some are born addicted to drugs or with deformities, and some just seem to be "different" in a vague sort of way.

These kinds of biological circumstances certainly can cause people to be short-changed when it comes to self-esteem.

Some people get shortchanged, or perhaps shortchange themselves, for other reasons. There are people, and this seems to be especially true of adolescent girls, who feel defective because they don't match up to what happens to be in vogue. If their hair is curly, they want it to be straight. They're too tall, too short, too heavy, too skinny—it goes on and on.

Children whose parents constantly expect more from them than they're able to achieve often are just as at risk for low self-esteem as those whose parents tell them they're unable to do anything.

Sometimes a family member is adversely affected by the deficiencies, real or perceived, of other family members. A teenager, for instance, might feel ashamed or helpless to do anything about a parent's substance-abuse problem or a sibling's sexual orientation.

Self-esteem can be challenged in many ways, both biologically and environmentally.

## Making Sure You Get What You Deserve

Many people tend to focus on negative aspects of themselves. Often, these things aren't even that important; for one reason or another, they just become focal points. Consider these examples:

➤ Roger weighs 190 pounds. He saw a height-weight chart that said his ideal weight is 178 pounds. Ever since seeing the chart, Roger is convinced that he's an overweight, lazy slob.

➤ Richard's SAT scores were too low for him to get into the prestigious private school he'd applied to, so he attended a state-run university near his home instead. He graduated and is doing fine, but Roger's convinced that he ruined his life by not scoring high enough on the SATs. He views himself as stupid and inferior.

➤ Barbara was born with one leg slightly shorter than the other, and she has a very slight limp. Her friends tell her they don't even notice it, but she's sure everyone is always staring at her and talking about her because of it. Barbara feels that she's not "normal" and is somehow inferior because of her leg.

We could go on and on with such examples. Whenever we focus on something negative about ourselves, we put our self-esteem at risk. That's not to say that we don't need to address negative qualities and try to overcome them, but when we obsess on them, we're getting into dangerous territory.

Before you decide that you're bad, or helpless, or defective based on one negative aspect of yourself, take a look at the big picture.

Barbara has a slight limp, but she also has a great smile and a beautiful singing voice. She's smart, and she makes people laugh. So does the limp make her defective? Of course not.

Another trap we set for ourselves is comparing ourselves negatively to others. We're not as pretty, not as macho, not as smart. We don't cook as well, we're not as athletic. When people make such comparisons, they often get down on themselves, and their self-esteem suffers.

If you think your self-esteem isn't as high as it should be, take a look at your social behaviors and attitudes. We don't mean going-out-to-parties social behavior. We mean, do you let people walk all over you? Are you everyone's doormat? Maybe you don't ever make your wants and needs known. Or maybe you're super aggressive and people resent you for it.

Any of these or similar factors could be affecting your self-esteem. If you think it's possible, be aware that you can change such behaviors. You'll learn a lot more about how to do that in later chapters of this book, or you can get professional help if you feel it's necessary.

**Personality Pointer**

Check out a book called *Your Perfect Right: A Guide to Assertive Living,* by Robert E. Alberti and Michael L. Emmons. It's full of good stuff.

**Notes and Quotes**

Stephen Hawking has Lou Gehrig's disease and is confined to a wheelchair. He can do little to take care of himself and can only communicate by tapping on a computer keyboard and using a voice synthesizer. Some people might question the worth of such a person, or the person may question his own worth. Just to set the record straight, Hawking is a genius in physics and was appointed Lucasian Professor of Mathematics at Cambridge—a position once held by Sir Isaac Newton. Despite his physical challenges, Hawking's outlook is positive. He once said, "My body may be confined to this chair. But with the Internet my mind can go to the ends of the earth."

# Everyone Has the Right to Say No

Some people—lots of people—have trouble saying no. They take on work and responsibilities they can't handle. They get overstressed because they try to take care of all of everyone's needs. They say yes to sex when they don't really want to. Or drugs. They go places and do things that aren't safe.

In these types of situations, people may feel they don't have the right to say no. That is rarely the case.

When people can't say no, it can result in a variety of problems, all of which mean trouble for their self-esteem.

Saying no isn't just okay, it's a right that every person has. Saying no is sometimes necessary to protect your own safety and health, and is absolutely crucial if you want to have honest and open relationships with others.

Don't feel that you need to offer excuses or a lengthy explanation when someone asks you to do something you'd rather not do. You can give the reason if you want to, or you can simply say, "Sorry, I won't be able to." You're perfectly within your rights to do so.

# Determining Your Self-Esteem Level

You probably have a pretty good idea of whether your self-esteem is high, low, or somewhere in the middle. Just in case you don't, you can find out all about it on the Web.

Here are a few of the many Web sites you can visit to find self-esteem quizzes and information. Go ahead and answer the questions and have fun, but remember, don't take these Internet tests too seriously. Many of them have questionable reliability and validity.

➤ www.psychtests.com/selftest.html

➤ www.wellnessnet.com

➤ www.mindlift.com

➤ http://members.tripos.com/Nadabs/self-esteem-test.htm

# Check Yourself Out

Here are several questions to help you reflect on what you've read in this chapter, and perhaps to take the information a step or two farther in your own mind:

➤ How do I measure my self-esteem?

➤ When I have a problem, do I feel like I can handle it?

➤ To what degree am I satisfied with what I've done and achieved in the past and hopeful about my future? Do I experience happiness in the present?

➤ How much do I interact with and feel connected to the people around me?

➤ Do I believe I have the right to say no?

You might benefit from discussing these questions with another person, or just thinking about them on your own.

---

### The Least You Need to Know

➤ Self-esteem is the measure we use when we assess ourselves.

➤ Your level of self-esteem affects your personality, your beliefs, and nearly everything you do.

➤ Both biological and environmental factors contribute to your self-esteem.

➤ Treating people fairly and with respect can help bolster their self-esteem.

➤ Some people get shortchanged on self-esteem due to biological or environmental factors.

➤ If you think your self-esteem isn't as good as it should be, ask yourself if there are certain behaviors or habits you exhibit that may be affecting how you feel about yourself and how others treat you.

➤ Saying no asserts your independence and boosts your self-esteem.

---

# States of Being

Up until now, we've been talking about relatively enduring aspects of personality. Core beliefs. Personality traits. Schemas. All of these are things we're either born with or we develop early in our lives. They're part of who we are and pretty much remain with us until we die.

In this chapter we talk about something different: temporary conditions. Depression. Anxiety. Panic. Stress. Fatigue. Although conditions like depression and anxiety can last for years (and to people suffering from it, it may feel like it's permanent), states are usually of relatively short duration. They are not considered to be enduring phases of personality.

By the end of the chapter, the difference between enduring traits and temporary *states* will be clear to you.

## Temporary Conditions

Traits—the subject of Chapter 10, "Personality Traits"—are enduring. As you just read, states are temporary conditions. When we talk about a state, we're mostly referring to moods and mood disorders—stress and fatigue, things that come and go, or perhaps occur only once.

A point to remember is that, while states (or moods) are temporary, someone can be born with the trait of moodiness, which is permanent. It's a tricky distinction.

We say that Amy is suffering from depression. She's in a state of depression. The state is affecting her personality and her mood, but she's getting counseling and the state seems to be improving.

**Personality Parlance**

A **state** is a temporary condition of the personality, as opposed to an enduring phase of personality. A state is similar to a mood.

Andy, on the other hand, was born moody. You just never know how Andy will react to a situation, and it can be pretty uncomfortable to be around him. Still, everybody knows that's how Andy is. He was born moody, and unless something spectacular happens, he will die moody. Moodiness for Andy is part of who he is. Andy's moodiness isn't a state or a mood; it's a trait.

States interfere with a person's normal traits or disposition. They alter the mood of the person who's suffering from them.

In addition to depression, some common states are anxiety, panic, adjustment disorder, stress, and fatigue.

# Where Do They Come From?

As with the enduring phases of personality, states are thought to be caused by several contributing factors, both biological and environmental.

Biological contributors include …

➤ Chemical imbalances in the brain.

➤ Genetics. There definitely is a genetic connection to moods; we know that states such as depression tend to run in families.

➤ Hormones. Conditions such as hypothyroidism can be a contributing factor to a state such as depression.

➤ Medications.

Environmental factors include …

➤ Poor diet.

➤ Being stuck in bad circumstances.

➤ Lack of exercise.

➤ Isolation.

A belief component can also contribute to states. If Kate fails an important test, for instance, she may feel very down and upset. She believes that she let herself, and perhaps others, down by failing the test. She fell short of the expectations she has for herself, and she's convinced that this failure will affect the rest of her life.

Kate's belief about her situation or circumstances could contribute to a state of depression. It wouldn't necessarily do so, but if there were other contributing factors, such as changes in brain chemistry or hormonal factors, it could.

There's no formula, no set combination of factors that can explain the onset, development, or duration of a particular state. It's very difficult to establish a cause-and-effect relationship between an occurrence and a state, even though a state often occurs when a chemical change is coupled with a disruptive or distressing event. While we know that many people who suffer from depression have an imbalance in brain chemistry, we don't definitively know that the imbalance *causes* the depression.

While the answer to "What causes states?" isn't perfectly clear, it's generally thought that several factors come together to cause the temporary condition. Ongoing research, we hope, will give us more definitive answers in the future.

# Living in an Altered State

Living with a condition such as depression or anxiety can be devastating. If the state lasts a long time, those affected may feel as though they will never be normal again. People in such a state may feel guilty for disrupting the lives of family members or for missing work. States affect millions of people each year and cost millions of dollars in medical and lost work expenses.

While states normally are of fairly short duration, they're not to be taken lightly. Psychologists treat states very seriously. If you think you may be suffering from a state such as depression or anxiety (two of the most common), you should see a professional for diagnosis.

When a state or mood is diagnosed, it's referred to as an *Axis I disorder*. Axis I is the first of a five-tiered

**Personality Pointer**

Our tendencies toward states are somewhat dependent on our overall enduring personality. People who are very stable (traits) are less likely to be thrown into a state (like depression) when something upsetting occurs. People who are fragile personalities are more likely to experience a state.

**Don't Go There!**

While there are many excellent sources of information available on states such as anxiety and depression, if you suspect that you may be suffering from a state, don't try to diagnose or treat it yourself. Seek professional help.

**161**

diagnostic tool, which you can read more about in Chapter 24, "Rewriting History." For now, here's a summary of the axis levels:

➤ **Axis I.** Lists the presenting problem or chief complaint, including mood disorders.

➤ **Axis II.** Lists personality disorders (refer to Chapter 24 for a full discussion).

➤ **Axis III.** Lists any type of relevant medical conditions.

➤ **Axis IV.** Lists social stressors, such as early childhood abuse, job loss, divorce, and so forth.

➤ **Axis V.** Gives a numerical rating between 0 and 100 of how well a person is functioning. This is called the *Global Assessment of Functioning* (GAF).

It's important to know that most states can be successfully treated; if you think you're suffering from one, don't lose hope.

Descriptions and symptoms of some of the most common states follow.

## Depression

Depression is a psychological condition that changes how you think and feel, and also affects your social behavior and your sense of physical well-being.

Depression is not "the blues," or a day or two of feeling sad. It's normal to feel tired or sad or worried in response to major stress, when someone dies, or when you're faced with a serious problem. These feelings normally last for a few days, or maybe a few weeks, and could be considered a state, but then they pass. If they persist, get worse, and start to interfere with your life, you should see a psychologist for diagnosis.

Symptoms of depression include …

➤ A persistently depressed, sad, anxious, or empty mood.

➤ Feeling worthless, helpless, or experiencing excessive or inappropriate guilt.

➤ Hopelessness about the future and excessively pessimistic feelings.

➤ A loss of interest and pleasure in usual activities.

➤ Decreased energy and chronic fatigue.

➤ Loss of memory, difficulty in making decisions, or an inability to concentrate.

➤ Irritability, restlessness, or agitation.

**Notes and Quotes**

More than 17 million people in the United States experience depression each year. Almost everyone is affected by depression at some time during his or her life—either directly by experiencing it, or indirectly by having a family member or close friend experience it.

➤ Sleep disturbances—difficulty in sleeping or sleeping too much.

➤ A loss of appetite and diminished interest in food, or overeating and weight gain.

➤ Recurring thoughts of death, or suicidal thoughts or actions.

Some people experience many symptoms, while others have just a few. Some symptoms could be severe while others may be mild.

## Anxiety

Everyone feels nervous, anxious, and scared sometimes for various reasons. If you have to make a speech, sing in public, or tell your spouse you want a divorce, you're likely to experience anxiety, big time.

Anxiety disorders cause people to feel scared, uneasy, and distressed. If not treated, an anxiety disorder can be very disruptive and cause all sorts of problems in a person's life.

Some of the common symptoms of different anxiety disorders include ...

➤ A need to constantly check and recheck actions.

➤ Constant and unrealistic worry about everyday occurrences and activities.

➤ Fear and anxiety that occur for no apparent reason.

Like depression, anxiety disorders can be treated quite successfully.

**Personality Pointer**

Anxiety disorders are the most common mental illnesses in America. More than 19 million people are treated for them each year.

## Panic Disorder

Panic disorder usually appears during the teens or in early adulthood. The exact cause of this state is unknown. Panic attacks can occur "out of the blue," but there also can be a link between panic attacks and major life events or transitions. The onset sometimes occurs when a person graduates from college, gets married, has a child, and so forth.

Those with panic disorder suffer from panic attacks—intense and sudden feelings of fear. These attacks come on with no apparent reason and can be extremely frightening and distressing.

Some symptoms of a panic attack include …

➤ A racing heartbeat.

➤ Difficulty in breathing, or feeling unable to get enough air.

➤ Intense terror.

➤ Dizziness, lightheadedness, or nausea.

➤ Trembling, sweating, or shaking.

➤ Choking, chest pains, hot flashes, or sudden chills.

➤ Tingling in fingers or toes.

➤ Fear of going crazy or of imminent death.

**Personality Pointer**

About one in every 75 people experience panic disorder.

Panic attacks can happen in perfectly normal, harmless situations. They sometimes even occur during sleep.

A panic attack is not dangerous in itself, but it's extremely disturbing and frightening, and it sometimes leads to other problems, such as phobias, depression, or substance abuse.

## Adjustment Disorder

Adjustment disorder occurs in response to an identifiable stressor. The symptoms, which may be emotional, behavioral, or both, occur within three months of the stressful event.

Adjustment disorder is interesting because it's so varied. One person's adjustment disorder can be triggered by nothing more than a friend moving out of town. Or it can be triggered in the residents of an entire region by a tornado, an earthquake, a major fire, or a similar disaster. Groups can also experience adjustment disorder after their company suddenly closes down, for example.

Even a continuous situation, such as caring for a disruptive child or being abused by a spouse, can trigger an adjustment disorder. So can a particular time of year, such as Christmas.

Other stressors could include getting married, retiring, having a child, being on strike, economic depression, war, famine, and illness.

Some symptoms of adjustment disorder include …

➤ Feeling sad or anxious.

➤ Regularly acting out of the ordinary without understanding why. This could include acts such as fighting, reckless driving, truancy, and vandalism.

➤ Sleep disruptions.

➤ Sexual difficulties.

### Don't Go There!

Don't ever avoid getting professional help if you need it because you're afraid doing so will be seen by others as a weakness. While there used to be something of a stigma associated with conditions such as depression and anxiety disorders, increased education has made people more aware and understanding of these and other states. Avoiding help out of pride won't solve your problem, and you're likely to end up in greater distress than is necessary.

The symptoms of anxiety disorder are generally far in excess of what you'd expect a normal reaction to a stressful event to be. They sometimes cause difficulty in social situations or work situations.

The states we've outlined are not the only ones, but they're some of the most common. Most are treatable with counseling, medication, or a combination of both.

# Working with the Hand Life Deals Us

For the most part, we have little or no control over our biological circumstances. We don't have a say in our genetic makeup, and we can't control—not without help, anyway—our brain chemistry or our hormones.

In addition, as kids, we had little control over our environments. We didn't get to choose the homes we grew up in or the families that raised us.

We do, however, contribute to our *schemas* (remember schemas from Chapter 11, "Schemas and So Forth?"), and we do have the opportunity to evaluate our beliefs, emotions, and values—and change them if we really want to.

You can learn much more about changing behavior and personality in Part 6, "Personality and Change," so for now, suffice it to say that by changing your thoughts and beliefs, it's possible to change your emotions and behaviors.

As mentioned earlier, moods are one example of a state. Traits are a part of one's overall personality.

### Personality Pointer

Changing your mood is a lot easier than changing your personality. Changing your mood, which is a temporary condition, requires developing different thoughts and assumptions, but changing your personality, which is more enduring and fixed, involves the altering of *core beliefs*.

For now, let's focus on mood changes, not personality changes. You can accomplish mood changes by developing alternative thoughts and assumptions.

To change your *automatic thoughts* and *assumptions,* you have to retrain them. It's sort of like being a tennis player who's developed a very bad habit with his backhand and has to be completely retrained to do the stroke properly.

Let's use Dorothy as an example. Dorothy has just broken up with her long-time boyfriend, Donald, and she's pretty depressed about it. Dorothy's automatic thought about this is, "This is awful. I can't make it without him. I don't know what to do."

A psychologist who's working with Dorothy to change her automatic thoughts and assumptions will ask Dorothy to re-evaluate those thoughts. The psychologist will help her to do so by asking her questions such as these:

➤ Has your relationship with Donald always been perfect?

➤ How did you get along in life before you and Donald were together?

➤ Were you happy every minute of your life while in your relationship with Donald?

➤ Did the relationship foster your personal growth?

These questions help Dorothy evaluate the actual strength of her relationship with Donald. By doing so, she may find out that life with Donald wasn't as great as she thought. It wasn't perfect bliss. Yes, now that she thinks about it, she did have a life before Donald, and quite a nice life at that.

The psychologist then might ask, "Is it literally true that you can't make it without Donald?"

**Personality Parlance**

A **schema** is the cognitive structure containing memories, emotions associated with memories, and core beliefs. **Core Beliefs** are basic concepts people have about "the way things are" with themselves, others, and the world. **Assumptions/Rules/Attitudes** are intermediate beliefs that affect the way people view certain situations which in turn affects the way they think, feel, and act. **Automatic Thoughts** are situation-specific reactions that affect emotions.

Hopefully, Dorothy now realizes that she can indeed make it without Donald. If she believes she can, it's possible for her to develop a new automatic thought concerning the situation. Her revised automatic thought might be something like this: *While it's true that I really relied on Donald and I'll miss him a lot, the fact is that I know I can get along without him. So, even if it's difficult, I know I'll survive this and eventually get along okay.*

If Dorothy is able to make that transition from *I can't do it, I can't make it* to *It will be hard, but I'll be okay,* her level of depression and anxiety will decrease, and her level of self-efficacy will improve dramatically. (Refer to Chapter 12, "The All-Important Self-Esteem Factor," for more on self-efficacy.)

Dorothy will still experience sadness about the loss of the relationship, but not to the degree that it will be emotionally crippling.

Rich is an example of how a person suffering from anxiety might change his automatic thoughts and assumptions.

Rich has been named valedictorian of his college class and will have to make a speech at his commencement ceremony in front of thousands and thousands of people. His automatic thought upon learning that he'll have to give the speech is, *I can't do that, I'll mess up.* His resulting emotions are panic and worry. He fantasizes about not showing up. Maybe he'll get sick and won't be able to attend; he may even get the physical symptoms of an illness. Maybe he'll have a car accident.

After working hard to modify his automatic thoughts, however, Rich replaces his original thought with a different one. He now thinks, *I know this will be difficult, but I've worked hard and I'm prepared to do it.*

Rich's new emotion is nervousness, as compared to panic and worry. His new behavior, however, is to fantasize about success. He imagines himself giving the best speech he's ever given. Upon changing his thought and behavior, his self-efficacy improves dramatically, and his chances for success increase.

Changing your mood isn't always easy. Sometimes you can't just "snap out of it"; it requires help and work on your part. It can be done, though. Knowing that should make the concept of moods, and states, a little less daunting.

# The Mind-Body Connection

The special edition of *American Psychologist* you read about in Chapter 12 also carried an interesting article about the connection between emotional and physical health. The article, "Emotional States and Physical Health," by Peter Salovey, Jerusha B. Detweiler, and Wayne T. Steward, all of Yale University, and Alexander J. Rothman of the University of Minnesota, reviews some of the literature on the topic and presents these findings:

➤ Depressed individuals report ailments more frequently than is normal.

➤ Depressed people think they're less healthy than those who aren't depressed, whether or not they really are.

➤ When psychological services are available through a health plan, patients' need for and use of medical services is reduced.

➤ The onset of a physical illness that interferes with pleasurable daily activities can result in a depressed mood.

➤ Negative emotional states are thought to be associated with unhealthy lifestyles, while positive emotional states are thought to be associated with healthier lifestyles.

➤ Negative moods increase a person's susceptibility to illness.

➤ The use of humor as a coping style is thought to increase levels of antibodies that fight the common cold.

➤ The more that older women cry as a coping method, the more health problems they report.

➤ People who are made to feel sad report more physical symptoms than those who are made to feel happy.

➤ Using humor, having a sense of self-efficacy, and having a social support network all are indicators for better physical health.

➤ Getting into a better mood is likely to help people avoid ill health or to improve their health.

➤ One way to improve an emotional state is through *downward social comparison,* or comparing yourself to someone who's worse off than you are.

➤ Exercise increases positive feelings and decreases negative ones.

➤ About 35 percent of patients report relief of symptoms when given a placebo.

➤ A positive mood results from the renewal of hope and can impact positively on physical health.

While these findings probably don't come as a great surprise, it's interesting to see them compiled into a single article.

You've no doubt had experiences in which your physical and emotional states were tied together. How many times have you developed a pounding headache after trying to finish a project you took home from work while your kids just wouldn't leave you alone? Or when it's two days before a major holiday and you've yet to start your shopping and decorating?

Psychological states take their toll physically—there's no doubt about it. Nor is there any doubt, as we assured you earlier, that most states are treatable.

# Check Yourself Out

Here are several questions to help you reflect on what you've read in this chapter, and perhaps to take the information a step or two farther in your own mind:

➤ How often do I experience extreme emotional states?

➤ Am I more prone to feeling depressed or anxious?

➤ What stressful events did I experience recently?

➤ What was the first thought I had about myself in the stressful situation?

➤ Has my physical health been affected by my emotional states?

You might benefit from discussing these questions with another person, or just thinking about them on your own.

---

### The Least You Need to Know

➤ States are different from enduring traits because they're temporary and cause changes to the overall personality.

➤ Temporary states can be debilitating and distressing, but they usually can be treated successfully.

➤ Some of the most common states are depression, anxiety, panic disorder, adjustment disorder, fatigue, and stress.

➤ There are some things we can't change, such as our biology and early environment, but we can work on changing our beliefs, thoughts, and assumptions.

➤ Psychological health and physical health are closely related.

---

# Part 4

# Personality Disorders

*Part 4 explores the fascinating topic of personality disorders. There are many kinds of disorders, and all can be extremely disruptive and distressing to the lives of those who suffer from them, as well as the people who love them.*

*The Diagnostical and Statistical Manual, considered to be the definitive guide to personality disorders, describes disorders like this:*

> *A personality disorder is an enduring pattern of inner experience and behavior that deviates markedly from the expectations of the individual's culture, is pervasive and inflexible, has an onset in adolescent or early adulthood, is stable over time, and leads to distress or impairment.*

*There are 10 recognized personality disorders, which are grouped into three clusters.*

*Cluster A includes the eccentric behaviors: paranoid, schizoid, and schizotypal personality disorders.*

*Cluster B includes the dramatic behaviors: antisocial, borderline, histrionic, and narcissistic personality disorders.*

*Cluster C includes the fearful behaviors: avoidant, dependent, and obsessive-compulsive personality disorders.*

*In this part, we also look at the symptoms, schemas, and treatments for each of these disorders.*

# Chapter 14

# Eccentric
# Behaviors

---

### In This Chapter

➤ Understanding the different meanings of "eccentric"

➤ Learning the difference between eccentric behaviors and eccentric people

➤ Exploring the paranoid personality disorder

➤ Looking at the schizoid personality disorder

➤ Working with someone who is schizotypal

---

It's not uncommon to refer to someone as "eccentric." We tend to use the word to describe people such as the elderly woman who comes to church wearing the same fur wrap and feathered hat that she did in the 1940s. Or the man who, despite the weather, rides around town on an old, yellow bicycle, his pet dog stashed in the basket on the handlebars.

We sometimes think of artists, writers, and musicians as being eccentric—Ernest Hemingway, Dorothy Parker, Vincent Van Gogh, and Michael Jackson come to mind.

The word "eccentric" comes from the Greek *eccentros,* which means "out of the center." The word has meanings relevant to astronomy, geometry, forestry, and machinery. It also is relevant to the discipline of psychology.

In psychology, *eccentric* describes a cluster of personality disorders:

➤ Paranoid

➤ Schizoid

➤ Schizotypal

In this chapter, we look at these personality disorders and talk about just what they are, how they manifest themselves, and what help or treatments might be available for them.

# Recognizing Eccentric Behavior

The woman in the 1940s-era fur and hat or the man on the yellow bicycle may be described as eccentric, but in the psychological sense, they may or may not be.

People with eccentric behaviors (in the clinical sense) very often act or appear odd. Just because they act odd, however, doesn't mean they're eccentric in the clinical sense.

### Don't Go There!

It's tempting to diagnose others or ourselves, but it can be a dangerous practice. It takes a lot of training to assess and diagnose a personality disorder, so it can only be done properly by a professional. By attempting to do so yourself, you could be delaying someone's treatment and jeopardizing their well-being.

The man on the yellow bicycle *could* be suffering from a personality disorder. Or he might just enjoy taking his dog for bicycle rides. Who knows? Maybe he rides the bike to keep in shape, or he enjoys being out in the fresh air, or he has a physical condition that keeps him from driving a car and forces him to bike instead.

The woman in the old fur coat and hat also *could* have a personality disorder. Or she may dress oddly for another reason. Maybe her husband gave her the fur coat and hat and died shortly afterward, making them his last gift to her. If so, she may wear them for sentimental reasons. Maybe she's poor and unable to buy a new coat, so she wears the old fur for warmth.

The point is that you can't just look at people, or be around them for a short time, and conclude that they're paranoid or schizotypal. You may correctly assess that there's something atypical or abnormal about certain people, but unless they're professionally evaluated, it's very difficult to determine what the problem might be.

# Paranoid Personality Disorder

"Paranoid" is another word we tend to use rather loosely. "Don't be so paranoid," we'll tell someone who's worrying about losing a job. Or we might say, "I'm really paranoid about why I was invited to that party tomorrow night." Unless we're psychologists, we tend to use the term "paranoid" when "worried" or "suspicious" is what we mean.

In psychological terms, *paranoid* has a different and highly specific meaning: A person with paranoid personality disorder will be worried and suspicious, but in an entirely different sense.

What we say about the personality disorders we look at in this and other chapters is based on descriptions of the disorders in several highly regarded and widely consulted books:

➤ *The Diagnostic and Statistical Manual of Mental Disorders,* Fourth Edition (DSM-IV), the American Psychiatric Association,1994.

➤ *Disorders of Personality: DSM III,* by Theordore Millon John Wiley & Sons, 1981.

➤ *Cognitive Therapy of Personality Disorders,* by Aaron T. Beck and Arthur Freeman, Guilford Press, 1990.

➤ *Cognitive Therapy for Personality Disorders: A Schema-Focused Approach*, Third Edition, by Jeffrey E. Young, Ph.D., Professional Resource Exchange, 1999.

## What Is Paranoid Behavior?

People with paranoid personality disorder, as described in the DSM-IV, suffer from a "pervasive distrust and suspiciousness of others." They tend to think that the motives of people they encounter are hostile and malevolent. *Paranoia,* which usually begins by early adulthood, is suspiciousness or mistrust that's not based on facts. If there is a cause for suspiciousness or mistrust, a paranoid person may greatly overreact.

People with paranoid personality disorder normally have four or more of the following characteristics, as listed in the DSM-IV. They ...

➤ Suspect, without sufficient basis, that others are exploiting, harming, or deceiving them.

➤ Are preoccupied with unjustified doubts about the loyalty or trustworthiness of friends or associates.

➤ Are reluctant to confide in others because of unwarranted fear that the information will be used maliciously against them.

➤ Read hidden demeaning or threatening meanings into benign remarks or events.

➤ Persistently bear grudges and are unforgiving of insults, injuries, or slights.

➤ Perceive attacks on their character or reputation that are not apparent to others, and they are quick to react angrily or to counterattack.

➤ Have recurrent suspicions, without justification, regarding the fidelity of a spouse or sexual partner.

**Personality Parlance**

**Paranoia** is suspiciousness or mistrust that's either highly exaggerated or completely unfounded and unwarranted. It's not based on any facts that would support it.

There's a big difference between paranoia and justified suspicion. (And, as former secretary of state Henry Kissinger once said, "Even paranoids have enemies.") Let's look at an example of each so that you can see the difference.

Mary suspects that her husband, Sam, is having an affair. He's been staying out later and later at night, claiming that he has to work. Prior to a couple of months ago, however, Sam never had to work past 5:30 or 6:00 P.M.

On the nights that Sam is home, he no longer reads or watches television or just sits and talks with Mary. Instead, he goes to bed early with a book. She's entered the room unexpectedly a few times, only to have him quickly hang up the telephone.

The most tangible reason for her suspicions is a charge for $109 at the Boulevard Café that showed up on Sam's VISA bill. Mary happened to notice the bill on Sam's desk and checked the calendar. Sure enough, the charge was made on one of those nights Sam said he was working late.

Mary's extremely upset and worried. She can't sleep at night and wakes up wondering if Sam is going to leave her. She looks at everything he says and does with suspicion, wondering if he's lying or telling the truth.

**Personality Pointer**

Statistics show that between 0.5 percent and 2.5 percent of the general U.S. population suffers from paranoid personality disorder.

Sheila also suspects that her husband, Bill, may be having an affair. In fact, she's pretty sure of it. Bill comes home from work at the same time he always has and stays home most evenings. Sometimes, though, he runs an errand or two. Sheila's very suspicious of those trips, even though Bill is usually only gone for half an hour or so and comes back with the items he went out to get.

Sheila is convinced that Bill buys the items on his lunch hour, stashes them in the car, and then goes out to meet somebody when he says he's running an errand. She's checked his car a few times, looking for packages that he'd hidden there, but has found nothing.

Bill also plays tennis with some buddies once a week at a local club. Sheila hates that time when he's gone. She's convinced that Bill's really meeting his girlfriend somewhere. Bill has repeatedly invited Sheila to go along and watch him play, and she declines, but she drives through the club's parking lot during his scheduled playing time, just to be sure his car is there. And twice she sneaked in and watched him play for a couple of minutes.

Sheila tells Bill that he's acting differently toward her, even though she can't really pinpoint how. She's sure that he's not as warm or thoughtful as he had been before he started his affair. Sheila is angry at Bill for betraying her and makes his life miserable every chance she gets.

So who's paranoid and who isn't? The answer's fairly obvious. Mary and Sheila are both suspicious of their husbands, but Mary's suspicions are based on facts, while Sheila's aren't. Sheila thinks that Bill's having an affair even though there's absolutely no evidence supporting her belief. His habits haven't changed, he invites her to come with him when he goes out, and his behavior toward her is the same.

Sam, on the other hand, actually is acting and behaving differently. Mary also saw the charge for the dinner on a night Sam claimed to be working. She has facts to base her suspicions on.

As you can imagine, people with paranoid personality disorder can be extremely difficult to get along with. Relationship problems are very common.

Paranoids may be very argumentative, complaining, or aloof. They may act secretive, devious, or cold toward others. Some keep constant vigil, and they can act hostile or sarcastic.

Most people with paranoid personality disorder are rather self-sufficient and have a strong sense of autonomy. They need a high degree of control, and they are rigid and critical of others. They generally have a difficult time accepting criticism and are quick to blame others. They can be litigious or have grandiose fantasies of power and rank.

Paranoids often use negative stereotypes of others, such as those of other races or cultures. They're often seen as fanatics, sometimes as belonging to way-out religious cults, survivalist groups, and the like.

## The Paranoia Schema

People with paranoid personality disorder—or any kind of personality disorder, for that matter—generally have predictable schemas, or processes they use to assimilate information and experiences. (Refer to Chapter 11, "Schemas and So Forth.")

Paranoids, and those with other personality disorders, have some characteristics that are overdeveloped and some that are underdeveloped.

With paranoid personality disorder, the overdeveloped characteristics are vigilance, mistrust, and suspiciousness. The underdeveloped characteristics are serenity, trust, and acceptance.

Here are some observations about the schemas of people with paranoid personality disorder:

➤ They believe all other people are potential adversaries.

➤ Their strategy is one of wariness.

➤ Their view of themselves is righteous.

**Personality Pointer**

Nearly everyone has personality characteristics that are developed to a greater extent than others. The overdevelopment and underdevelopment, however, are far more pronounced in people with personality disorders.

➤ They view others as being interfering, discriminatory, abusive, and malicious toward them.

➤ Their main belief is that the motives of others are suspect. They need to be on guard at all times, looking for hidden motives.

➤ They are accusatory and make counterattacks against those whose motives they distrust.

The early environments of people suffering from paranoid personality disorder aren't well-known. In large part, this is due to the questionable reliability of the paranoid person supplying the information.

Hypothetically, at least, it fits that paranoid people were brought up in truly dangerous or hostile environments, with lots of ridicule, lying, and deceit.

## Getting Help for Paranoid Personality Disorder

Working in therapy with a paranoid person is not an easy task.

Fortunately, therapists sometimes can help people with paranoid personality disorder by getting them to understand that their vigilance isn't balanced and, along with other aspects of their behavior, produces side effects.

The vigilance of paranoids tends to be very one-sided. They watch very closely for what they perceive to be suspect motives. They need these motives to support their belief that the person they're watching can't be trusted. Paranoid people won't, however, watch for behavior that indicates the person *can* be trusted.

A paranoid person overreacts to small slights from others and is very quick to counterattack.

**Personality Pointer**

If a therapist can't earn or loses the trust of a paranoid person, treatment becomes extremely difficult, and the chances for success are limited. This is one of the major problems with treating paranoia.

If Lisa's boss reminds her that her report is late, for instance, Lisa may perceive the reminder to be ridicule because she didn't finish her work, or badgering from a boss who doesn't like her.

Lisa may come back at her boss, claiming that the lateness of the report is his fault for giving her too much work to do, or accusing him of picking on her or treating her unfairly.

By acting this way, Lisa puts off her boss and others, and discourages them from trying to be nice to her. When people aren't nice to Lisa, it supports her beliefs that they don't like her or are out to get her.

If those who are paranoid are able to understand that process, altering their thinking and behavior may be possible.

Therapists also address and try to improve the coping skills of paranoid patients and their ability to realistically perceive others.

# Schizoid Personality Disorder

As you know, there are all kinds of people with all kinds of personalities. Some people tend to be excitable, while others are mellow. Some people have a lot of energy, while others move more slowly and do less. Some are loving, sharing, warm people, while others are selfish and cold.

People with schizoid personality disorder, however, are very different. They're not like most people, in that their personality traits are subdued and flat. They sometimes seem to be almost without personality.

## What Is Schizoid Behavior?

According to the DSM-IV, someone with *schizoid personality disorder* suffers from "a pervasive pattern of detachment from social relationships, and a restricted range of expressions of emotion in interpersonal settings."

People with schizoid personality disorder normally have four or more of the following characteristics, as listed in the DSM-IV. These people …

➤ Neither desire nor enjoy close relationships, including being part of a family.

➤ Almost always choose solitary activities.

➤ Have little, if any, interest in having sexual experiences with another person.

➤ Take pleasure in few, if any, activities.

➤ Lack close friends or confidants other than first-degree relatives.

➤ Appear indifferent to the praise or criticism of others.

➤ Show emotional coldness, detachment, or flattened affectivity (a person's emotional responses).

**Personality Parlance**

**Schizoid personality disorder** is a strong and constant pattern of detachment from social relationships. A schizoid person has great difficulty in interpersonal relationships, caused by the inability to effectively experience and express emotions.

People with schizoid personality disorder have difficulty expressing anger, even in response to provocation. They seem to lack emotion on all levels. They react passively to adverse circumstances, sometimes even showing no emotion when a family member dies or when witnessing an accident.

Schizoid people have difficulty responding to life events, so they tend to avoid them. They date infrequently, if at all, and often remain unmarried.

They're likely to experience job problems if interpersonal communication is required, but they may do okay in jobs that are fairly isolated. People with schizoid personality disorder may seek out and do all right in a warehouse job, or as a computer operator or programmer, or a forest ranger. They see themselves as loners.

Schizoid people rarely seek treatment for the condition because they don't feel there's anything wrong. They don't suffer distress because of their condition—they simply seem not to care about it, or much of anything else.

**Notes and Quotes**

We know that schizoid personality disorder is uncommon, but we have no way of knowing how many people actually have it. That's because it's very unusual for someone who is schizoid to seek treatment, and we don't get an indication of the frequency of the condition.

**Notes and Quotes**

In 1981, Theodore Millon described those with schizoid personality disorder as having "defective perceptual scanning." That means they lack the ability to pick up the details of life.

## The Schizoid Schema

As with people who are paranoid, those with schizoid personality disorder tend to have predictable schemas and characteristics.

A schizoid person has the overdeveloped characteristics of autonomy and isolation, and the underdeveloped ones of intimacy and reciprocity.

Here are some observations about the schemas of people with schizoid personality disorder:

➤ They believe they need plenty of space.

➤ Their strategy is to achieve isolation.

➤ They view themselves as being self-sufficient or a loner.

➤ They view others as being intrusive.

➤ They believe relationships with other people are unrewarding, messy, and unpleasant.

➤ Their main strategy is to stay away from others.

➤ Schizoids look at themselves as observers rather than participants. They're seen by others as dull and uninteresting. They tend not to contribute to what's happening around them, and often are ignored.

Schizoids miss the subtle details of life. According to Theodore Millon, they don't pick up the details that other people do; because of that, they never get the cues that produce emotional responses. As a result, they show very little emotion. Schizoids are lethargic, with unexpressive movement, poor social skills, and slow speech.

The poor social skills of those with schizoid personality disorder predisposes them to fail, which makes it even more likely that they'll withdraw even further.

Millon suggested that there are biological explanations for schizoid behavior. He thought there could be autonomic hyperactivity, which means that there's so much inward activity that outward activity is extraneous and unnecessary.

Another explanation, according to Millon, is a deficit in the *reticular formation*. The reticular formation is the system that gets you up and moving. If it's not working properly, sluggishness and excessive slowness could result.

People with schizoid personality disorder formulate schemas of social isolation and alienation early on. They stay on the outside of group activities and stay away from people. They tend to disapprove of others' beliefs, behaviors, and values.

**Personality Pointer**

If the autonomic hyperactivity theory sounds familiar, it's because you read something similar as related to introverts and extroverts. It's been theorized that introverts have more going on inside of them, so they seek less exterior stimulation.

## Getting Help for a Schizoid Person

As we pointed out earlier in this chapter, people with schizoid personality disorder don't tend to recognize their condition or seek help for it.

It's possible that someone with the condition would look for help with a mood disorder, such as depression, at which time the schizoid condition could also be diagnosed and addressed. In general, however, schizoids are not motivated to change their personalities.

**Don't Go There!**

If you know someone who you suspect has schizoid personality disorder and you try to help, be careful. You're likely to be seen by the person as irritating and intrusive. Remember that one of the goals of a schizoid person is to avoid relationships and personal interaction. Unless the person's behavior is putting him or her—or someone else—at risk, it's probably better not to intervene.

If schizoid people would seek treatment, therapists could try to reduce their level of isolation. It's difficult to do that, however, because the typical automatic thought of people with the disorder is that they'd rather do it alone. Or they may think, *I have no motivation, so why should I bother to change? Nobody cares, anyway.*

Doctors also could help people with schizoid personality disorder to develop the ability to empathize with others, and to consider what others may be thinking. Doctors would probably offer social skills training and encourage patients to look for and attend to details, so that they could, perhaps, experience emotion.

# Schizotypal Personality Disorder

Of the three personality disorders in the eccentric behavior cluster, the schizotypal personality disorder is the most eccentric.

As with someone who's schizoid, a schizotypal person also has trouble with relationships. And, as with someone who's paranoid, a schizotypal person may be suspicious and experience paranoia. In addition to those things, however, someone with schizotypal personality disorder also may experience odd or magical thoughts and illusions.

## What Is Schizotypal Behavior?

People with *schizotypal personality disorder,* according to the DSM-IV, experience "a pervasive pattern of social and interpersonal deficits marked by acute discomfort with, and reduced capacity for, close relationships as well as by cognitive or perceptual distortions and eccentricities of behavior."

**Personality Parlance**

**Schizotypal personality disorder** is the most serious of the disorders in the eccentric behavior cluster. It is evidenced by great discomfort with close relationships, as well as oddness and eccentricities of behavior and thinking.

A person with schizoid personality disorder normally has five or more of the following characteristics, as listed in the DSM-IV. The characteristics begin by early adulthood.

➤ Ideas of reference—thinking people do things because of them or that things happen because of them.

➤ Odd beliefs or magical thinking that influences behavior and is inconsistent with subcultural norms (for example, superstitiousness or belief in clairvoyance, telepathy, or "sixth sense"; in children and adolescents, bizarre fantasies or preoccupations).

➤ Unusual perceptual experiences, including bodily illusions.

➤ Odd thinking and speech (for example, vague, circumstantial, metaphorical, overelaborate, or stereotypical).

➤ Suspiciousness or paranoid thoughts.

➤ Inappropriate emotions or a narrow range of emotions.

➤ Odd, eccentric, or peculiar behavior or appearance.

➤ Lack of close friends or confidants other than first-degree relatives.

➤ Excessive social anxiety that does not diminish with familiarity and tends to be associated with paranoid fears rather than negative judgments about self.

A person with schizotypal personality disorder is not likely to seek treatment for the condition but may look for help with Axis I disorders, such as depression or anxiety.

The schizotypal condition is treated very seriously for many reasons. It's a very distressing condition, both to the people suffering from it and to their family and friends.

There's also the risk that, in response to stressful situations, a schizotypal person could pass over to having symptoms of a psychosis, such as schizophrenia. If that occurs, there's the risk of hallucinations or delusions—both very serious symptoms.

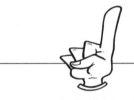

**Personality Pointer**

About 3 percent of the general population in the United States has schizotypal personality disorder.

## The Schizotypal Schema

Unlike people with paranoid or schizoid personality disorders, who tend to have similar thought processes, there's nothing typical about what schizotypals might think or believe. This makes it very hard to form a schema for a schizotypal person.

Four themes are common among schizotypal people, however:

➤ They are suspicious or have paranoid thoughts.

➤ They have *ideas of reference,* which means they think people do things because of them or that things happen because of them.

➤ They have odd, sometimes magical beliefs. They might believe for instance, that a dead person is present, that other people can hear their thoughts, or that they can hear what others hear or feel what they feel.

➤ They have illusions or think they see things differently from other people.

A peculiarity of schizotypal people is that they tend to go off on seemingly meaningless tangents. They're very vague about things, which makes it difficult to understand what they're trying to convey. It's very difficult to pin down their thoughts because of their odd emotions and affect.

Schizotypal people sometimes behave inappropriately, perhaps laughing about someone's death or crying about a happy event. They often have great social anxiety and are awkward and uncomfortable around others. These feelings of anxiety and awkwardness cause them to avoid relationships.

People with schizotypal personality disorder know that they're odd, and they feel odd.

Unlike schizoid people, those with a schizotypal personality disorder desire closeness but have so much anxiety they avoid relationships.

Schizotypal people experience cognitive distortions. They think they cause things to happen, such as earthquakes, fires, or floods. They feel very strongly about what they believe, and because of that, they're sure their feelings must be right.

Schizotypal people also may believe they have a sixth sense or can see what will happen in the future.

The automatic thought of people with schizotypal personality disorder is that they're defective or misfits.

## Getting Help for a Schizotypal Person

People suffering from schizotypal personality disorder desperately need social contacts in order to avoid losing contact with reality. Unlike schizoids, schizotypals find isolation painful. They may be aided by learning social skills so that they're more comfortable in social situations.

**Personality Pointer**

If you know people who have been diagnosed with schizotypal personality disorder, you may be able to help by getting them out and broadening their social network. The contact with others may be welcome, which would lessen their isolation and the pain that goes with it.

Therapists may challenge the automatic thoughts of schizotypal people in attempts to shake their belief that they're defective. Therapists may use role playing to help teach social skills.

People with schizotypal personality disorder may need help with learning to disregard some of their thoughts. If Charles thinks that a dead person is sitting with him, he needs to develop (with help from his therapist) a coping strategy. He'll be trained to think, *Even if I think there's a dead person here, that doesn't mean that there is one.* If Charles can understand that, he may be able to change his behavior by not acting as though there's a dead person at the table with him.

I'm sure you can imagine after reading this chapter that personality disorders can be extremely disruptive and distressing. They not only affect the person suffering with them, they have a ripple affect on families, friends, and co-workers as well.

# Check Yourself Out

Here are several questions to help you reflect on what you read in this chapter, and perhaps to take the information a step or two farther in your own mind:

➤ How does a personality disorder differ from a "normal" personality?

➤ When do personality disorders usually appear in a person's life?

➤ How would you describe paranoid personality disorder?

➤ Do you think the best way to motivate people with schizoid personality disorder is to appeal to their emotional side?

➤ Does a person with schizotypal personality disorder like being alone?

You might benefit from discussing these questions with another person, or just thinking about them on your own.

---

### The Least You Need to Know

➤ The personality disorders in the eccentric behaviors cluster are paranoia, schizoid behavior, and schizotypal behavior.

➤ Paranoid personality disorder makes a person view others with great mistrust and suspicion, even when there are no facts or circumstances to warrant it.

➤ People with schizoid personality disorder generally have no interest in relationships, have little or no response to provocation or adverse circumstances, and are emotionally flat.

➤ Schizotypal personality disorder causes people to suffer great anxiety in social situations, even though they really want social contact.

➤ The symptoms of most personality disorders occur by late adolescence or early adulthood.

➤ Those suffering from personality disorders usually can benefit from professional treatment.

---

# Chapter 15

# Dramatic Behaviors

## In This Chapter

➤ Defining dramatic behaviors

➤ Looking at antisocial personality disorder

➤ Understanding the seriousness of borderline disorder

➤ Histrionic behavior and where it comes from

➤ Identifying and working with a narcissistic person

In the last chapter, we discussed the difference between someone who is eccentric in the common sense, such as the man who rides the bicycle with the little dog in the basket, and someone who is eccentric in a psychological sense.

In this chapter, you can learn what it means for someone to have a dramatic behavior in the psychological sense, as opposed to merely behaving in a dramatic manner. As with eccentric behaviors, there's a big difference.

When we think of drama, or of something or someone being dramatic, we usually think of plays, melodramas, operas, and movies; and the people who perform in them.

We also use the word "dramatic" to describe a person who is highly emotional, or who tends to speak or act in an exaggerated manner.

In the psychological sense, "dramatic" describes a cluster of personality disorders, including these:

➤ Antisocial

➤ Borderline

➤ Histrionic

➤ Narcissistic

In this chapter, we discuss what each of these personality disorders is. You'll learn the characteristics of those who suffer from the disorders, and what help or treatments might be available for them.

# How Dramatic Behavior Is Identified

As with any personality disorder, professional diagnosis is necessary. You may think someone seems odd or different, but it's really not possible to pinpoint what's going on with people unless they are tested and given a professional evaluation.

Sometimes people who suffer from personality disorders have associated features such as depression or anxiety. It might be tempting to say, "Well, she's depressed," when in fact, the problem is much different from depression.

As we did in Chapter 14, "Eccentric Behaviors," in this chapter we base our text on descriptions of the disorders and treatment issues in these books:

➤ *The Diagnostic and Statistical Manual of Mental Disorders,* Fourth Edition (DSM-IV)

➤ *Disorders of Personality: DSM III*

➤ *Cognitive Therapy of Personality Disorders*

➤ *Cognitive Therapy for Personality Disorders: A Schema-Focused Approach,* Third Edition

Let's get started by looking at the antisocial personality disorder.

# Antisocial Personality Disorder

We sometimes refer to someone who doesn't seek out or enjoy the company of others as being *antisocial.* "That John is so antisocial," Jessica complains. "I called him three times and asked him to meet me for a drink, and he had a different excuse every time."

While that's a widely accepted use of the word "antisocial," it by no means is the definition in the psychological sense.

A person who suffers from antisocial personality disorder is much different from John, who prefers staying home with a good book to meeting Jessica for drinks.

## What Is Antisocial Behavior?

A person with antisocial personality disorder, as described in the DSM-IV, suffers from a "pervasive pattern of disregard for and violation of the rights of others."

This behavior usually begins in childhood.

A person with antisocial personality disorder normally has three or more of the following characteristics, as listed in the DSM-IV:

➤ Failure to conform to social norms with respect to lawful behaviors, as indicated by repeatedly performing acts that are grounds for arrest

➤ Deceitfulness, as indicated by repeated lying, use of aliases, or conning others for personal profit or pleasure

➤ Impulsiveness or failure to plan ahead

➤ Irritability and aggressiveness, as indicated by physical fights or assaults

➤ Reckless disregard for the safety of self or others

➤ Consistent irresponsibility, as indicated by repeated failures to sustain consistent work behaviors or to honor financial obligations

➤ Lack of remorse, as indicated by being indifferent to or rationalizing having hurt, mistreated, or stolen from another

Those with antisocial personality disorder tend to be career criminal types. They lack empathy, are cynical, and are contemptuous of the feelings, rights, and sufferings of others. They're exploitive, especially in a sexual manner. People with antisocial personality disorder may have many sexual partners but rarely maintain monogamous relationships.

If you were to meet someone at a party who has antisocial personality disorder, at first you might think the person to be charming. Many antisocial people have a superficial charm that allows them to get away with a lot in social situations. As you got to know the person, however, you'd soon realize that the charm was only on the surface.

Antisocial people are likely to have inflated opinions of themselves and act very self-assured. They are highly opinionated but not considerate of the opinions of other people. They have trouble controlling impulses and are unable to tolerate boredom.

**Personality Pointer**

Many people are deceitful from time to time, or they fail to plan ahead, or they act irresponsible by forgetting to pay a bill or phone a friend. These occasional acts are much different from the actions of someone with antisocial personality disorder. Such actions must be repeated and consistent to be considered symptoms of a personality disorder.

**Don't Go There!**

One of the things that makes people with antisocial personality disorder so dangerous is that they often can be extremely likeable when you first meet them. It's only after you get to know them that you understand what they're really like.

People suffering from antisocial personality disorders generally are irresponsible as parents, and they often experience depression.

## The Antisocial Schema

People with antisocial personality disorder, like those with other types of disorders, generally have predictable schemas. The processes they use to assimilate information and experiences tend to be pretty much the same, and they have many of the same overdeveloped and underdeveloped characteristics.

With antisocial personality disorder, the overdeveloped characteristics are combativeness and the tendency to exploit others. The underdeveloped characteristics are empathy and social sensitivity.

Here are some observations about the schemas of people with antisocial personality disorder:

**Personality Pointer**

Characteristics of antisocial behavior usually begin early in life and are displayed in different ways. Children with the disorder often are bullies and may be physically cruel to other people or to animals.

➤ Their main belief is that people are there to be taken.

➤ Their strategy is to attack others by robbing them, deceiving them, and so forth.

➤ Their avoidance strategy is to stay away from other people, or, sometimes, to try to compensate for their behavior by acting socially adept and flirtatious.

➤ They view themselves as loners and as being autonomous and strong.

➤ They view others as being vulnerable and open to exploitation.

➤ They believe they're entitled to break rules and that other people are patsies.

The early environments of people with antisocial personality disorder usually include abuse or neglect. The environments are unstable, with erratic parenting and unpredictable discipline.

## Getting Help for an Antisocial Person

Antisocial personality disorder is difficult to treat for various reasons. Antisocial people may seek treatment if they're looking for help for another problem, such as depression or substance abuse. Often, however, those with antisocial personality disorder don't see that, for example, hurting or robbing another person is any reason to seek treatment. They don't see that their behavior is a problem.

If treatment is started, antisocial people often won't continue with it.

The first thing therapists do with antisocial people is to try to get them to see how their behavior is likely to lead to restrictions on their freedom. Therapists try to make such patients understand that they may be facing jail, or losing their children, or confronting some other similar calamity.

Therapists focus on the patients' losses at first, because at the beginning of therapy, patients are interested only in matters that affect their own well-being, not that of others. In later therapy sessions, if things go well, therapists will be able to get them to focus on the effects their actions have on others.

Therapists also try to make their clients appreciate that something may be available in the future (such as freedom) but is not available at the time. They try to help their clients learn to curb their impulsiveness, and they try to teach them how to have empathy for others.

If all goes well, the antisocial person eventually will start to develop a sense of responsibility or caring for others, and to consider the welfare of others.

# Borderline Personality Disorder

Another of the cluster of dramatic behaviors is the borderline personality disorder. This is an extremely complex and serious condition, which unfortunately, involves a high rate of suicide among those suffering from it.

People who suffer from borderline personality disorder frequently seem to sabotage themselves or to ruin their chances for succeeding at something. They drop out of school during the last semester, for instance, or do something to destroy the one personal relationship they have that seems to be working out.

**Notes and Quotes**

It's estimated that between 1.8 and 4 percent of the general U.S. population suffer from borderline personality disorder. Statistics show that 23 percent of all inpatients in psychiatric care are borderline, as are 11 percent of all outpatients.

## *What Is Borderline Disorder?*

A person with borderline personality disorder, as described in the DSM-IV, suffers from a "pervasive pattern of instability of interpersonal relationships, self-image, and effects; and marked impulsivity beginning by early adulthood."

People suffering from borderline personality disorder usually have five or more of the following characteristics, as listed in the DSM-IV:

➤ Frantic efforts to avoid real or imagined abandonment

➤ A pattern of unstable and intense interpersonal relationships characterized by alternating between extremes of idealization and devaluation

**Notes and Quotes**

There's a book about borderline personality disorder called *Eclipses: Behind the Borderline Personality Disorder*. What's really interesting about the book is that the author, Melissa Ford Thornton, has had the disorder for years. The book was published in 1997 by Monte Sano Publishing and is available online at www.Amazon.com or www.BN.com.

➤ Identity disturbance—a markedly and persistently unstable self-image or sense of self

➤ Impulsivity in at least two areas that are potentially self-damaging, such as binge eating, reckless driving, sex, spending, or substance abuse

➤ Recurrent suicidal behavior, gestures, or threats; or self-mutilating behavior

➤ Affective instability due to a marked reactivity of mood (severe mood swings), such as intense episodes of *dysphoria* (a general sense of ill-being), irritability, or anxiety that usually last a few hours and rarely more than a few days

➤ Chronic feelings of emptiness

➤ Inappropriate, intense anger or difficulty controlling anger (could result in recurrent physical fights, frequent displays of temper, or constant anger)

➤ Paranoid thoughts, and on-again, off-again feelings of being disconnected from oneself

People with borderline disorders may experience hallucinations and ideas of reference during stress. They tend to be more secure with objects or pets than with people.

**Personality Pointer**

Relationships with people who have borderline personality disorder usually are extremely difficult because of the tremendous pressure a borderline person exerts. Therapists and doctors have the same relationship troubles, in that borderlines often idealize caregivers at first, placing them on a pedestal. When patients begin to realize that their caregivers are only human, they become disillusioned and often treat the caregivers poorly. If you have a relationship with someone with borderline personality disorder, it's good to be aware of these tendencies so that you can better understand the person.

As stated earlier, many borderlines commit suicide, mutilate themselves with razor blades or knives, or burn themselves with cigarettes. They experience recurrent job losses, broken relationships, and highly charged relationships with others. There's a desperate need among those with borderline personality disorder to be in a relationship. They need to feel that they're wanted and needed.

Despite the terrible fear of abandonment typical to this group of people, they tend to push others away because they don't trust them.

Cindy is in a relationship with Paul, and though things seem to be going along fairly well, she worries constantly that he'll leave her.

Paul reassures Cindy constantly, but she can't trust him, so she doesn't believe what he says. She ends up making life so miserable for Paul that he eventually does leave her. His leaving confirms Cindy's fears of abandonment.

## The Borderline Schema

The borderline schema is very complex, because people with borderline personality disorder often have combinations of all schemas running at once. Many people suffering from this disorder feel unlovable, overly vigilant, and defective—all at the same time.

The overdeveloped area of people who are classified as borderline is multiple negative schemas. The underdeveloped area is positive schemas.

Here are some observations about the schemas of people with borderline personality disorder:

➤ Their main belief is that they don't deserve to have their needs met, and that they're bad and unworthy. People with borderline disorder think they must have a very serious need before they will ask for something.

➤ Their main strategy is to display extreme behaviors to get attention or have their needs met. This might include cutting or burning themselves, or making an accident happen. They may burn down their house, stalk someone, or do something to injure themselves or make themselves sick.

➤ Their view of themselves is that they're unworthy and failures.

➤ Their view of others is one of extremely unrealistic expectations in terms of time and attention. People with borderline personality disorder feel a desperate need to have someone, but they put such demands on the other person that it very often makes a relationship impossible.

➤ Their schema maintenance is to behave erratically and in an extreme manner, but they often compensate by trying to keep their behavior under control while in public.

➤ Their schema avoidance patterns are often in conflict with one another. To avoid one schema, such as mistrust, which leads to being hurt, they may push away a person they're close to. This action triggers another schema of abandonment.

The early environment of a person with borderline personality disorder is usually one of abuse and neglect.

## Getting Help for a Borderline Person

Treatment for people with borderline personality disorder is a very difficult process. Therapists try to connect with such people in a therapeutic process and to establish a trusting relationship.

Therapists set very clear, specific treatment goals and try to keep their patients moving toward those goals. They teach patients to cope with emotions and situations, and help them resolve issues of dependence and autonomy.

Some doctors think that borderline personality disorder is a problem of emotion regulation. That is, they think that there's a physiological cause for the inability of borderlines to control their emotions. If that is true, one thing doctors try to teach borderlines is impulse control. This helps patients slow down and not react so quickly to things that happen to them.

As you no doubt realize from reading this section, borderline personality disorder is very disruptive to a person's life and makes relationships with others extremely difficult.

**Personality Pointer**

When in treatment, people with borderline personality disorder tend to dwell on bad things that have happened to them and, if permitted, would spend entire therapy sessions talking about those things. Therapists work hard to keep them focused on treatment and try to avoid having them focus on past events.

# Histrionic Personality Disorder

Chances are that if you've ever met a person suffering from histrionic personality disorder, you remember the experience.

A person with histrionic personality disorder, as described in the DSM-IV, displays a "pervasive pattern of excessive emotionality and attention seeking."

This behavior begins by early adulthood.

## What Is Histrionic Disorder?

People suffering from histrionic personality disorder usually have five or more of the following characteristics, as listed in the DSM-IV:

➤ They are uncomfortable in situations where they are not the center of attention.

➤ Interaction with others is often characterized by inappropriate sexually seductive or provocative behavior.

➤ They display rapidly shifting and shallow expressions of emotions.

➤ They consistently use their physical appearance to draw attention to themselves.

➤ Their speech is extremely emotional, and lacks detail.

➤ They display self-dramatization, theatricality, and exaggerated expressions of emotion.

➤ They are suggestible—that is, they are easily influenced by others or circumstances.

➤ They consider relationships to be more intimate than they actually are.

People with histrionic disorder have a great need to be the center of attention—all the time. They often have trouble with same-sex relationships and achieving intimacy.

They act out roles in a relationship, imagining themselves to be, for example, a victim, or perhaps a prince or princess. They crave novelty, stimulation, and excitement. Those with histrionic personality disorder are easily bored with routine. They look for immediate satisfaction and have little interest in the long term. They may make a suicide attempt to get attention.

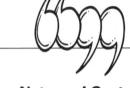

**Notes and Quotes**

Between 2 and 3 percent of the general U.S. population suffer from histrionic personality disorder.

## The Histrionic Schema

The overdeveloped characteristics of people with histrionic personality disorders are exhibitionism, expressionism (the open, unrestrained expression of feeling), and impressionism (the use of exaggerated expression of emotion, lacking in factual detail).

The underdeveloped characteristics are control and reflectiveness.

Here are some observations about the schemas of people with histrionic personality disorder:

➤ Their basic beliefs are that they need to impress others.

➤ They believe that other people are there to serve or admire them, and that others have no right to reject or deny them.

➤ Their main strategy is to be dramatic, use charm, cry, or perhaps even attempt suicide to get what they want.

➤ Their view of themselves is glamorous.

➤ Their view of others is that they're seducible, receptive, and admiring.

People with histrionic personality disorder most likely come from early environments that didn't give them the nurturing and acceptance they needed.

They were taught that they need other people in order to have their needs met. When they didn't get the attention they wanted from others, they learned to act in dramatic ways to get that attention and to have their needs met.

People who are histrionic assume that they're inadequate and unable to handle life on their own. Because they believe that they can't make it on their own, they look for others to carry them through.

They have a strong fear of rejection, and because they believe that others should always do what they want them to do, when others reject them it is particularly devastating.

Long-term relationships rarely work for histrionic people. They need—and demand—constant reassurance from their partners and are extremely demanding in other areas, as well.

> **Personality Pointer**
>
> For reasons that are unclear, histrionic personality disorder affects many more women than men. This also is true for borderline personality disorder. Men tend to get the antisocial label.

People who have histrionic personality disorder try to avoid self-knowledge. They're shallow but can have very intense moods. They usually employ "all or nothing" thinking, overgeneralizations, and emotional reasoning.

## Getting Help for a Histrionic Person

Treating people with histrionic personality disorder isn't an easy task. Because they often initially view the therapist as their rescuer, the therapist must see that the patient becomes actively involved in treatment right from the beginning. Histrionic people must be made to understand that they have to take responsibility for their treatment and that the therapist can't do it for them.

Therapists try to get histrionic people to focus on one issue at a time, which is difficult, because they quickly lose interest. They often drop out of therapy because they become bored and unwilling to work.

Because of their short attention span, histrionic patients are typically given homework by the therapist seeking to keep them active and involved between sessions. Before therapists can enlist the aid of their histrionic patients in their own treatment, they generally challenge their patients' basic assumption—that they're helpless and need others to take care of them.

# Narcissistic Personality Disorder

You've probably seen narcissistic people in movies or on television shows. They're usually portrayed as being extremely pompous, haughty, and self-absorbed; and often are used as comic characters. But there's nothing funny about narcissistic personality disorder; it can be a disabling condition that causes major problems in people's lives.

A person with narcissistic personality disorder, as described in the DSM-IV, displays a "pervasive pattern of grandiosity (in fantasy and behavior), need for admiration, and lack of empathy." The behavior begins by early adulthood.

## *What Is Narcissistic Disorder?*

Someone suffering from narcissistic personality disorder usually has five or more of the following characteristics, as listed in the DSM-IV:

➤ A grandiose sense of self-importance, as evidenced by exaggerating achievements and talents, or expecting to be recognized as superior without commensurate achievements

➤ A preoccupation with fantasies of unlimited success, power, brilliance, beauty, or ideal love

➤ The belief that they are special and unique, and can only be understood by, or should associate with, other special or high-status people or institutions

➤ A need for excessive admiration

➤ A sense of entitlement, or unreasonable expectations of especially favorable treatment or automatic compliance with their expectations

➤ Interpersonally exploitative, with a tendency to take advantage of others to meet their own ends

➤ A lack of empathy and an unwillingness to recognize or identify with the feelings and needs of others

➤ The tendency to envy others or believe that others envy them

➤ Arrogant, haughty behaviors or attitudes

People with narcissistic personality disorder have a vulnerable self-esteem. They have a very difficult time accepting criticism, which often leads to problems at work or with relationships. If criticized, they may react with disdain, rage, or defiant counterattacks. Or they may withdraw.

**Notes and Quotes**

Less than 1 percent of the general population suffers from narcissistic personality disorder.

Interpersonal relationships also are difficult for narcissistic people because of their constant need for admiration and their sense of entitlement.

## The Narcissistic Schema

The overdeveloped characteristics of people with narcissistic personality disorder are self-importance and competitiveness.

The underdeveloped characteristics are sharing and group participation.

Here are some observations about the schemas of people with narcissistic personality disorder:

➤ Their main belief is that they're special. They believe they deserve special rules or are above rules, and that they are better than other people.

➤ Their main strategy is self-promotion and competition, as well as using and manipulating other people while disregarding rules.

➤ They view themselves as special and better than other people.

➤ They view other people as being inferior.

➤ They think the task of other people is to admire and praise them.

The early environments of most narcissistic people are permissive and overindulgent. Their parents inflate their sense of self-worth to an unrealistic and unhealthy level, and they develop a lack of direction and a destructive sense of superiority.

The early maladaptive schema is one of entitlement and grandiosity. To maintain the schema, people with narcissistic personality disorder act superior. The schema avoidance is to withdraw when hurt. Schema compensation is to reinforce the sense of self-superiority.

**Personality Pointer**

When treating narcissistic people, trained therapists look for destructive behavior—particularly the possibility of cocaine use. For whatever reason, cocaine is a popular drug with narcissistic people.

## Getting Help for a Narcissistic Person

In order to be helped, narcissistic people must learn to deal with the fact that they're not really superior to everyone around them. Therapists try to help patients understand this, while at the same time helping them to cut down on any destructive habits they might have, such as drug abuse.

Therapists also work with patients on relationship issues, because as you might imagine, there is much conflict in that area. As long as narcissistic people believe they're superior, it's not possible for them to have equal, sharing relationships with others.

If you try to help someone who has narcissistic personality disorder, be aware that the slightest suggestion of criticism is likely to be received with anger, or the narcissistic person may withdraw.

As you can see, these dramatic behaviors are not to be taken lightly or dismissed. They're real personality disorders, and people suffering from them require understanding, empathy, and most often, professional help.

# Check Yourself Out

Here are several questions to help you reflect on what you've read in this chapter, and perhaps to take the information a step or two farther in your own mind:

➤ How would you know if you had the characteristics of any of the personality disorders discussed in this chapter?

➤ If you were in a relationship with someone who had one of these personality disorders, how would your life be affected, and how would you deal with the person?

➤ What are the types of dramatic behavior you see in each of the disorders discussed in this chapter?

➤ Would you consider getting professional help for yourself if you had one of these disorders?

You might benefit from discussing these questions with another person, or just thinking about them on your own.

---

### The Least You Need to Know

➤ Dramatic behaviors include the following personality disorders: antisocial, borderline, histrionic, and narcissistic.

➤ Antisocial behavior is present among criminals or others who fail to conform to social norms with respect to lawful behaviors.

➤ Borderline personality disorder is extremely serious, and often entails suicide or suicide attempts.

➤ Someone displaying histrionic behavior typically desires to be the center of attention and often displays inappropriate sexual or provocative behavior.

➤ Narcissistic people think they're better than everyone around them and hold other people in disdain.

➤ Dramatic behaviors interfere with relationships, employment situations, and other areas of life.

---

# Chapter 16

# Fearful Behaviors

> ## In This Chapter
>
> ➤ Identifying fearful behavior
>
> ➤ Making the distinction between fearful and shy
>
> ➤ Understanding avoidant personality disorder
>
> ➤ The characteristics of a dependent person
>
> ➤ Looking at obsessive-compulsive personality disorder

We've probably all known people who we would describe as fearful. They're timid and hesitant. Many of them don't like to make decisions or call attention to themselves. Often we associate shyness with fearful behavior. It's important to understand, however, that while shyness is a personality trait, it's in no way a personality disorder.

Mary is shy. She's always been shy. She sometimes must attend business-related functions at which she's expected to socialize with people she doesn't know. Mary doesn't look forward to these events, and she always feels relieved when they're over. Because it's part of her job, however, she attends the functions and does the best she can. Although she doesn't feel entirely comfortable, she introduces herself to people, hands out her business cards, and makes appropriate conversation.

Adam, on the other hand, is way past shy. Adam would never take a job in which he'd be expected to socialize with people. He barely nods when the delivery guy drops off a package to his home office, where he designs computer programs.

Adam doesn't belong to any clubs or professional organizations because that would require him to interact with other people. He pretty much stays at home because he's afraid that if he does go out or join a group, other people will make fun of him or not like him.

There's a big, big difference between Mary and Adam. While Mary has the characteristic of shyness, Adam suffers from a personality disorder. Mary is able to function normally, even if she's not always comfortable. Adam, on the other hand, is hindered by his behaviors.

Someone who truly has fearful behavior is not a person who happens to have the personality trait of shyness. Fearful behavior is much different than shyness.

Let's take a look at what fearful behavior is and the personality disorders it encompasses.

As we did in Chapter 14, "Eccentric Behaviors," in this chapter we base our text on descriptions of the disorders and treatment issues in these books:

➤ *The Diagnostic and Statistical Manual of Mental Disorders,* Fourth Edition (DSM-IV)

➤ *Disorders of Personality: DSM III*

➤ *Cognitive Therapy of Personality Disorders*

➤ *Cognitive Therapy for Personality Disorders: A Schema-Focused Approach,* Third Edition

# How Fearful Behavior Is Identified

Fearful behavior describes a cluster of personality disorders:

➤ Avoidant

➤ Dependent

➤ Obsessive-compulsive

Again, it's important to remember that, while many people may display mild avoidant, dependent, or obsessive-compulsive behaviors from time to time, a true personality disorder is something much different and far more serious.

Lots of people "obsess" over a presentation they have to make, or what they're going to wear, or how to act on their first date with someone intriguing.

Many people "depend" on others for moral support, or for help in getting through difficult times, or for practical matters, such as fixing a computer when it goes haywire.

And many people occasionally use "avoidance" techniques—perhaps to avert being trapped by the chatty neighbor or to dodge what's sure to be an unpleasant situation.

None of these behaviors indicate a personality disorder. Let's examine each of the personality disorders that fall under the fearful behavior blanket. You'll easily see the difference between occasional behaviors and disorders.

# Avoidant Personality Disorder

Although most of us occasionally go out of our way to avoid unpleasant or uncomfortable situations, people with avoidant personality disorders take the practice to the extreme.

Those suffering from this disorder avoid many basic parts of life, mainly because of their fear that they'll be laughed at or ridiculed. They have a very low opinion of themselves, and avoid involvement in any new situations, or in relationships, fearing rejection or ridicule. In short, people with avoidant personality disorder avoid, and miss, a lot of life.

## *What Is Avoidant Personality Disorder?*

A person with avoidant personality disorder, as described in the DSM-IV, suffers from "a persistent pattern of social inhibition, feelings of inadequacy and hypersensitivity to negative evaluation." The disorder begins by early adulthood.

People with avoidant personality disorder are watchful. They closely observe and appraise the expressions and movements of others. They act fearful and tense, which sometimes causes others to ridicule them.

People with avoidant personality disorder usually have four or more of the following characteristics, as listed in the DSM-IV:

➤ They avoid activities that involve interpersonal contact.

➤ They avoid getting involved due to a fear of not being liked or accepted by others.

➤ They practice restraint in intimate relationships due to fear of shame or ridicule.

➤ They have a marked preoccupation with being rejected or criticized by others.

➤ They stay away from new, interpersonal situations due to feelings of inadequacy.

➤ They view themselves as inferior, socially inept, or personally unappealing.

➤ They take few, if any, personal risks in the engagement of new activities for fear of embarrassment.

**Personality Pointer**

The behaviors and demeanors of people with avoidant personality disorder sometimes make them the objects of ridicule. When that happens, it confirms their self-doubts and makes them even more fearful and apprehensive.

**Notes and Quotes**

Avoidant personality disorder affects 0.5 to 1 percent of the general U.S. population.

People with avoidant personality disorder are terribly afraid that they may blush or cry in public or in front of others. They're shy, timid, lonely, and isolated. These characteristics cause problems with social and occupational functioning.

Melissa has a very small social support network, and although she desires acceptance and affection from others, she has very restricted interpersonal contact. She'll be uncertain and clingy in the relationships that she does have. Her desire for acceptance and affection from others leads her to fantasize about being popular and having people like her and seek her out.

She has very low self-esteem.

## The Avoidant Schema

People with avoidant personality disorder have the overdeveloped characteristics of vulnerability, avoidance, and inhibition. The underdeveloped characteristics are self-assertion and the ability to be outgoing or gregarious.

Here are some observations about the schemas of people with avoidant personality disorders:

➤ Their main beliefs are that they may get hurt, that it's terrible to be rejected, and that they're unable to tolerate any unpleasant feelings.

➤ Their main strategy is one of avoidance, especially in situations in which they'd be evaluated. They try to avoid all unpleasant feelings.

➤ They view themselves as vulnerable, socially inept, and incompetent.

➤ They view others as being critical, demeaning, and superior.

➤ They maintain their schemas by remaining on the outside of situations. Their schema avoidance is to avoid other people.

➤ To compensate for their behavior, they try to keep up with work or projects.

➤ They assume that they must be bad or defective because they make other people treat them badly.

Most people who suffer from avoidant personality disorder probably were treated badly early on in their lives. They most likely were told that they weren't worthwhile. Because of those early beliefs, they're unable to acknowledge that they could be treated well.

Avoidant people are extremely self-critical. They think they're stupid—losers. Because of their beliefs, they're afraid to let anyone get close to them, lest that person discover how bad and fearful they are. Even if people treat them okay, their schemas don't let them believe that it's happening, so they may perceive that they're being ridiculed.

Those with avoidant personality disorder go overboard to avoid confrontation. They turn down promotions and refuse invitations to social events to avoid being in the position of having to confront, or even just be around, other people.

If Dave's boss tells him he'd better crank up his production a little bit because he's falling behind, Dave will assume he's being criticized because he's defective or bad.

On the other hand, if Dave's boss tells him that he's a good worker and he's glad to have him on his team of employees, Dave will discount the praise. He'll think that, if his boss knew him better, he wouldn't have complimented him. Or he may think that he's been able to fool his boss by making him think that he's a good worker. Dave's schema won't allow him to believe that he may be worthy of the praise his boss has offered.

## Getting Help for an Avoidant Person

In order for avoidant people to be helped, they must be willing to encounter unpleasant feelings. That is difficult, because fearful people have a tendency to try at all costs to avoid any sort of unpleasant feeling.

Therapists or others trying to help avoidant people have to get them to interact with others. They also need to address and challenge the avoidants' thoughts and beliefs that they are unlikable and defective. It's very difficult to get avoidants to address these unpleasant issues until they demonstrate their willingness to experience unpleasant feelings.

# Dependent Personality Disorder

As mentioned earlier in this chapter, we all are, to some degree, dependent on other people. People with dependent personality disorder, however, take

**Personality Pointer**

Avoidant people become isolated because social situations are so uncomfortable for them. They tend to seek out jobs that allow them to work in fairly solitary conditions, such as driving a truck, fixing or operating machinery, or working on a computer.

**Don't Go There!**

If someone you know has avoidant personality disorder but isn't interested in professional treatment, don't try to push him or her into it. The best thing you can do is provide information about the disorder and its treatment, and show the person that you care.

dependency to a higher level. These are people who can't make decisions without extensive consultation with others and are terrified of not having close relationships because they don't believe they'll be able to care for themselves.

## What Is Dependent Personality Disorder?

A person with dependent personality disorder, as described in the DSM-IV, has a "pervasive and excessive need to be taken care of that leads to submissive and clinging behavior and fears of separation."

The behavior starts by early adulthood.

People with dependent personality disorder usually display four or more of the following characteristics, as listed in the DSM-IV:

➤ They have difficulty making everyday decisions without an excessive amount of advice and reassurance from others.

➤ They need others to assume responsibility for most major areas of their life.

➤ They have difficulty expressing disagreement with others because they fear loss of support or approval (this doesn't include realistic fears of retribution).

➤ They have difficulty initiating projects or doing things on their own, due to a lack of self-confidence in judgment or abilities, not a lack of motivation or energy.

➤ They go to excessive lengths to obtain nurturing and support from others, to the point of volunteering to do things that are unpleasant.

➤ They feel uncomfortable or helpless when alone because of exaggerated fears of being unable to care for themselves.

➤ They urgently seek another relationship as a source of care and support when a close relationship ends.

➤ They are unrealistically preoccupied with fears of being left to take care of themselves.

People with dependent personality disorder typically are pessimistic and filled with self-doubt. Similar to those with avoidant personality disorder, dependent people will belittle or dismiss their abilities and assets. When they're criticized, or if someone expresses disapproval of something they do, the negative remark confirms dependents' feelings of worthlessness about themselves.

They'll seek overprotection and look for someone who will dominate the relationship. They become very anxious when faced with making decisions and generally try to get others to make decisions for them.

## The Dependent Schema

The overdeveloped characteristics of a person with dependent personality disorder are the tendency to be clinging and help-seeking.

The underdeveloped characteristics are self-sufficiency and mobility.

Here are some observations about the schemas of people with dependent personality disorder:

➤ Their basic beliefs are that they're helpless and they need other people in order to survive.

➤ Their basic strategy is one of dependence and of forming dependent relationships.

➤ They view themselves as being needy, weak, and helpless.

➤ They idealize others and see them as nurturing and supportive.

➤ To maintain their schemas, dependent people rely totally on others. The schema avoidance is to procrastinate, and the schema compensation is to do things without help.

**Personality Pointer**

Interestingly enough, some dependent people overcompensate and act fiercely independent. They won't accept help from anyone and become indignant and upset when someone offers help.

Generally, dependent people are underassertive to the extreme. They assume, based on the beliefs formed in their early environments, that they're inadequate and helpless. The only solution, they think, is to find somebody to take care of them.

## Getting Help for a Dependent Person

The job of therapists treating those with dependent personality disorder is to try to move them toward autonomy and self-reliance. The dependents need to learn to make decisions for themselves.

The basic beliefs of dependent people that must be addressed are those that deal with their perceived inadequacies. They need to learn to recognize their capabilities and to not dwell so much on what they believe they're unable to do or incapable of doing.

Dependent people, as you might expect, more often than not are perfectly willing to go into treatment for their personality disorder. The problem is, they often can become dependent on the therapist, who they view as someone else to help them and take care of them.

A common example of a dependent personality is a woman who lives in an abusive situation. She knows her situation isn't what it should be, but she's severely hampered by her belief that she's inadequate and unable to care for herself. She feels she needs someone to take care of her, even if that person beats or otherwise abuses her. It's a very difficult cycle to break, but dependent people can be treated successfully.

# Obsessive-Compulsive Personality Disorder

The closets and drawers in Karen's house are works of art. Everything in them, right down to the smallest object, is perfectly arranged in neat rows, according to size and color.

Peter volunteers to organize his community's Fourth of July parade. He's so rigid about the order in which participants must march, what each person should wear, and other details, that many people decide not to participate. The parade eventually is cancelled.

**Notes and Quotes**

People with obsessive-compulsive personality disorder sometimes are unable to complete a task or project because of the impossibly high standards they set. They're so concerned with doing every aspect of the job perfectly that the job never gets finished. Others are very compulsive about getting things done right down to the last detail.

Joe hasn't taken a day off from work in four years, and he thinks nothing of working 14 or 16 hours a day. His preoccupation with work has led to the breakup of his marriage.

Karen, Peter, and Joe share the personality disorder of obsessive-compulsiveness, which can be extremely disturbing and disruptive.

As with the other personality disorders we've discussed, many people display mild obsessive behaviors or tendencies. Susan might always check three times to make sure she unplugged the iron, just because it's something she worries about. Ted might insist that the interior of his car be kept immaculate and in perfect order.

On their own, these behaviors don't mean that the people who display them are obsessive in the psychological sense, or that they suffer from obsessive-compulsive personality disorder.

## *What Is Obsessive-Compulsive Personality Disorder?*

A person with obsessive-compulsive personality disorder, as described in the DSM-IV, experiences a "pervasive preoccupation with orderliness, perfectionism, and mental and interpersonal control, at the expense of flexibility, openness, and efficiency."

These behaviors begin by early adulthood.

People with obsessive-compulsive personality disorder usually have four or more of the following characteristics, as listed in the DSM-IV:

➤ They are preoccupied with details, rules, lists, order, organization, or schedules to the extent that the major point of the activity is lost.

➤ Their perfectionism interferes with task completion. (They are unable to complete a project because their own overly strict standards aren't met.)

➤ They are excessively devoted to work and productivity to the exclusion of leisure activities and friendships (this doesn't include someone who needs to work all the time for economic reasons).

➤ They are overly conscientious, scrupulous, and inflexible about matters of morality, ethics, or values.

➤ They are unable to discard worn out or worthless objects, even when they have no sentimental value.

➤ They are reluctant to delegate tasks or to work with others unless those people submit to their exact way of doing things.

➤ They adopt a miserly spending style toward themselves and others. They view money as something to hoard for future catastrophes.

➤ They exhibit rigidity and stubbornness.

**Notes and Quotes**

About 1 percent of the general U.S. population suffers from obsessive-compulsive personality disorder.

People with obsessive-compulsive personality disorder need rules and established procedures in order to operate effectively. They have trouble setting priorities and get upset and angry when they can't control their physical and interpersonal environments.

They are excessively deferential to authorities they like and excessively resistant to authorities they don't like.

Sheila just loves her new boss, Donna. She thinks Donna's the best thing that ever happened to the customer service department, and she's willing to do anything for her. Sheila shows up at work early in the mornings, stays late to work on extra tasks, and skips her lunch hour regularly to help Donna catch up with extra projects.

Unfortunately for Sheila, the higher-ups in her company also like Donna, and after a year, Donna gets promoted out of Sheila's department. Frank is Sheila's new boss, and Sheila doesn't have one good thing to say about him.

She criticizes him constantly to her co-workers, although she doesn't confront Frank directly. She does only the jobs that she absolutely has to, refuses to stay a minute past five o'clock, and tells Frank that she won't help with planning the company picnic, though she always did so when Donna was her boss.

It's not that Frank isn't a good boss; it's just that Sheila doesn't like him because he took Donna's place. In Sheila's mind, Donna was great and Frank is awful. Obsessive-compulsive personality disorder tends to generate all-or-nothing thinking, along with great intensity of emotions. Sheila doesn't confront Frank directly, however, because she doesn't like emotional expressiveness.

People who are obsessive-compulsive are not spontaneous; they're preoccupied with the logical and intellectual aspects of things. They tend to restrain themselves—to remain completely silent—until they can say exactly the right thing.

## The Obsessive-Compulsive Schema

The overdeveloped characteristics of an obsessive-compulsive person are those of control and responsibility. The underdeveloped characteristics are those of spontaneity and playfulness.

Here are some observations about the schemas of people with obsessive-compulsive personality disorder:

➤ Their basic beliefs are that mistakes are bad and they must not make any. They think they know what's best in all situations. They view details as crucial and think that people should do better than they actually do.

➤ Their main strategy is perfectionism, applying rules, and exerting control.

➤ They view themselves as responsible, accountable, and competent.

➤ They view others as irresponsible, casual, incompetent, and self-indulgent.

➤ Their schema maintenance is the pursuit of perfection, and their avoidance mechanism is to just drop out.

➤ Obsessive-compulsive people may compensate by doing something that is fun, or at least something they perceive to be fun.

**Personality Pointer**

When obsessive-compulsive people compensate for their disorder by having fun, the decision to do so isn't entirely conscious. They don't think, *I know I'm a real stuffed shirt, so today I'm going to go out and have a lot of fun.* Going out and doing something fun is more a way for obsessive-compulsive people to trick themselves into thinking they're okay.

The early environment of someone with obsessive-compulsive personality disorder usually is one in which parents set impossibly high standards. The parents most likely were unrelenting in their expectations, and the child was not allowed to make any mistakes.

Obsessive-compulsives are rigid and intense, and they can lose their sense of connection to the world because they think they need to do everything themselves or it won't be done properly. They feel very strongly that there are right and wrong ways of doing things, and right and wrong decisions.

They believe that, to be worthwhile people, they must avoid mistakes at all costs, because to make a mistake is to fail.

## Getting Help for an Obsessive-Compulsive Person

Obsessive-compulsive people need to alter or reinterpret their underlying assumption that there are right and wrong ways of doing things, and that they need to avoid making mistakes at all costs.

Therapists who work with obsessive-compulsive patients might teach them relaxation techniques, help them learn about decision-making, and teach them how to consider multiple possibilities rather than assume that the only possibilities are "right" and "wrong."

Therapists try to get their obsessive-compulsive patients to experiment a bit, and to be more flexible in how they perform tasks.

Working with obsessive-compulsive people can be challenging, because they have a difficult time accepting that the way they've been doing things isn't necessarily the best way. Excellent progress, however, is possible with the proper counseling.

People with fearful behaviors generally aren't violent or terribly threatening in an overt manner. Relationships with fearful people, however, can be extremely difficult and disheartening.

As with all personality disorders, a professional diagnosis probably is necessary.

# Check Yourself Out

Here are several questions to help you reflect on what you've read in this chapter, and perhaps to take the information a step or two farther in your own mind:

➤ Can you explain the difference in the behaviors of people with erratic behavior patterns versus fearful patterns?

➤ What are some typical behaviors of people with fearful personality disorders?

➤ If you decided to make some personal changes, how long would you give yourself to make progress?

➤ How easy would it be for you to be around someone with a fearful personality disorder?

➤ After reading about all the personality disorders, how has your view/opinion of people who display different behaviors been affected?

You might benefit from discussing these questions with another person, or just thinking about them on your own.

**The Least You Need to Know**

➤ Fearful behaviors include avoidant, dependent, and obsessive-compulsive personality disorders.

➤ Fearful behavior, which is a disorder, is much different than shyness, which is simply a personality trait.

➤ A person with avoidant personality disorder is socially inhibited, feels inadequate, and is overly sensitive to criticism.

➤ Relationships with dependent people are extremely difficult because they typically are extremely demanding and clinging.

➤ People who are obsessive-compulsive are very rigid, often setting impossibly high standards for themselves and assuming that their way of doing something is the only "right" way.

# Chapter 17

# The Addictive Personality: Myth or Reality?

> ### In This Chapter
>
> ➤ Debating the categorization of addictive behaviors
>
> ➤ Viewing addiction as learned versus biologically based behavior
>
> ➤ Exploring different types of addictions
>
> ➤ Looking at the characteristics of addictive behavior
>
> ➤ The similarities and differences between addictions and personality disorders
>
> ➤ Determining whether you're at risk

We've probably all known a person with an addiction.

Maybe your parent, aunt or uncle, or spouse was addicted to alcohol. Or a brother or friend lost all his money, along with his job and family, because he couldn't stay out of the casinos or away from the horseracing track.

Maybe you've known someone who was addicted to cocaine, methamphetamines, or heroin. Or someone who felt compelled to run 18 miles every day, or someone who couldn't get away from the television set, or who ruined her credit when she spent far more money than she had on repeated shopping sprees.

Addictions are common in our society, and they have profound and sometimes devastating effects on individuals, families, and communities.

While nearly everyone recognizes that addictions exist, there's great disagreement about how they should be classified and considered.

In this chapter, we look at how theorists and psychologists view addictive behaviors, and at some of the types of addictions. You'll learn when a habit may mean trouble, and how to get help if you think you or someone you're close to may have an addiction.

# The Debate About Addictive Behaviors

One of the most controversial topics today in theoretical circles is that of how to classify addictive behaviors.

The argument, basically, comes down to whether addictive behaviors are diseases or learned behaviors.

Some addictive behaviors—gambling, substance abuse, and problem eating—are classified in the *Diagnostic and Statistical Manual of Mental Disorders,* Fourth Edition (DSM-IV) as individual disorders. The dispute, then, is not whether these behaviors are disorders, but whether the disorders are diseases or learned patterns of behavior.

Consider alcohol dependence as an example. If alcohol dependence is a disease, it isn't proper to list it as a personality disorder. Other diseases, such as diabetes and cancer, would never be considered personality disorders—why would alcohol dependence?

If alcoholism is a learned behavior, on the other hand, perhaps it could qualify as a personality disorder. To complicate the alcohol dependency question even further, we sometimes say that a person who engages in one or more addictive behaviors has an *addictive personality.*

Alcohol dependency, as you might imagine, is one of the most hotly debated issues in the addictive behaviors spectrum. Just what is it? Is it a disease, a behavioral disorder, or an addictive personality problem?

Some professionals feel very strongly that alcoholism is a disease, while others insist it's a behavioral disorder. Some think it falls under a pattern of addictive behavior that includes, along with substance abuse, addictions to things such as work, sex, television, and exercise.

While the issue of alcohol abuse is controversial, it's much more clearly defined and studied than some other addictive behaviors that aren't even listed in the DSM-IV. There are all sorts of addictions, many of which haven't received much attention or been the subject of much research.

### Notes and Quotes

As we continue to research and learn about alcohol abuse and other addictive behaviors, you can expect that the debate about how to classify them will become even more intense. It doesn't appear that the controversy over addictive behaviors is going to let up anytime soon.

What does it mean, exactly, to be addicted to something? We often use the word loosely, saying things like, "Oh, yes, I'm addicted to chocolate," or "He's addicted to that television set when football season rolls around."

We don't think anyone really disagrees that people can be addicted to watching television, surfing the Web, exercising, or working. None of these things, however, are classified as addictive behaviors in the DSM-IV.

So, what *does* addiction mean? As with other questions we've discussed throughout this book, there's no single definitive answer.

Webster's dictionary describes *addiction* as being "devoted or given up to a practice or habit, especially a bad habit."

While that definition is okay and widely accepted, it's not without flaws. If a priest is devoted to his habit of frequent and fervent praying, for example, does that mean he's addicted to prayer?

**Personality Parlance**

**Addiction** is widely thought of as being devoted or given up to a particular practice or habit, as Webster's dictionary states. You need to remember, however, that the word is described differently by various professionals, depending on whether they consider an addiction to be a disease or a learned behavior.

If Betsy watches television for 10 hours every day, you certainly could say she's devoted to a particular practice. You can't necessarily say, however, that she's addicted to television. Maybe she simply has nothing else to do, likes to have the television turned on for company, or enjoys the drone in the background.

On the other hand, John, who watches television for 10 hours a day while ignoring his family's needs, misses work because of his behavior, and wants to stop but doesn't seem to be able to, may be addicted.

As you've no doubt figured out by now, "addiction" means different things to different people.

Consider an article called "Gambling: Disease or Excuse? High Rollers Suffer from an Illness," published in the August 1989 issue of *Journal of Drug and Alcohol Dependence*. The article was written by Sheila Blume, a former scientific director for the National Council on Alcoholism and director of the Alcoholism and Compulsive Gambling Program at South Oaks Hospital in Amityville, New York. Blume, who considers gambling an addiction, offers this definition of addiction: "A condition in which bodily health is seriously attacked, deranged, or impaired; sickness, illness." In other words, addiction is a disease.

According to the disease model, addiction is inbred and biological. The solution to it is medical and spiritual, much as it would be for another type of disease.

### Notes and Quotes

The Alcoholics Anonymous program is based on a disease model and strongly stresses a spiritual component. AA has more than two million members. Rational Recovery is a self-help program based on the principles of rational emotive therapy, which fits the social learning model. It is not as well-known but has helped many people.

In contrast to Blume's definition of addiction is one from the social learning perspective, which states that addiction is learned behavior, not genetic.

Stanton Peele, a social psychologist who has worked in the addictions field for many years, describes addiction in his 1975 book, *Love and Addiction,* as "an experience that grows out of an individual's routinized, subjective response to something that has special meaning for him—something, anything that he finds so safe and reassuring that he can not be without it."

Those who subscribe to the social learning model say that addiction is a way of coping, and that recovery requires coping skills and changes in the environment of the addicted person.

As you can see, the disease model definition of addiction is definitely at odds with that of the social learning model.

Let's look at some of the other views of the disease model and the social learning model so that you can compare the differences.

## The Disease Model

Those who subscribe to the disease model as it pertains to addiction believe that these statements are true:

➤ Addiction is all or nothing. You can't be just a little bit addicted. You either are or you aren't.

➤ Addiction is a primary disease. It's not caused by anything else.

➤ Addiction is permanent. That doesn't mean it can't be treated and controlled, but the disease remains.

➤ People who are addicted are in denial. Denial is a defense mechanism people use to protect themselves from the truth. This means that the truth is too painful or too scary for the person to face or accept. People who lose jobs or get arrested may deny that it was because of their addictions and say instead that it was just bad luck, or it happened because the boss or the cops or someone else didn't like them.

➤ People trying to stop an addiction should associate primarily (until the addiction is under control) with other recovering addicts. This is to ensure they'll have support, be with people who have similar goals, and avoid being with people who are using drugs or alcohol.

## The Social Learning Model

The social learning model, on the other hand, holds that the following statements are true and accurate. Compare them with those of the disease model, and note the strong differences.

➤ Addiction is a means of coping with circumstances or situations.

➤ Recovery requires that those who are addicted develop better coping skills, and that their environment be changed. They have to remove themselves from places and situations that contribute to their addictions. Alcoholics need to avoid bars; drug addicts need to avoid places and people they associate with drug use.

➤ Addiction is not all or nothing—it's a continuum, and it can be outgrown.

➤ Addiction stems from life problems.

➤ People without addictions are the best role models for addicts and should be the primary contacts of those trying to overcome addictions.

➤ Recovery requires addicted people to develop their own power, not to rely on a higher power.

The two models are very different, and the debate concerning them continues. Biological or learned? Disease or behavior? Should addictions be included in the DSM-IV and other publications that deal with personality disorders and conditions?

One thing we can be sure of is that the debate will continue.

# Different Kinds of Addictions

Everyone knows there are people who are addicted to drugs, alcohol, or gambling. The word "addiction," however, is being used to include an increasing number of substances, activities, and behaviors.

In addition to widely known and recognized addictions, you may recently have heard of other kinds of addictions:

➤ Relationships

➤ Sex

➤ Eating

➤ Spending

➤ Buying

➤ Working

➤ Self-mutilation

➤ The Internet

➤ Exercise

➤ Television

You might question how something like exercise, which we're constantly told is good for us, can be an addiction. An addiction to exercise is commonly called a *positive addiction,* and some people argue that, if something is positive, it can't be a problem.

**Notes and Quotes**

It's hard not to see the irony in the fact that there's a Web site established for people who are addicted to the Internet.

We disagree, however, and believe that any activity that is the frequent or constant cause of a problem must be considered a problem in itself.

If Charlie insists on running four hours every day, despite the constant protests of his family, who object to his giving up all the leisure time they might have together, then running is a problem.

Another set of problems has sprung up due to expanding technology, which provides such things as the Internet and Nintendo for people to get addicted to.

The addictions we've mentioned so far are by no means the only kinds of addictions out there. The list is long, and the distinctions between what's really an addiction and what isn't aren't always clear.

# Characteristics of Addictive Behaviors

Generally speaking, addictive behaviors cause problems— for the addicted people, the people around them, or both.

Because there are so many types of addictive behaviors, many of which aren't addressed in the DSM-IV, it's difficult to pinpoint specific characteristics for all of them.

While the DSM-IV doesn't cover many addictive behaviors, it does address and list characteristics of substance dependence.

Substance dependence, the manual says, is a "maladaptive pattern of use leading to clinically significant impairment or distress." The DSM-IV goes on to say that people with a substance dependence have three or more of the following symptoms. These symptoms occur at any time within the same 12-month period:

➤ They build up a tolerance, which means they need more of the substance to achieve the same effect.

➤ They go through withdrawal symptoms when they stop using the substance.

➤ Over time, they drink more or use larger amounts of the substance.

➤ They have a persistent desire to, or make unsuccessful attempts to, cut down on or control their substance use.

➤ They spend a considerable amount of time getting, using, and recovering from the use of alcohol or other substances.

➤ They give up or reduce important activities (social, occupational, or recreational) because of the substance use.

➤ They continue to use the substance, despite the problems this causes.

In the DSM-IV, substance dependence categories include alcohol, marijuana, nicotine, cocaine, and others.

The DSM-IV also lists gambling as a behavior disorder in its "Impulse Control Disorders" category. Eating disorders have their own category in the DSM-IV, but addictions to things such as television, work, and exercise aren't listed at all.

The reason is that there's not enough evidence in these types of behaviors to support calling them disorders in themselves. The behaviors displayed are usually thought to be explained by another, larger disorder the person has. Excessive behaviors, for example, may be explained by the fact that a person has a bipolar (excessive mood shifts between depression and manic phases) disorder, an antisocial personality disorder, or an impulse control (an urge to do something harmful to oneself or someone else) disorder.

The reality is that it is very confusing and very difficult to evaluate addictive behaviors because there's no overall, comprehensive system for doing so. Unlike recognized personality disorders, such as the avoidant, borderline, and schizoid types, addictive behaviors don't come with a clearly spelled-out set of characteristics and symptoms. Addictions may fall into many different categories, depending on whose opinion you ask or which source you consult.

# When Does a Habit Become an Addiction?

Identifying the point at which a habit becomes an addiction is extremely difficult. The factors involved in answering that question—if there are any at all—often are conflicting. What may be true in one person's case may not be true in another's.

To add to the problems associated with differentiating a habit from an addiction, there is no general agreement among professionals on what the terms mean.

**Personality Pointer**

Be aware that some of the characteristics associated with substance dependency show up in other types of addictive behaviors as well. Someone may continue to shop, for instance, even though the act of shopping is causing serious problems, just as someone may continue to drink or use drugs. There are many overlaps.

**Don't Go There!**

To say that a behavior isn't a problem until it manifests itself as a physical illness is considered by many to be an extreme point of view. People have many types of problems in their lives besides physical illness. To dismiss problems caused by some behaviors— problems in relationships or finances, for example—seems to minimize and even discount some serious considerations.

In one school of thought, addiction is a disease. That means people can engage in a particular behavior until they become physically ill; at that time, their behavior is re-defined as an addiction.

A commonly accepted axiom is that if something causes a problem, that thing in it-self is a problem.

Suppose that John drinks only two drinks after work every night. However, this drinking causes him to be nasty toward his family and then fall asleep and miss his son's baseball games and his daughter's soccer games. In this case, John's drinking is a problem.

If Sharon goes shopping every Friday night, that's not necessarily a problem. If she overspends dramatically, and the shopping causes big trouble between her and her husband, however, it's a problem.

Regardless of what someone does (drink, gamble, watch television), if it causes prob-lems in life, that behavior is a problem.

The factors that indicate a substance dependency problem apply to some other addic-tions as well, but not to all of them.

For example, a research report in the American Psychological Association publication, the *APA Monitor,* concludes that people who are addicted to television experience the same sort of symptoms as people with alcohol addiction. They need to watch more and more television to get the same satisfaction from it; they tried to cut down on their watching and couldn't. They were not, however, neglecting other things be-cause of their excessive viewing habits.

**Personality Pointer**

Many groups help people who have addictions. Here are the Web sites of three of the best known:

**Debtor's Anonymous**
www.debtorsanonymous.org

**Alcoholics Anonymous**
www.alcohols-anonymous.org

**Gambler's Anonymous**
www.gamblersanonymous.org

Currently, no official set of criteria exists for each ad-diction, but it's possible to come up with criteria for a specific addiction if you've a mind to do such a thing. You probably can piece together some criteria from the Internet, but a word of warning: Be very careful with Internet tests that claim to be measures for ad-dictive behavior. Many of these tests are not scientific or valid; they're just out there. There are some good ones, though, and you might find them useful. Look for tests that include information about their validity and reliability, and explain how they were developed. Or, try to find questionnaires that have been used as part of a legitimate research project.

If you think you have a habit that is becoming, or has become, an addiction, there is likely to be an organi-zation that can help you. Your physician or a licensed counselor also can help you determine the degree of the problem and steer you toward the kind of help you may need.

# How Addictions and Personality Affect One Another

Just as personality has biological, psychological, and social components, so does addiction. You heard over and over again in earlier chapters that our personalities are influenced by all those factors. Each of us is the sum of our *biopsychosocial characteristics*. Addiction, too, is the result of biopsychosocial characteristics.

Addiction and personality are closely tied together, and as you might suspect, one almost always affects the other. Let's look at how the two are related:

**Personality Parlance**

**Biopsychosocial characteristics** are those that are influenced by biology, psychological factors, and social factors. Both personality and addiction have biopsychosocial roots.

➤ Addictive behavior sometimes starts as a way of coping with a personality problem, and it can be a method of coping with emotional pain. Amy has avoidant personality disorder. This makes social contact extremely difficult. She has not been successful with relationships, and she has a lot of trouble keeping jobs because she's so reluctant to interact with others. Amy knows she has problems. She also knows that after a couple of glasses of wine, or sometimes many more than a couple, those problems don't seem to bother her as much. She drinks every night to make herself feel better.

➤ Some moods or states (temporary conditions) are so distressing that addictive behavior begins as a way to get through them. John has been diagnosed with depression, and he's terrified. His mother suffered off and on with depression for years, and he's terribly afraid the pattern is repeating itself with him. He begins supplementing the prescription antidepressant drugs he's been taking with lots of alcohol, because the whiskey makes him feel a bit better and helps him to not worry so much about the diagnosis of depression.

➤ On the flip side, if a person has an addiction, it can produce changes in mood. Addictions can cause depression and anxiety where they didn't exist before.

➤ Addictions can make a change or adjustment not only in one's mood, but in one's personality. You may have heard someone say something like, "Carl's a nice guy until he starts drinking, and then he gets really mean."

➤ An addiction can disguise itself as another disorder. Someone buying and using drugs, for instance, may behave like someone who has antisocial personality disorder.

➤ Some people engage in excessive behavior during certain periods in their lives. It could be while they're in college, after the breakup of a relationship, or after the death of a loved one. They use a particular behavior as a coping method in a particular type of situation, which may lead to addictive behavior.

As you can see, personality and addictions are tied together, but the connection isn't clear-cut. Addiction can lead to depression, anxiety, and antisocial behavior. And it seems clear that those same conditions can cause people to engage in behavior that may lead to addictions.

## Do Addictions Count as Personality Disorders?

Do addictions count as personality disorders? Good question. The DSM-IV, considered the definitive source when it comes to diagnoses, says no. It has not, to date, included a category on addictive personality because there is no single set of criteria to show that addictive personality is sufficiently similar to—or distinct from—other personality disorders.

**Don't Go There!**

While drinking has long been considered a collegiate rite of passage, it's recognized today as one of the most serious problems facing campuses and in no way should be taken lightly. College and university officials are addressing the matter of binge drinking, which has become an epidemic on campuses across the country. Excessive use of alcohol while in college can lead to addiction.

Consider the following questions, which generally are used when diagnosing personality disorders. We've adapted them to see if they also apply to addictive behaviors, and we've inserted our opinions along with each answer. Take a look and see what you think:

1. Does the addict exhibit patterns of belief, emotion, and behavior that deviate markedly from society's expectations?

   We believe these patterns are present. Addiction deviates. The answer to this question is a partial yes. Addiction is an enduring pattern, but while other personality disorders start by early adulthood, this is not necessarily so with addiction.

2. Does addiction affect cognition? Does it alter how people perceive themselves, others, and events?

   Yes. Addiction affects self-esteem, interpersonal relationships, and the prioritization of valued activities.

3. Does addiction affect people's emotional responses and the way they act?

   Yes. Addiction affects these things by increasing the addict's range of moods. They are more unstable during withdrawal, and their emotional responses are not always appropriate.

4. Does addiction affect the ability to function in interpersonal relationships?

   Definitely. Intimate relationships suffer from addictions; and family, work, and social relationships are affected.

5. Does addiction affect impulse control?

   Yes. Addiction lessens control, and addicts may engage in very risky and impulsive behavior. They may steal or rob in order to get a drug, charge items they can't pay for, gamble with borrowed money, or take risks when driving.

6. Is addiction an enduring pattern? Is it inflexible and pervasive across a broad range of personal and social situations?

   Yes. Addiction affects social relationships, jobs, and families. Although an excessive behavior can be stopped abruptly, the underlying maintenance structure of an addiction takes years to unravel.

7. Is clinically significant distress caused by addiction?

   Yes. Addicts could suffer from depression, anxiety, or paranoia caused by their addiction. Addiction can produce a broad range of maladaptive behaviors and greatly affect the addict's level of functioning.

8. Is addiction constant, and does it have a long duration that goes back to adolescence or early adulthood?

   Not necessarily. From beginning to end, an addictive cycle usually takes many years, but addictions can start at different life stages.

9. Can addiction be accounted for by another disorder?

   No. Other disorders may precede the addiction, which may be initiated to cope with the preexisting condition, but there is not a direct causal relationship between other disorders and addictions.

10. Is addiction due to the physiological effects of a general medical condition?

    No. Again, medical conditions may precede a pattern of excessive behavior (an addiction), but no causal relationship exists between them.

As you can see, addiction has many—but not all—of the characteristics of a personality disorder. Some of the factors don't fit, but more do than do not.

Addictions have biopsychosocial components, just as disorders and diseases do. That's controversial but is becoming more widely recognized and accepted.

There are biological components to every personality disorder, but as with addictions, there's no medical procedure to test them or treatments for them. Medications can treat some of the symptoms of the various disorders, but they cannot treat the personality disorder or addiction itself. In that way, addiction is not like other diseases.

The question remains: Can addictions be considered personality disorders? We think that instead of putting addictions in the same category as personality disorders, a new classification should be added to the DSM-IV to cover addictive behavior. It may be best to have a category called "Addictive Disorders," with its own general classification system and specific criteria for each type of addiction.

It will be interesting to see what happens in the coming years as more studies examine the causes and other aspects of addiction.

# Determining If You're at Risk

If you think you may be addicted to drugs, alcohol, gambling, or any other behavior or substance, the best thing you can do is to get all the information you can about addictions and addictive behaviors.

All sorts of assessments are available on the Internet to help you determine the seriousness of your problem. (See Appendix B, "Additional Resources," for recommended sites.) One thing to remember is that if you think your behavior is a problem, there's a real possibility that it is.

Recognizing that you may have a problem is taking a big step on the road toward recovery. The next step is to ask your physician or therapist to assist you in finding help. If you go to a church or synagogue, you can talk to your minister or rabbi.

Check out Internet sites such as Alcoholics Anonymous or one that pertains to the addiction you're wondering about. Professional sites such as schematherapy.com explain the kinds of therapy that can help with the recovery process. AA and many other sites offer questions you can answer privately to explore whether your behavior is a problem.

Addictive behavior continues to be an area of intense study. If you have questions about your behavior or that of someone you care about, get some reading material or talk to somebody you trust.

# Check Yourself Out

Here are several questions to help you reflect on what you've read in this chapter, and perhaps to take the information a step or two farther in your own mind:

➤ What are your own thoughts about whether addictions are diseases or behavioral problems?

➤ How much difference does it make to you that a problem is categorized as a disease or a behavioral problem?

➤ How bad does a problem have to be before someone should do something about it?

➤ Who is the person you trust most to talk to about this?

➤ If you were concerned about your own behavior, what would you do?

You might benefit from discussing these questions with another person, or just thinking about them on your own.

---

### The Least You Need to Know

➤ Whether addiction should be categorized as a disease or a learned behavior is a real source of debate among people who study addictive behaviors.

➤ There are common addictions, such as alcohol abuse and gambling, and uncommon ones, such as Internet or shopping addictions.

➤ Many addictions have some common characteristics, but there's no definitive source that lists the characteristics of each type of addiction.

➤ There are similarities and differences between the symptoms of addictions and those of personality disorders.

➤ Certain methods can help you determine whether you have an addiction or a potential addiction, and many places offer help.

---

# Part 5

# For Love and Money

*Have you ever wondered why you find some people so attractive, while others do nothing for you at all?*

*Or why it is that you've always dreamed of being a professional tour guide, while your older brother always wanted to work in a bank like your dad did?*

*In Part 5, we cover at length how your personality affects your love life and your career. We also look at how your personality affects the kind of parent you are or will be, and what you can do to be the best parent you can possibly be.*

*You'll learn in these chapters why some people are as compatible as can be, while others don't like each other from the instant they meet. Is there such a thing as love at first sight? Or is that strictly the stuff of romance novels?*

*What about your personality and the job scene? Are you the kind of person who'll be a high-profile supervisor six months after you start with a company? Or are you destined to be a rank-and-file employee? Will you seek out a job that puts you in contact with lots of people and demands that you regularly give talks and presentations? Or will you be happier sitting alone in the cab of a truck as you coast along the nation's highways?*

*You'll find out in this section how your personality goes a long way in determining the type of the job you'll have and the kind of worker you'll be.*

# Your Personality and Your Love Life

If you think your love life is ruled by the stars or by destiny, you might want to step back and consider another factor—your personality.

Your personality, with its biological and learned components, is directly related to whom you'll be attracted to. It also affects how you'll expect a partner to treat you, how you'll treat your partner, and many other aspects of love and relationships.

This doesn't mean that you have no control over how your relationships will go, or who you'll choose to marry. It simply means that, because of your personality, you're inclined to choose certain types of people when establishing relationships and to expect certain things of those relationships.

Your personality affects how you'll act while you're in a relationship and what you might do if a relationship starts to go bad.

## Love at First Sight

Maybe you think you were attracted to that guy you met at the gym because he was nice about helping you adjust the weights, or because he has great biceps, or because you discovered while having coffee together afterward that the two of you seem to have a lot in common.

Or maybe you fell head over heels for the new woman who started working in your office because she has a wonderful smile, or is very efficient and well-organized, or always goes out of her way to say something nice to you.

All of those things may have been factors in your attraction, but let's take it a step further and see if we can figure out why. Why do some people like those who are outgoing and gregarious, while others are attracted to more quiet, reserved folks?

Why do some people enjoy being around others who are relaxed and laid back, while others prefer to be with somebody who's more serious and driven?

Believe it or not (and we know that some of you would prefer not to believe it), we tend to re-create the family environment in which we grew up.

This is great if you grew up like the Waltons, safe and secure in a loving, well-directed environment. On the other hand, it's pretty awful if you grew up being whacked around whenever your dad got drunk, or you were screamed at and told you were stupid if you forgot to close the garage door or turn off the kitchen light.

**Personality Pointer**

Remember that we learn better from what we observe than from what we're told. If your dad tells you as a child that cheating is bad, but you observe him over the course of 20 years cheating his clients or customers, you're more likely to be influenced by his behavior than by his words.

At one point or another, practically all kids swear that they'll never—not in a thousand years—be anything remotely like their parents. They won't act like their parents do, they won't marry a person like either of their parents, they won't do the same work their parents do—you get the picture.

Well, guess what? Most of us not only end up marrying someone with characteristics similar to those of our parents, but we get more like mom and dad every year.

Why? Because it's what we know. It's what's inside of us, in our genes and in the beliefs and attitudes we acquired early on. If you were raised by your biological parents, you've got a strong dose of genetics working in you along with the effects of the environment in which you grew up.

Even if we don't have good feelings about how we grew up or were treated as kids, we still tend to be pulled toward people with whom we can create similar situations.

When you're attracted to someone, chances are it's a person who will be able to help you re-create the family environment in which you were raised. It's one of the reasons why we tend to marry people whose backgrounds and socioeconomic levels are similar to our own.

Once we're in relationships, we tend to act like our parents did in their relationships. This occurs because we model the behavior we observed while growing up. If your parents yelled at each other when they argued, you're more likely to yell at your partner than is someone who grew up in a household where nobody ever raised their voice. Even if there are aspects of our parents' relationships that we didn't like while growing up, we tend to act in a similar manner.

Of course, this isn't always bad. If your parents were respectful, helpful, and loving toward each other, you'll be more inclined to act in that manner toward your partner than you might be if your folks had acted differently.

When we meet somebody with a similar background, we hit a comfort level. We feel at home with that person.

Say that Barb and Brad meet while playing tennis at the community park. They get to know each other a little better, go out on a few dates, and find that they like each other very much.

When they start talking more seriously about themselves, they discover that one of the attitudes they share is that they don't want to be like their parents.

Barb's parents were screamers, and she grew up fearing that every small argument would turn into an ugly, upsetting screaming match. Brad's parents didn't have much money while he was growing up, and he's sworn to himself that he's going to work hard and be financially successful.

Barb and Brad also discover that neither of them wants to remain in the small town where they're living. They want to move to a large city.

**Personality Pointer**

If you can, try to remember how your grandparents related to one another, and then think about your parents' relationship. Or think about how the parents of a close friend acted together, and then how that friend handles his or her own relationships. It's easier sometimes to spot similarities in a relationship when the relationship isn't your own.

Their shared desire to change their situations gives Barb and Brad something in common, and it makes their relationship seem very special to them. They become infatuated with each other, thinking that they're meant to be together. When infatuation occurs, it becomes difficult to see the other person's shortcomings.

For example, Barb doesn't notice that Brad is incredibly cheap. She thinks that he's admirable for saving money and working toward his goal of financial success. Brad, on the other hand, doesn't notice that Barb is practically incapable of expressing an opinion about anything. He thinks that she's mild-mannered because she's determined to not be like her screaming parents.

*Infatuation* is often interpreted as love at first sight. As you probably know, it seldom lasts.

**231**

While Barb and Brad think that they're going to break out of their parents' molds by avoiding screaming matches or making lots of money, they're mistaken. They may do what they say they'll do, but they're merely changing behavioral aspects of their relationship. They'll still have the beliefs and values they grew up with.

People often are attracted to each other because they fill each other's needs.

Sharon grew up in a home where she was abused by her father. Because of that, she believes that she's unlovable, and she expects that she'll be hurt. Tom also grew up in a home with an abusive father. He also believes that he's unlovable.

When Sharon and Tom first get to know each other, neither is particularly trustful. They don't expect someone to love them. They both fantasize about having a relationship unlike the one they experienced with their father: They want to live without hurt and pain. Their shared fantasy pulls them together, but the fantasy soon ends, because neither of them has had the modeling to know how to build a loving, respectful relationship, nor do they have the beliefs to support one.

As much as we might like to deny it, we're all products of our genes and environments, and we've all learned from what we've observed and heard. Our genetic and environmental backgrounds give us the material from which we form our beliefs. Those beliefs are about ourselves, our self-esteem, how we treat others, and how we expect to be treated by others in close relationships.

Our beliefs, coupled with the behavior we've observed from our parents, give us extremely strong messages about relationships and marriage.

## Personality Types That Attract—or Don't

You've probably heard people say or have said yourself, "I really like a guy with a good sense of humor." Or "It's really important to me that whoever I end up with is intelligent."

While physical appearance is a very important factor in why people are attracted to one another, personality is important as well. Certain personality types seem to be attracted to, or, decidedly not attracted to, certain other personality types. Some women can't stand the thought of a man who bosses them around, while other women might see being told what to do as a way of being taken care of, and find it comforting.

In this section, we look at what types of people are attracted to one another, and why.

# I'd Like to Get to Know You

Many personality combinations have proven over time to work very well. In some of the combinations, the personality characteristics of both people are very similar; in others, their characteristics seem to be very different.

Likes attract, mostly because their backgrounds are similar and they have a level of comfort with one another. Many people tend to marry within the same, or similar, educational, socioeconomic, and religious backgrounds.

Many people marry someone they met in college, at work, in church, or at a social event. People you'd meet at those kinds of places generally have a background that's not too different from yours.

On the other hand, people who are seemingly opposite from one another also can find themselves attracted to each another. That's because some personality types complement others.

Here are some examples of complementary personality combinations:

➤ **Introvert and extrovert.** Jack is an introvert, and Jean is an extrovert. Jack is generally quiet, preferring to spend his time making wood furniture in his workshop, painting landscape scenes, or playing cards with a small group of close friends.

Jean, on the other hand, is extremely outgoing and vocal. She's chairwoman of three committees in town, stops at the local coffee shop every morning to catch up on all the latest gossip, and loves big parties.

People still think it's amazing that Jack and Jean ended up together, much less that they recently celebrated their fiftieth wedding anniversary. The secret to their long and successful relationship is that Jean talks and Jack listens.

➤ **Impulsive and serious.** Mark is a serious guy. As much as others try to get him to loosen up a little bit, he almost always remains solemn. He's thoughtful and

**Notes and Quotes**

Psychoanalyst Carl Jung said that when we seek a mate, we look for someone who matches our archetype. Our archetypes are the shared images, patterns, and motifs within all of us. That means that somewhere there's a perfect match for each of us—a soul mate. When we meet our archetypal match, Jung said, we'll know it, and there will be instant love.

**Don't Go There!**

While there's no question that opposites attract, the complementary characteristics of two people can cause problems down the road. That take-charge attitude that was so appealing to the woman when the couple first met, for example, could turn out to be a source of resentment and trouble later in the relationship.

**233**

deliberate, and thinks ahead about what he'll say or do. Planning is a big deal with Mark; he does very little without careful consideration.

Sue, on the other hand, is quick to laugh, fun, and impulsive. She loves to act on the spur of the moment and thinks nothing of changing plans if something more appealing comes along.

Mark and Sue drive each other crazy sometimes because of their differences, but they have complemented each other through more than 15 years of marriage.

➤ **Dependent and strong.** Doris was never given much of an opportunity to make decisions while she was growing up. Her parents told her what to do, what to wear, what to say, where to go to school, and who to spend her time with. As a result, she grew up pretty much unable to fend for herself.

Don, on the other hand, is a take-charge kind of guy. If there's a problem, he fixes it. If there's an emergency, he knows what to do. He's assertive and smart, and always seems to know what to do.

Doris and Don were attracted to each other the first time they met. Don's been taking care of Doris, and Doris has been depending on Don, since they were married nearly 10 years ago.

Other opposites that attract include relaxed and tense, shy and outgoing, and fearful and brave.

Even though opposites attract and can have successful relationships, the couples that seem to be most successful in the long run are those that are most alike—both in personality and in background.

People with good self-esteem, for instance, seem to feel more comfortable around others with good self-esteem, rather than around people who are very dependent.

**Personality Pointer**

Unlike animals, we're not totally controlled by our instincts. We're able to make choices that affect our behavior and to negotiate our instincts with the other factors in our lives.

## Oil and Water

While it's clear that there are personality types that are attracted to one another, it's equally clear that some people just aren't meant to be together.

People at opposite ends of a continuum generally are not suited as mates. While Jean is an extrovert and Jack an introvert, they're not at opposite ends of the introvert versus extrovert continuum. Jean is far more to the extrovert end than Jack, but neither is introverted or extroverted to the extreme.

People who are at the opposite ends of a continuum might be attracted to each other and have a fling, but chances are that neither will be able to tolerate a relationship for long. The closer to each other's opposites people are, the less well they mix in the long term.

We talk about couples being opposites, but they probably really aren't. Jean may fall at about 7 on the introvert/extrovert continuum, and Jack at 3, and that works out okay. If Jean were at 10 and Jack at 0, however, they probably would not have stayed married for 50 years. That's not to say that Jean and Jack haven't had some ups and downs in those 50 years. You can be sure there have been many times when Jean has said, "I knew he was quiet when we married, but now he never talks to me." Jack, on the other hand, has no doubt muttered many times, "She never shuts up."

These kinds of problems normally can be worked out if both partners are willing to address them and work on them, and the relationship is otherwise stable.

## Trouble in Paradise

All relationships have ups and downs. You probably will never meet a couple who hasn't experienced some sort of problem during the course of their time together. Fortunately, most problems are resolvable if both people want them to be.

Couples run into bigger problems, however, when the foundation of their relationship is on shaky ground.

Each person brings assumptions to a relationship when it first starts. Those assumptions concern ...

➤ Their behavior within the relationship.

➤ Their partner's behavior within the relationship.

➤ What life will be like, now that the relationship has started.

➤ What the relationship will be like.

> **Notes and Quotes**
>
> Statistics show that nearly one of every two marriages will end in divorce, with 60 percent of all divorces occurring in the 25-to-39 age group.

Unfortunately, while Mary may have certain assumptions and expectations concerning the relationship, Joe's assumptions and expectations might be very different.

Sometimes important issues aren't discussed. Mary and Joe might assume that they understand the other's assumptions and expectations, while in reality, they don't.

Or perhaps they don't want to risk upsetting the other or causing trouble in paradise by talking about what they expect and want from their relationship. If this sounds surprising, it really shouldn't. Many couples rarely talk about much of anything.

If the couple's assumptions and expectations remain unaddressed, both people usually find out later on that the relationship isn't what they thought it would be.

**Personality Pointer**

While many couples try hard to make their relationships work, there are some who look to divorce as a quick fix for their problems. For them, there's the "Do It Yourself Divorce Kit," available online or through the mail. It's a bargain at only $39.95, and you can use MasterCard or VISA to pay for it. Go figure ...

As you can imagine, that realization can lead to great disappointment and disillusionment. If that occurs, the couple needs to go back to the basics and sort things out from the beginning. They need to talk about all the things they should have addressed in the first place. They need to be willing to make a firm commitment to the relationship and have a genuine willingness to work very hard to make things better.

Couples disagree, argue, and fight about all sorts of things. Some common issues are finances, how decisions are made, and sex. These can be tough issues to sort through and resolve, and they often are cited as irreconcilable differences.

In addition to the everyday problems that tend to get in the way of relationships, problems of one person's personality also can wreak havoc.

Let's look at how problems with someone's personality can place a great strain on that person's relationship:

➤ Jessica, due to things that happened while she was growing up, believes that she's unlovable. Even though her husband, Joe, loves her very much, Jessica can't get over her core belief that she's unlovable. One day Joe comes home from work with a beautiful bouquet of yellow roses. He saw them in the shop window on his way home and thought how much Jessica would like them. He wants the flowers to tell Jessica how much he loves her. Jessica, because of her core belief that she's unlovable, assumes that Joe is up to something, and that he brought her the flowers because he feels guilty and is trying to make himself feel better. She accuses him of having an affair and throws the flowers on the floor.

➤ Carl has the core belief that he's unlovable. He's been married to Sharon for six years, and they've had their ups and downs. He often gets jealous, is suspicious, and gets upset when Sharon has to work late or go out on her own. So far they've managed to work through their problems, but things haven't been very good lately. One day Sharon comes to Carl and admits that she's had a brief affair with someone she met at work. She feels awful that it happened, and she'll do anything she can to make her marriage work. To Carl, who has the core belief that he's unlovable, Sharon's affair merely confirms what he's thought all along. He's always expected that she would leave him because she doesn't really love him, and the affair she's had proves that he's right. He tells her to pack up and get out of the house.

A common source of problems in relationships stems from *mind reading*. Mind reading is a cognitive distortion that occurs when one partner believes that he or she knows what the other person is thinking.

Mind reading leads to all kinds of trouble. Consider these examples:

➤ Jack and Jenny have a date at 7 P.M. Jack breezes in at about 7:25, apologizing profusely for being late. Jenny, a mind reader, knows that Jack isn't really sorry. She knows that Jack has been out having fun with his friends and didn't really want to go out with her at all. He just feels sorry for her. Jack, by the way, was running late because he wanted to finish up some work before his date with Jenny.

➤ Rachael buys Rick a beautiful gold watch for his thirtieth birthday. She has saved her money for years to buy it. Rick, a mind reader, knows that Rachael's intentions aren't sincere. He knows that she only bought him the watch to make up for some problems they've had and to force him to remain committed to her.

**Personality Parlance**

**Mind reading** is a cognitive distortion that can lead to big problems in a relationship. Mind reading occurs when someone assumes they know what the other is thinking, even though they haven't bothered to ask that person about it.

As you can see, mind reading is a dangerous and potentially destructive practice. It's far better to express your feelings and give your partner a chance to respond to them than to assume you know what someone is thinking.

## How to Tell If You Have a Problem

Contrary to what storybooks and movies might tell us, there's no such thing as a match made in heaven, where a couple never disagrees, never argues, and lives in perfect bliss.

Every person has core beliefs, automatic thoughts, cognitive distortions, and so forth. All of those things can have a profound effect on a relationship. Our beliefs and thoughts cause us to have varying levels of commitment to our relationships; they affect the roles we play in relationships and how our relationships work out.

When two people disagree about the rules or guidelines of their relationship, problems can crop up.

**Personality Pointer**

If you think your relationship is in trouble, it will take a certain amount of courage to address the matter with your partner. Just remember that avoiding or ignoring a problem won't make it go away.

Although every relationship experiences problems from time to time, most of them aren't all that serious and can be worked out. Some warning signs, however, signal potentially serious problems:

➤ Anger or resentment over something that happened years ago. If you're still upset because your husband didn't take you away for your tenth anniversary, and now you've been married for 14 years, it's time to do something about it.

➤ If you find yourself snapping at your husband for not picking up his socks or closing the cabinet door, but the real source of your anger is the missed anniversary trip, there's a serious problem in your relationship.

➤ If you haven't talked to your wife for three years about anything except who will pick up the kids, you have a serious problem. If you can't interact on an emotional level, you need to find some help.

Of course, any sort of abuse in a relationship certainly signifies big trouble and should be addressed. No relationship is perfect, but some problems are bigger and more serious than others.

## What to Do When Problems Occur

In most relationships, one partner is usually the first to recognize that a problem exists. That is the first step toward fixing it. Then the partner who recognizes the problem needs to address it with the other person.

**Personality Pointer**

Before you try to talk to your partner about a problem, it's helpful to articulate it to yourself. Think about what is happening and how you might characterize the problem to your partner. This will make it a lot easier when the time comes to sit down and talk it out.

Many people have difficulty initiating a conversation about a problem. Certainly, it's often easier to ignore it and hope it will go away. Communication, however, is extremely important in a relationship. When you're ready to talk, you might start by saying something like this:

"You know, Debra, I'm worried about something. We seem to have trouble talking about money, and the situation seems to be getting worse."

By expressing yourself that way, you're not blaming Debra for the problem; you're expressing concern about a problem and indicating that you want to do something about it.

Ideally, Debra also will acknowledge the problem and be equally concerned. You'll discuss the money issue as a couple, do some problem solving, and keep your relationship on track.

Here are some suggestions for what to say if you have a problem in your relationship. Remember that "I" statements are usually much better than "you" statements.

➤ I feel upset when you overspend on our credit card.

➤ I feel angry when you put me down in front of other people.

➤ I feel sad when you tell me that we'll do something together, and then you go out with your friends instead.

I + how you're feeling + a brief description of the situation that's causing the problem: It's not a magic formula, but it's far more effective than some of the alternatives.

If you say, for instance,

"You make me so angry when you go out with your friends instead of doing something with me,"

you immediately put your partner on the defensive. You're making the other person responsible for your feelings, which isn't true. Your partner may be responsible for the situation that caused you to feel angry, but your partner can't control your feelings. Those are your own.

Blaming your partner for the problem does not encourage communication, and communication is absolutely necessary if you're going to resolve the problem.

Here are some steps to help keep communication open and solve a serious problem:

1. Describe the situation that led to a problem for you.
2. Identify your automatic thought that pertains to the situation. For example, *I can't stand this any longer.*
3. Evaluate your automatic thought and develop an alternative belief.
4. Describe your perspective or intentions concerning the situation.
5. Clarify your intentions, and apologize for any miscommunication that may have occurred on your part.
6. Recommit to working on the relationship.
7. Start over with a sort of courting period.
8. Commit to spending time together, and start talking again.

If you and your partner need to make decisions concerning a problem, there's a way to make it easier. The following chart is a tool you can use to make decisions, weigh possibilities, or initiate discussion. In fact, this chart has proven very helpful to individuals and couples when they need to make decisions of any kind. You could use it when discussing whether to buy that new house or car, whether to continue using drugs, or whether to stay in a troubled relationship. This chart helps you conduct your own cost benefit analysis for difficult-to-make decisions.

### Sample Cost/Benefit Analysis

|  | Advantages | Disadvantages |
| --- | --- | --- |
| Staying in relationship | Security | Boring |
|  | No first dates | No understanding |
|  | Comfort | Little support |
|  | Love | Little in common |
| Ending relationship | End fighting | Have to start over |
|  | Can pursue own interests | Need to find support system |
|  | Feel free again | Feel lonely |

If you've really tried to work things out on your own, but your relationship still seems to be in trouble, you should consider getting counseling. It's important to know when counseling is necessary. If you wait too long, you run the risk of losing any emotional connection to your partner. At that point, your commitment to one another suffers, and the relationship is likely to fail.

# Making the Most of Counseling

If you do opt for counseling to help you fix the problems in your relationship, there are some things you can do to make the most of it:

**Don't Go There!**

Don't wait until the relationship has been seriously breached; it will be very difficult to get it back together. The best time to enter counseling is when there's still a strong commitment to the relationship. Resist the temptation to be too proud or too stubborn to suggest counseling if you think it's necessary.

➤ Remember that the more you put into counseling, the more you'll get out of it. If you're willing to work and cooperate with one another and the counselor, your chances of solving your problems increase.

➤ Find a therapist both of you feel comfortable with. Most counselors will spend a few minutes talking to you about how they work before scheduling an appointment.

➤ Be willing to work on the relationship between counseling sessions. Do your homework.

➤ Don't use the cost of counseling as an excuse not to go. Some agencies work on a sliding-scale basis. If there's a money problem, consult a social services resource agency in your community for more information.

If you want to go to counseling but your partner doesn't, you might still find it useful. Counseling may help you figure out what to do and whether you want to remain in the relationship. An excellent adjunct to counseling is Aaron T. Beck's *Love Is Never Enough*.

# Check Yourself Out

Here are several questions to help you reflect on what you've read in this chapter, and perhaps to take the information a step or two farther in your own mind:

➤ What characteristics are most important to you in a relationship?

➤ In what ways do you resemble your parents?

➤ How good are you at discussing problems without blaming your partner (or your close friend, if you're not in a romantic relationship)?

➤ If you and your partner were in trouble in your relationship, would you both go for counseling?

➤ What reasons would cause you to end a relationship?

You might benefit from discussing these questions with another person, or just thinking about them on your own.

---

### The Least You Need to Know

➤ Attraction to another person consists of both biological and learned components.

➤ People with similar backgrounds and personalities often are attracted to one another, and such matches generally tend to be the most successful.

➤ People with opposite personality characteristics also are attracted to one another, but their differences can lead to problems down the road.

➤ While all relationships experience resolvable problems from time to time, there are some signs that indicate your relationship may be experiencing more serious trouble.

➤ If serious problems occur in your relationship, it's important to address them promptly.

➤ If you decide to get counseling, your chances of it being successful increase if you are willing to work and cooperate, and you feel comfortable with your counselor.

---

# Chapter 19

# Personality on the Job

---

### In This Chapter

➤ Understanding how personality affects your career

➤ Picking a career that will make you happy

➤ Understanding traits and job aptitude

➤ Getting along with bosses and co-workers

➤ Dealing with a problem employee

➤ Coping with workplace violence

➤ Understanding how personality, along with other factors, contributes to your career aptitude

---

For most people, the important things in life are our family, friends, work, and leisure activities. These are the things that consume most of our time and energy, and shape our lives. Work can take up a significant amount of time and energy, and often, we do it because we have to when we'd rather be doing something else.

Just as personality affects your love life, it also significantly affects your career. Your personality plays a big part in the type of job you get, how you function in the job, and how you interact with people on the job.

## How Personality Counts in Your Career

It's widely recognized and accepted that people with certain types of personalities are better suited to certain types of jobs than they are to others.

A person who is extremely shy and reserved, for instance, probably wouldn't be an effective street cop. On the other hand, somebody who's brash and pushy would be a poor choice for a counselor or religious leader.

The factors that influence our careers are ...

➤ **Personality.** Everyone has traits and habits that make them better suited for some jobs than others. Your temperament, or general disposition, is an extremely important factor in your career.

➤ **Early environment.** How you were raised also affects your career. If your parents were very demanding, for instance, you might be very good in a fast-paced, highly demanding job. If you were raised in a loving and nurturing environment, you may do well in a career such as teaching or nursing.

➤ **Cultural, social, and educational exposure.** These factors affect our specific interests and often influence which careers we choose.

➤ **Likes and interests.** Many people look for careers that reflect their likes and interests. People who love music and have been involved in music their entire lives might train to be a music teacher, a musician in an orchestra, or a conductor.

People who love animals and have good organizational skills might aspire to be the manager of a zoo. People who love fabrics and clothing may go to school to learn to be a fashion designer, tailor, or model.

If food and cooking are your passions, you might decide to go to a culinary school and learn to be a chef, or get into another area of food service. If you love gardening and being outdoors, a career as a landscape architect might make sense.

➤ **Talents and training.** Unfortunately, having an interest in something doesn't guarantee that you'll be successful at it as a career. Most of us will never end up as professional musicians or athletes, no matter how much we love to play the violin or swing a tennis racket. Having the talent for a career and getting the training we need are major factors when it comes to career success.

A personality profile that's given to help determine career aptitude will reveal whether someone's

**Personality Pointer**

The days of having one career throughout your life are over. Multiple careers are now the norm. If you're considering a career change, check out *The Complete Idiot's Guide to Changing Careers,* by William Charland, or *Shifting Careers: How to Master Career Change and Find the Right Work for You,* by Carole Hyatt.

personality is compatible with certain types of jobs. It won't reveal anything about that person's likes, training, and experience, however. For that reason, profiles might tell you that you'd be good at things that don't seem to be related to each other. They might suggest that you'd be good at careers that you've never even considered. Career aptitude tests, however, while they're not foolproof, can present some possibilities and give you some ideas. They also might give you some interesting insights into your personality and how it will affect your career decisions.

# A Butcher, A Baker, A Candlestick Maker

Most people begin considering different jobs and careers while they're still children. Boys and girls test out different jobs in their play. They're police officers, doctors, cowboys, movie stars, teachers, models, stockbrokers, and lawyers before they turn six years old.

Adults fuel children's interests in careers by asking them what they want to be and by talking about their own jobs. Work and careers are central to our society. Think about how often adult conversation centers around them. Go almost anywhere, and you'll hear people talking about their jobs. Work is a big deal. That's why it's important to use good judgment when choosing a career.

Here are some things to consider if you're looking for a job or thinking about a career change:

➤ Will the job you choose make you happy? Will you find the work to be interesting and rewarding?

➤ What type of training and how much of it will you need for a particular job or career?

➤ If you're thinking about changing careers, why? What don't you like about the job you have now?

While some people are lucky enough to have jobs they really love, many people are perpetually dissatisfied with the work they do. They chase after what they think will be the ideal job, only to discover six months later that they don't like it, despite the high salary and three-week vacation package. This phenomenon is noted in the October 1999 edition of *American Psychologist*. An article by Mihaly Csikszentmihalyi, "If We Are So Rich, Why Aren't We Happy?" points out that the only goal we seek that is a goal in itself is happiness. It's not true, he asserts, that increased affluence leads to happiness.

It could be that you become dissatisfied with your job because of the excessive pressure placed on you to meet productivity levels. Even if you love the work, it no longer seems enjoyable or rewarding. It's very important to choose a career that's suited to your personality, because your chances of happiness on the job increase. So in this case, instead of looking for a career change, you'd look for another job in the same field.

Some people know from early on in their lives what they want to do. Maybe they are exposed to a particular job at an early age and decide that's it. They're lucky enough to have fewer decisions to make down the road. Most of us, however, need some help in deciding what career to pursue.

### Notes and Quotes

*We're living at unprecedented levels of prosperity, but we've found out that having more money hasn't improved the quality of our lives, as a society. We've never before seen so many violent crimes. The breakdown of the family continues, we have high rates of drug dependency, and a rapidly growing rate of the use of anti-depressant and anti-anxiety medications.*

—Mihaly Csikszentmihalyi, in *American Psychologist*

## Choosing a Career That's Right for You

Let's say you've decided to make a career change. You know you've had enough of the advertising business, but you don't know which field to move on to.

### Personality Pointer

Check out the Keirsey Temperament Sorter and the Keirsey Temperament Sorter 2 on the Internet. You can find them at http://keirsey.com.

You know that you need to make at least $50,000 a year, so you can rule out the areas that don't pay that much. You know that you're not willing to go back to school for any more than one year, so you know you're not going to be a surgeon or a genetic engineer.

Once you've used your personal criteria to narrow down career possibilities, you can use a career aptitude test to help you further narrow your choices.

Some tests, such as the *Minnesota Multiphasic Personality Inventory* (*MMPI*) and the *Sixteen Primary Factor Inventory* (*16PF*) can only be administered professionally by psychologists. Other tests, however, such as the Myers-Briggs and the Holland Self-Directed Search are available from career counselors and human resource people.

Another good test, the Keirsey Temperament Sorter, is available on the Internet.

Many other career aptitude tests are available. They ask questions about your interests, your way of handling situations, and so forth. The Myers-Briggs test is one of the most popular personality tests used for employment and business purposes. It's often used in setting up teams of workers in a company to help determine which personality types might work best together.

Also, you can find professionally scored tests on the Internet that may be useful. Some are free, while others require payment. (See Appendix B, "Additional Resources," for a list of sites.)

**Personality Pointer**

If you're considering a career or a career change, one of the best resources is still *What Color Is Your Parachute?*, written by Richard Nelson Bolles in 1970 and revised since then for the thirtieth consecutive year.

## Matching Traits with Jobs

Personality tests give you a report on your temperament and match your answers to the most similar responses of members of various professions. The people you most closely match hold the jobs you should be best-suited for. If your answers line up with those of many teachers, for instance, the test suggests that you may be suited for teaching. Or truck driving, or law, or whatever.

From your profile, you learn that your personality can work for you in a variety of jobs. Once you have the test recommendations on which jobs you're suited for, you can consider other factors, such as how much education is necessary.

We know that certain traits lend themselves better to some jobs than to others. Let's consider a few.

Someone who's shrewd might make a very good businessperson. Someone who's particularly shy probably shouldn't pursue a career in marketing. People who think on their feet, have a high energy level, and are good at handling emergencies might look at jobs such as police officer, news reporter, or emergency medical technician. People who constantly seek adventure shouldn't go into the postal service but may be suited to be tour guides. Those who are extremely emotional or neurotic probably wouldn't make good chief executives or military officers.

**Don't Go There!**

If you abhor the thought of eating animals, don't even think about getting a job in the meat-packing industry! Your values also are an important factor in the kind of work you choose to do.

Personality traits and temperament are indeed important when you're thinking about careers. Be sure you consider all factors when you're thinking about what you want to do.

# Learning to Live with Co-Workers and Bosses

Sometimes finding a job is the easy part. Once you start, you may find that it presents all sorts of challenges. Your personality affects not only the type of career you choose, but how you respond to various situations once you're in a job.

So what happens if you end up with the job you want, only to discover that your boss seems to be from another planet? Or suppose you find that several of your co-workers seem to have it in for you? Or that most people in your department appear to be totally inept, not to mention incredibly lazy?

Your personality largely determines how you'd react to these and other situations—or at least how you might like to react. If you're an outgoing, assertive type, you may tend to react to situations that bug you more quickly and decisively than someone who's more shy and reserved. Regardless of your personality type, however, it's very important to understand what is—and isn't—appropriate behavior in the workplace. You need to deal with certain people in certain ways, and understanding what those ways are, and why, is extremely important.

Suppose that you have a problem with your manager, Helen, and you know you're going to have to talk to her about it. If you're an impulsive type, you might be tempted to rush in and speak your piece without thinking it through, first. If you're hesitant or timid, you may find the thought of encountering your boss under these circumstances to be daunting, and try to avoid the situation altogether.

The best thing to do, regardless of your personality type, is to practice your social and assertiveness skills before making your approach. You first need to identify the problem in your own head and be clear about it when you approach your boss.

Decide when and where you'll talk to Helen. Be sure it's a time and place that's mutually convenient. Don't stop her when she's on her way to an important meeting and ask to have a chat. You could ask her early in the morning if she might have a few minutes later in the day when you could talk to her. Whatever you do, don't attempt to talk to Helen about a problem when other workers are around. These discussions should be held in private, unless circumstances warrant including another person.

**Don't Go There!**

One of the most self-defeating things you can do in a work situation is to complain about your manager to co-workers. What you say will no doubt get back to your manager, and your unprofessional behavior will diminish that person's respect for you as an employee.

Once you and Helen are together, begin by explaining to her what you perceive the problem to be. If you're the type of person who is easily intimidated, or you're uncomfortable when dealing with authority, it may be difficult for you to do this. Having thought through what you want to say ahead of time will give you a real advantage.

Your comments to Helen should be presented respectfully and calmly, giving her a chance to respond once you've made your point. Don't, however, be afraid to stand your ground. Some personality types find this easy to do, while for others, it's more difficult.

You should pretty much follow these same guidelines if you find that you're having a problem with a co-worker. Always be respectful, don't cast blame, and make sure you let the other person know how the situation is making you feel.

# Dealing With Difficult Employees

If you're a supervisor who's having trouble with an employee, follow the same general guidelines discussed in the preceding section.

The offensive behavior might be inappropriate social behavior, low productivity, or poor-quality work.

Let's say that Jack hasn't been doing his share of the work for the past few weeks. You've heard other employees complaining about it. They've had to take on Jack's work in addition to their own, and several important jobs assigned to Jack have simply not been done. The whole department is falling behind because Jack's not pulling his weight.

The first thing you need to do is identify the problem. Then tell Jack how you and his co-workers are affected by his behavior. Be as specific as you can. Don't just say, "You know Jack, you haven't been very productive lately." Use specific examples. Mention the report that Jack never finished and how it held up the entire department's presentation, or the phone calls from a prospective customer that he left unreturned, consequently losing a sale.

Be sure that you talk to Jack reasonably: Nobody likes to be yelled at. Explain what the consequences of his behavior have been on the rest of the department. Try to remain calm, and be sure to give Jack a chance to explain himself. Who knows? Maybe he hasn't been feeling well for the past couple of weeks. Maybe he's having serious problems at home—his wife announced she's leaving him, or he's just had a death in his family.

**Personality Pointer**

If you find that, as a supervisor, you're unable or unwilling to deal with difficult or problem employees, you'd better consider letting somebody else take on the supervisory role. Hardly anyone likes confrontation, but you'll jeopardize the morale of your entire work group if you don't deal with problems.

Give Jack a chance to respond. If he acknowledges that he hasn't been doing his best work, decide together what can be done to improve the situation. Maybe you can suggest—or Jack will—that he come in an hour early every day for the next two weeks to make up for the work he let slide. Or maybe he'll offer to take work home, or come in to the office for half a day on Saturday.

If he doesn't offer any solutions to the problem, then you'll have to suggest some. Be willing to be flexible and work with him, but make sure he realizes the seriousness of his behavior, and encourage him to do something to improve it. If he refuses to work with you, is arrogant and disrespectful, or the problem persists, you'll have to begin a formal disciplinary process.

By knowing and understanding your own personality and following the advice in this section, you can develop your on-the-job skills and deal effectively with others.

# When Violence Hits the Workplace

It's a sad fact, but we live in an extremely violent society.

Kids kill other kids in their schools. They're gunned down as they play on city streets—hit with stray bullets from drive-by shootings.

Domestic violence is at an alarming level. A man shoots and kills his long-time girlfriend after accusing her of taking too much money out of their bank account. A woman kills her elderly mother because she's tired of taking care of her.

Violence has also invaded the workplace. News stories tell of employees crouching under their desks in terror as crazed co-workers run through the halls shooting people indiscriminately. The possibility of violent behavior at work is real, and we need to be aware of that and recognize the warning signs.

**Notes and Quotes**

According to the National Institute for Occupational Safety and Health, each week an average of 20 U.S. workers are murdered, and 18,000 are assaulted while on the job. Most of these are robbery-related crimes, such as convenience store hold-ups.

## *Recognizing the Warning Signs*

Remember the axiom that the best predictor of future behavior is past behavior?

People occasionally do something that's completely out of character, but not very often. Those with histories of violence are more likely to act out at work than people who have never exhibited violent behavior.

Employers can use various tests to try to screen out employees who are potentially violent or have other problems. The tests are helpful, but they're not foolproof.

Kurt Helm, an industrial psychologist from Dallas, spent 20 years writing tests to assess applicants' personalities, job skills, and work ethics. Now, according to a story that appeared recently in the *Wall Street Journal,* he's developed a test designed to assess an applicant's potential for violence, theft, drug use, and sexual harassment.

Helm admits that, while such tests are useful, they're not 100 percent dependable.

"Nothing is foolproof," Helm says. "There are some people there—we call them sociopaths—who are very good at fooling everyone."

Nobody's good at predicting violence. Remember, though, that it's better to act today in response to some indicator that a person has the potential to be violent than to wish too late that you'd done something that may have prevented it.

Whether or not you know that somebody has acted violently in the past, if you think that person is behaving in a way that may indicate imminent violent behavior, you can't afford not to take action. If Bruce tells you he's going to kill the boss, for example, you can't necessarily ignore the comment or pass it off as a joke.

Every threat or potential act of violence needs to be treated seriously. Some warning signs that a co-worker may be violent include …

➤ Displays of angry or hostile moods.

➤ Threats of violence.

➤ A history of violent behavior.

➤ Bragging about owning weapons.

➤ Impulsive behavior.

➤ Substance abuse.

➤ Depression accompanied by panic.

➤ Recent problems with co-workers or management.

➤ Feelings of desperation.

No one factor, by itself, predicts violence. These warning signs, however, can make people more aware of behaviors that could indicate potential violence.

**Notes and Quotes**

Businesses are advised by the National Institute for Occupational Safety and Health to come up with workplace violence-prevention policies and to have plans in place in case violence does occur.

## Coping with It Once It Happens

It's terribly unfortunate, but violence happens. Nobody wants it to, but when it does, it's better to have a plan in place than to be totally unprepared. Such a plan also can be used to deal with other critical incidents, such as the death of a co-worker from natural causes, or the occurrence of a serious accident. If such an incident does occur, *defusing* and *debriefing* processes are usually the most effective and useful tools.

Defusing is an informal process in which all affected persons meet to discuss their roles in the event, their perspectives on it, and the impact it's had on them. In most cases, defusing is enough.

Debriefings are usually conducted by formally trained professionals who take everyone involved through the incident step by step.

If you are an employer or your job involves crisis prevention and postcrisis follow-up, you should be in contact with a crisis center or employee assistance program for assistance in handling violence or other traumatic incidents that may occur in your workplace.

# Check Yourself Out

Here are several questions to help you reflect on what you've read in this chapter, and perhaps to take the information a step or two farther in your own mind:

> ➤ What type of work is most appealing to you?

> ➤ Do you have or are you willing to get the training and education needed for the work you want to do?

> ➤ Do you have the assertiveness skills needed to deal with conflict in the workplace?

> ➤ Do you, or does your employer, have policies and procedures in place to avoid violence in your workplace?

> ➤ What would you do if violence occurred in your workplace?

You might benefit from discussing these questions with another person, or just thinking about them on your own.

---

### The Least You Need to Know

➤ Several factors, including personality, help to measure your career aptitude and determine which jobs and careers you're suited for.

➤ You're more likely to be happy and successful if you choose a job that suits your personality than if you don't.

➤ Personality traits, such as shyness, aggressiveness, and determination, can affect not only the job you choose, but how you'll perform in that job.

➤ Your personality affects how you deal with people while on the job.

➤ Workplace violence is a reality, and everyone should be prepared to deal with it.

---

# Chapter 20

# Molding the Future

---

## In This Chapter

➤ Learning how personality affects how we parent

➤ Modeling good behavior for our kids

➤ Understanding how bad parenting happens

➤ Expecting great things of our children

➤ Spanking—not a good idea

➤ Setting your kids on the right path

---

We know that personality affects just about everything we do—including parenting. The type of parents we are is very much affected by our personalities and how we were raised by our own parents.

Being a parent is an awesome responsibility. It's without a doubt one of the most important tasks we'll ever undertake. And yet, most people get very little training to be parents. We don't go to parenting classes or take parenting courses in school. Most of our training occurs on the job.

Because of this, mistakes are bound to happen. Nobody's perfect, and as any parent knows, parenting is as difficult a job as there is. If you mess up a report at work, you can do it over. If you mess up with your child, it could have far-reaching consequences.

In this chapter, we look at how our personality affects the way we parent. Why are some people such great parents, while others never seem to get the knack of it? We also take a look at the discipline issue and how we deal with it as parents.

# Your Personality and Parenting

Parenting, as any parent knows, brings out some of our best and worst features. A mother sits up all night with her sick son, washing his hot face with cool cloths and reading to him when he can't sleep.

A father comforts a daughter who's just been scared by a large dog, holding her on his lap and assuring her that the dog won't hurt her.

Parents listen patiently as Jimmy, their seven-year-old, practices—again, and again, and again—the poem he must memorize for school. They spend hours on the sidelines of a soccer field on cold, drizzly spring mornings, or sit for the entire Saturday before Christmas at a swim meet, trying not to think about the work that's not getting done at home.

Parents do all these things gladly, because they're doing them for their children.

There's another side to parenting, however—a dark, ugly side.

A father becomes enraged because his son wets his bed for the fourth night in a row, and he beats the little boy with his fists.

A mother is so upset and frustrated because her baby has been crying nonstop for three hours that she repeatedly shakes her baby until it is still.

A child looks for comfort during a thunderstorm, only to be told to go back to bed and leave the parents alone—they're watching television.

How we respond to different parenting situations depends on our personalities, which as we know, are greatly affected by our core beliefs. Parenting triggers our core beliefs, and the way we parent is greatly affected by the core beliefs we have.

### Notes and Quotes

In April 2000, the U.S. Department of Health and Human Services reported that incidents of child abuse in the U.S. had decreased for the fifth consecutive year. Statistics reported by states for 1998 (the most recent available) showed 903,000 cases of abuse or neglect—down from a record high of more than one million cases in 1993. Fifty-four percent of all victims suffered neglect, while 23 percent were physically abused. About 12 percent of the victims were sexually abused. The number of child fatalities caused by maltreatment remained unchanged at about 1,100—or about three children every day.

If your core belief is that you're unlovable, for instance, you'll probably face more challenges in parenting than someone with a more positive core belief.

When you're parenting your children, you're sure to be reminded of events from your childhood. You'll remember how your parents treated you and what they said to you. Sometimes those memories can trigger very intense emotions, which can affect how you act toward your children.

Core beliefs can be challenging, but they don't have to be insurmountable impediments to good parenting. We can learn to recognize and develop alternative beliefs so that our old ones don't get in the way of our being effective parents.

In our experiences working with families, we've learned that children, regardless of their age or circumstances, in almost every instance desire approval from their parents. We don't know if it's an innate desire, but it seems to hold true almost all the time.

We've worked with families in which parents and children have been estranged for many years. Maybe there was a disagreement about where the child would go to college. A rift occurred that wasn't mended until 15 or 20 years later. After all that time, the child still wants the parents' approval. If the parents are receptive, and someone is willing to make the first move, there's a good chance for reconciliation.

We recently met a 29-year-old man, Wes, who had just moved back to the East Coast from Los Angeles, where he'd been working in an animation studio. Wes hadn't seen his parents for 10 years. He had been determined to be an artist, and they were set on his being a lawyer like his father and older brother. When push came to shove, at age 19, Wes took off and hadn't been back since.

One day Wes got a completely unexpected phone call from his mother, who told him that his father had just been diagnosed with Alzheimer's disease and wanted to see him. Within two weeks, Wes had moved back to New York and was staying with his parents, extremely grateful to be back at home with them.

Something to remember is that a parent always remains in a parent's role. Children can't make reconciliation happen, no matter how hard they may try, if the parent is unwilling to do so.

Wes's case is pretty extreme, although plenty of families find themselves in similar situations. Most people, however, don't have that degree of strain and animosity in their relationships with their kids.

**Personality Pointer**

Wes's story is a happy one of reconciliation after many years, but keep in mind that reconciliation doesn't happen magically, and it's not done without effort. You can be sure that Wes and his parents will have some rocky times ahead. They're all eager to make their relationship work, however, and we think their reconciliation will be successful.

# Why Some People Are Great Parents

We believe that, in nearly all cases, parents do the best they can, given their own personalities and circumstances.

Almost all people want what's best for their children. Obviously, however, some people are better parents than others. What is it, then, that makes some people great parents, while others fall short?

Let's get it straight from the start: Even really good parents make mistakes. As we said earlier, parenting is pretty much a learn-as-you-go proposition, and mistakes are bound to occur. Be assured, however, that making some mistakes doesn't make you a bad parent. In fact, parents can use the opportunity to show their children the best way to respond to making mistakes if they face up to and admit that they made the mistake, apologize if necessary, and work to fix any problems the mistake caused. Modeling desirable behavior for their kids is what successful parents do.

**Personality Pointer**

If you've made some mistakes as a parent, don't despair. It takes a lot of repetition of undesirable behavior on your part to produce really undesirable behavior in your children. On the flip side, don't expect good modeling on your part to produce immediate good behavior in your kids. You'll see long-term results, positive or negative, but don't look for anything to happen immediately.

If we're parents, we have to model the behavior we want our children to have. We can tell our kids how to act, what to think, and how to feel until we're blue in the face (and they're sick of hearing it). Without seeing us doing what we tell them, however, it doesn't work as well.

You may have told your children a hundred times that it's important to be respectful to other people. But if they see you screaming and making obscene gestures at the guy who takes your space in the parking lot, they're learning an entirely different lesson. Think about it. Which would impress *you* more? Actions go much further than words when it comes to setting an example. We're always teaching our kids through the modeling we do, so wise parents step back from time to time and take a good hard look at what they're teaching their kids through their actions.

If we want our children to be moral, productive, well-balanced human beings, it pays to periodically ask ourselves if we're doing enough to *show* our kids how they should live. Do you just talk about the ideals you have and behave in another way entirely? What's your ideal compared to what you model for your kids?

If you don't want your kids to smoke, drink, overeat, lie, yell, or cheat, then don't model those behaviors. If you want your children to be polite, work hard, be considerate of others, and have fun, then those are behaviors you need to model.

And if you want your children to be polite and respectful toward you, you've got to be polite and respectful toward them. Try to imagine how children must feel when a

**256**

parent gets in their face and screams at them to be polite and respectful. Talk about your mixed messages!

Our self-images and our beliefs about ourselves, other people, and the future have developed from repeated messages we've received throughout life. Through our actions, we're giving our kids the same messages and the same beliefs. Parents who constantly are frightened, defensive, hurt, or angry influence their children to feel the same way. Successful parents learn to deal with their own emotions and beliefs, and then model the behaviors they want their children to emulate.

Kids face many challenges today. Many of them have to deal with their parents getting divorced. They hear of children their own age being killed in their own schools, and they face peer pressure concerning drugs, alcohol, sex, and other potentially harmful situations.

The fact that something bad happens to children doesn't automatically mean they'll be scarred for life. How parents handle a situation largely affects how children will deal with it and to what extent they'll recover from it.

If Becky is in the next classroom when her friend is killed by a gun-toting student, she obviously is facing a rough time and most likely will have some problems because of what she's been through.

**Personality Pointer**

While parents are their kids' primary role models, other adults serve in that role as well. Adults in a caring, nurturing religious community, a neighborhood, or a social group can be great influences on your children. On the other hand, adults who don't act in a desirable fashion can be undesirable role models.

Great parents will support Becky in every way but won't let their own fear and anger spill over into Becky, making her fear and anger even more intense.

Though it sometimes can be difficult, great parents are able to keep the best interests of their children in focus, and to model the behavior they believe is ideal for them to emulate.

## Why Others Aren't Great Parents

Based on what we read in our newspapers and hear on the news every night, it can be difficult to believe that parents are doing their best. When we hear about a father who shoots his three children because he's upset with their mother for leaving him, it's extremely difficult to empathize or understand.

We truly believe, however, that nearly all parents care about their kids and about parenting, and try to do the best they can. So, why then, do some parents hurt their kids, or ignore them, or sexually abuse them, or tell them that they're worthless and will never amount to anything?

### Don't Go There!

Many people don't report suspected child abuse because they don't want to be nosy or meddle in the affairs of others. With an average of more than three children dying each day due to neglect or abuse, it's everyone's duty to report abuse if they're aware that it's happening. Don't neglect your duty if you know that a child is being abused. Call a child abuse hotline or child protective agency.

Here are a few of the most common reasons:

➤ Sometimes parents are totally emotionally unprepared to deal with a child. Parents who are dealing with all kinds of unresolved hurts and issues from their past will have a very difficult time dealing with the demands of a young child.

➤ Sometimes a complete breakdown occurs between what parents want for their kids and what they're able to provide. The parents may be totally unprepared emotionally, financially, culturally, or in other ways to adequately care for their children.

➤ Because we tend to parent the way we were parented, we often repeat our parents' mistakes—sometimes hardly realizing that we're doing so.

A young father who was slapped and beaten regularly by his own father knows that hitting isn't a good way to deal with his child. When he's at the end of his rope, however, the child has been crying for hours, he has no help, and he doesn't know what else to do, he may revert to the behavior he grew up with. We all tend to repeat what our parents did and to treat our children the way we were treated.

A woman whose father was standoffish and cold most likely will have a more difficult time showing love and affection to her own children than a woman who grew up in a loving, demonstrative home.

Parenting is a much greater challenge for some people than others, due to personalities and circumstances.

## *Personality Traits That Challenge Good Parenting*

Dr. Jeffrey Young, the developer of schema-focused therapy, first offered these possible dimensions of temperament in 1993. They're based on the following five scales:

➤ Shy↔outgoing

➤ Passive↔aggressive

➤ Emotionally flat↔emotionally intense

➤ Anxious↔fearless

➤ Sensitive↔invulnerable

Although Young did not propose these scales specifically for parenting issues, we believe that being on either extreme of any of these scales can cause problems in parenting.

A mother who's too shy will find it difficult to show the world to her child. A father who's too aggressive may fall short in respecting the rights of others.

Many people recognize that they fall to one side of the scale, and that before they have children, they can work on becoming more centered. It's best to be toward the center in all of these dimensions. Nobody is perfectly balanced, but being at any of the extremes can spell trouble for parents.

People who don't realize that they're at the extreme end of the temperament scale and don't work toward changing will have great challenges as parents. When parenting gets too challenging, some people are inclined to take out their frustrations on their children.

While certain temperaments can make being a parent more challenging, negative core beliefs can do the same.

Let's say, for instance, that a mother has asked her son Bruce five times to clean up his room. Finally she turns off the television and says something like this: "I know that you'd rather watch television than clean your room, but cleaning it is what you need to do right now."

Bruce, being a kid, comes back with, "You're mean and that's not fair. You don't care about me. You don't love me, and I don't love you."

If Bruce's mother has good self-esteem, she'll chalk up his comments to a strategic attempt on his part to manipulate the situation. She'll stick by her mandate that he needs to clean his room. If Bruce's mother has a core belief of being unlovable, however, his statement could be devastating.

While there are many challenges for parents, and some of them are very serious, most are not insurmountable. A parent who really wants to change and overcome some negative beliefs and thoughts usually can, with help.

**Personality Pointer**

Words from our kids can be extremely hurtful, even to a parent with good self-esteem. Remember that kids usually end up feeling sorry for what they've said in anger. Ultimately, responsibility will fall on you, the parent, to set the proper mood to discuss things.

# What We Expect of Our Kids

As a society, we seem to be all over the board on the question of what we expect of our kids, and what we want for them. Consider these examples:

➤ One segment of the population pushes its kids into the spotlight, dressing six-year-old girls up like movie stars, complete with makeup, jewelry, and cover-girl poses.

➤ Another group pushes its kids into athletics, telling them they've got to be better than the next kid and that winning is the only option.

➤ Some parents don't expect anything of their kids. As a result, the kids grow up not expecting much of themselves.

How much we expect of our children, and how we convey our expectations to them, have a long-term impact.

If parents push too hard, children learn to set extremely high standards. If children fall short of those standards, they may be vulnerable to depression or anxiety problems.

If parents set no expectations, limits, or rules and continually tell their children how great they are, the kids are likely to develop overly high levels of self-esteem, which can create problems. (See Chapter 12, "The All-Important Self-Esteem Factor," for more on the subject of self-esteem.) These children have learned that all they have to do to receive praise and rewards is to be there.

Your expectations for your children align with your personality and your expectations for yourself. If you're optimistic and fun-loving, and you expect great things from your own life, you'll probably expect great things for—and from—your child as well.

If you think the world is out to get you, chances are that's what you'll convey to your kids, too. And chances are that that's what they'll expect from their lives.

The very most that you can hope for, or expect from, your children is what you model for them. You may not see the results of your modeling for 10 or 15 years, but be assured that the lessons you're giving them through your actions are being heeded.

**Personality Pointer**

Parents tend to encourage their kids to have personalities that are similar to their own. A mother who is generous and caring toward strangers probably wants her children to be the same way, even if she never voices that wish. A father who is smart and hardworking probably would like to see his children grow up to have those same characteristics.

# Teach Your Children Well

What is it that you hope for your children? Do you want them to be wildly successful in business? Or known the world over for their generosity and kindness? Perhaps you'd like for them to be president, or a religious leader, or a famous painter or musician or actor.

Most people want their children to be happy and content. Smart parents understand that happiness doesn't come from working all the time or obeying orders from higher-ups or always being overly serious. Nor does happiness come from living a life of complete leisure, being expected to do absolutely nothing. Happiness comes from somewhere in between those extremes, and good parents model that behavior for their kids. The happiest people have lives outside of work. They spend time with family and friends, and have other interests and commitments. You can show your children how to do that.

Remember that more than anything, your children are looking for your approval. When you let them know that they have it, by giving them praise, a small gift, or just a hug, they tend to repeat the behavior that helped them get it.

Even if you're using all your parenting skills— modeling, positive reinforcement, discussion— to teach your children behaviors, don't expect them to get it all at once. Sometimes they aren't able, or willing, to display the entire behavior at once. If that's the case, be sure to reward any effort they make. Doing that will make them want to try again.

> **Notes and Quotes**
>
> An elementary school principal in Shillington, Pennsylvania, stands in the hallway with little cards that say "I caught you being good" on them. When he observes children walking quietly to class or helping a friend, he hands them a card and thanks them for their good behavior. The kids collect the cards and see who can get the most.

# To Spank or Not To Spank?

The answer to the question to spank or not to spank is easy. Don't. No good comes from spanking or otherwise using physical force on children.

As a rule, people spank their kids because of their own feelings of frustration; it may serve the parent as an immediate emotional release. It also may evoke some short-term compliance from the child. In the long run, however, spanking produces negative results for the child and affects the child's view of the parent.

Hitting a child is a form of punishment, and it's demeaning. A great deal of evidence indicates that punishment is far less effective than positive reinforcement, which makes children feel good about themselves and encourages them to act in a positive manner.

Punishment might be quicker and easier to practice than positive reinforcement—maybe that's why it's so often used. In the long term, however, even though positive reinforcement requires more thought and effort than whacking a kid does, it works a whole lot better.

### Notes and Quotes

A recent *American Psychological Association (APA)* Presidential Task Force addressed the issue of spanking in a report on violence and the family. It says that "Spanking demonstrates to the child that the person who is supposed to love him or her the most, who has social authority over the child, and who is the most responsible for the child's well-being, also has the right to physically hurt the child .... In other words, spanking a child increases the likelihood that when the child becomes an adult, he or she may use physical force for control or discipline."

# Remembering What's Important

Being a parent involves many compromises and trade-offs. There are highs and lows that sometimes can be extreme. There are good days and bad days, hopes and fears, dreams and disillusionment. On the bad days, remember the successes you've had with your children, and keep in mind that parenting is a long-term enterprise that can be one of the most rewarding experiences in life.

Much of your success as a parent will depend on the hopes and expectations you have for your children, your ability to model something close to the ideal that you want for them, and your diligence in positive reinforcement of their behaviors. These are the most important things you can do for your child. If you're experiencing personality problems that make it difficult for you to be the kind of parent you want to be, read on to the last section of this book and you may want to consider seeking help.

Our children can be unpredictable and infuriating, and often leave us wondering if we're doing a good job as a parent. Children can also be fun, smart, and very loving. Do your best, trust in yourself, and remember that your children look to you for love and approval.

# Check Yourself Out

Here are several questions to help you reflect on what you've read in this chapter, and perhaps to take the information a step or two farther in your own mind:

➤ What do you remember most about the way your parents treated you as a child?

➤ What is one thing your parents did that you promised yourself you'd never do?

➤ How does your personality affect your parenting?

➤ When you feel out of control, what do you do?

➤ How can you begin using more positive reinforcement to teach your child?

You might benefit from discussing these questions with another person or just thinking about them on your own.

---

## The Least You Need to Know

➤ Your personality factors into and affects the kind of parent you'll be on many levels.

➤ Great parents treat their children respectfully and model the behavior they want their kids to display.

➤ People who have trouble with parenting may be emotionally unprepared and lack parenting skills.

➤ What we expect of our kids and how we convey those expectations largely affects how they'll grow up.

➤ Punishment might be easier than positive reinforcement, but in the long run, it's far less effective.

➤ Modeling good behavior and reinforcing it in your children are the best things you can do to ensure they'll grow up to be happy, productive people.

# Part 6

# Personality and Change

*In the earlier parts of this book, we talk about theories—why we are how we are, how we assess personality, and how personality affects different aspects of our lives. We switch our focus in this part from talking about personality to telling you what you can do to change it. You'll discover what you can—and can't—change and how you can change aspects of your personality that may be causing distress in your life.*

*If there's an aspect of your personality that is causing you distress or discomfort, you'll learn how to begin working on changing it. We present some strategies for you to use and tell you how to put them into action.*

*Some things are much harder to change than others, but it's possible to change your behaviors, automatic thoughts, and even your core beliefs. This can greatly help you to reduce the distress levels in your life.*

*The ideas of many clinicians and researchers have been helpful in writing this section, but no one has been more influential on the content than Aaron T. Beck, M.D. You'll find Beck's important ideas about cognitive therapy and changing beliefs throughout Part 6.*

# Chapter 21

# Can a Leopard Change His Spots?

## In This Chapter

➤ Recognizing when we want to change

➤ Changing our beliefs and behaviors

➤ Going through the stages of change

➤ Using cognitive therapy for change

➤ Understanding time variables in making changes

There's probably not a person in the world who wouldn't change something about him- or herself if given the opportunity.

We know lots of people who would shave off 10 or 20 pounds, change the color of their hair, and make it curly instead of straight while they're at it. Then there are the resolution-type changes that we hear so many people talking about around New Year's:

"I'll get more organized."

"I won't eat as much chocolate."

"I'll exercise for three hours every day."

"I'll read Shakespeare's complete works before February 1."

"I'll never raise my voice at my kids again."

Many people, though, at some point in their lives, recognize that they need to make more profound changes than these. For some people, those who live in great pain due to aspects of their personality, change is not an option; it's a necessity.

In this chapter, we discuss the kinds of change that are possible and how we can make the changes we want to make. If you feel there are aspects of your personality you need to change, have hope. It doesn't happen overnight, but it can be done.

# What We Can or Can't Change

Some of the preceding chapters deal with our biological/evolutionary temperaments, and the environmental influences that affect our personalities. We're all, to a great extent, products of our biology and our environments. We had nothing to say about it, and we're pretty much stuck with the cards we were dealt. We are who we are, biologically speaking, and we grew up in the environments we grew up in, with the people who lived there with us. All that is in the past.

To return to the present, we know that if we don't like some of the things that are happening in our community or the world at large, we can get involved in working to change them. We can help change laws, make our streets safer, and clean up our rivers and roadways. Helping to bring about these kinds of changes, however important they may be, won't guarantee us greater happiness. For that, we need to address the aspects of our personality that are giving us pain.

So if we can't change our biology or our early environments, just what can we change? Can we make significant enough changes to improve the quality of our lives?

As we explained in Chapter 11, "Schemas and So Forth," we all create schemas, or cognitive structures, which we use to develop our own, unique belief systems. Our belief systems, which consist of our core beliefs, assumptions, and automatic thoughts, affect not only what we believe, but how we behave as well.

If your beliefs and behaviors are causing you grief, don't despair; it is within your control to change them. By doing so, you can greatly improve the way you feel and better the quality of your life.

**Personality Pointer**

We know that mental health and physical health are closely related. People who are emotionally distressed suffer many more physical health problems than do those who are emotionally sound. Improving mental health can greatly improve physical health.

# Time for a Change?

Nearly everyone feels the need to make some changes from time to time. Maybe you feel that you've got to get more organized, stop being so moody, or be more outgoing when you meet new people.

The need to change can become more intense and serious, however, if you're experiencing distress and encountering problems because of something related to your personality. That's when most people start thinking seriously about making some changes.

Distress and problems come in many forms and at many levels. Here are some of the most common:

➤ Mood conditions, such as depression and anxiety

➤ Behaviors that conflict with one's values, or behaviors that the person can't control

➤ Interpersonal problems that occur when family and friends become upset about what they see a person doing or how he or she is acting

➤ Deteriorating physical health

➤ Being in conflict with society due to illegal or unethical behavior

These signs can occur suddenly and serve as a wakeup call for the person with the problem. They are the main reasons people start looking for help to make changes in their personality.

Bob gets arrested for selling drugs. Janet's husband leaves her and takes the kids because she screams at them constantly. These types of circumstances can force people to confront their problems and decide whether to act on them.

Or problems can go on for years before people's distress reaches the level at which they decide they must make changes.

### Don't Go There!

Sometimes we mistake being ready to change for wanting other people to change. We think, *If only Mark would come home on time, then I wouldn't get upset and scream at him.* Hoping that someone else will change isn't productive and does nothing to help you. If you want to change, you have to take responsibility for the problem and be willing to work it through.

If you're reading this chapter, perhaps you're considering making some changes yourself. If that's true, good for you. It takes courage to admit that you need to change. If you are considering it, the first thing to do is identify exactly what it is you want to do something about.

# Identifying the Problem

Sometimes people will just feel lousy, without really knowing why. They say they want to change, but they're not sure what changes they should make.

Sometimes people look to others to change them, or to change for them. That doesn't work. If you feel that you need to change, you've got to specifically identify the problem that's making you feel lousy.

What part of your personality is causing problems for you? It could be thoughts, feelings, or behaviors.

Are you so shy that it's causing problems for you at work or in your social life? Are you so aggressive that you're beginning to alienate even friends and family members? Are you feeling too depressed to even get out of bed some mornings?

Once you've identified the problem, you can ask yourself some questions to help you better define it. Consider each question and the possible answers, and then rate your response from 0 to 10. In most cases, the higher you rate your response, the more distressing the problem is to you, and the more willing you'll be to work at changing it.

**Don't Go There!**

Change doesn't work if you're doing it for somebody else. If your wife is constantly telling you to cheer up because you're no fun anymore, so you act happy and bubbly just to keep her quiet, you're in for a long, tough road ahead. If you genuinely want to change so that you feel better, however, your chances greatly improve.

➤ How often does the problem bother me?

Rate your answer from 0 to 10, with 0 being not at all and 10 being unbearable. Along the continuum are infrequently, sometimes, every few days, most days, every day, and most of the day.

➤ How much distress does the problem cause when I experience it?

Rate your answer from 0 to 10, with 0 being not at all and 10 being a great deal.

➤ How much do I want to change?

➤ Rate your answer from 0 to 10, with 0 being not at all and 10 being a great deal.

Answering these questions as honestly as you can will give you an idea of your distress level and may help you realize whether a change is needed. Remember that the measure of distress necessary to make a person want to change varies from person to person. Not everybody is ready to change at the same time or at the same rate of speed.

Generally, the more distress the problem is causing you, the greater the likelihood you'll decide to change. If your desire to change is very strong, there's a good chance that you'll be successful.

# The Stages of Change

Change doesn't happen overnight. You can't decide before you go to bed one night that you won't be shy the next day. In fact, research indicates that change occurs in progressive stages.

James Prochaska and Carlo DiClemente have done a great deal of research concerning behavior change, and in 1982, they identified five stages people go through when making changes in their behaviors. We have adapted them here for use with personality changes.

Let's look at these stages using Jack as an example. He has a fiercely bad temper, is angry much of the time, and has no qualms about lashing out at whoever happens to be around.

1. **Precontemplation.** At this point, Jack has no idea that there's a problem and no plans to make a change. His wife and co-workers have certainly noticed Jack's shortcomings, and they mention them from time to time. Jack, however, thinks that everything is just dandy.

2. **Contemplation.** Jack now believes that there might be a problem. This is largely due to the fact that his four-year-old son told him, "I wish you lived someplace else. When you yell at me, I get scared." Jack tentatively asks his wife if the kids are afraid of him, and she says yes.

3. **Preparation.** Jack intends to take action to reduce his anger and improve his temper. He's thinking about what to do, but he hasn't made a firm decision yet about the course of action he'll take.

4. **Action.** Jack asks his wife to help him find a therapist who will work with him on his anger problem. He begins seeing the therapist once a week and actively working to change his behavior.

5. **Maintenance.** Jack has finished six months of therapy and has made significant changes in his personality. His kids snuggle on the

**Notes and Quotes**

Prochaska's and DiClemente's change model is considered user friendly because it accommodates relapses or backsliding. They contend that it's quite normal for a person to require several trips through the stages in order to achieve lasting changes. While backsliding isn't desirable, they recognize that it's not unusual and doesn't mean that the person who is trying to change is failing.

couch with him instead of crouching near the door, ready to run when he yells. Jack realizes that things are better, and he's working to maintain the changes he's made.

While Prochaska and DiClemente set up a concise model for change, it doesn't always happen exactly the way it did in Jack's case. For one thing, people remain in the different stages for different amounts of time. While Jack may have spent only two weeks in the preparation stage, Cheryl may be stuck there for two years.

If you're thinking about a change for yourself, try to evaluate at which point you fall on the change model. Perhaps you're in the contemplation stage or the preparation stage.

The next few chapters of this book tell you how you can help yourself make changes. If you're in the precontemplation or contemplation stage of change, you may benefit most from putting off any planning for specific changes, and simply reading through the next few chapters. Just keep your mind open to the information you'll find in these chapters.

If you're in the preparation, action, or maintenance stage, the next few chapters will help direct you in making or maintaining changes.

# Cognitive Therapy: The Basic Tool for Change

So far, most of this book has dealt with learning where your beliefs come from and how they're formed. Here you can learn how cognitive therapy can help you to change your beliefs.

**Personality Parlance**

**Cognitive therapy** is the most widely researched form of psychotherapy. It's been proven effective in the treatment of many conditions, including depression, anxiety, and personality disorders. Cognitive therapy teaches a patient to recognize and change thought distortions.

Cognitive therapy is a present-oriented psychotherapy. It proposes that thought distortions exist with all psychological problems. Through evaluation and modification of the thoughts, people make positive changes in their moods and behaviors.

By working with a cognitive therapist to evaluate their automatic thoughts and develop alternative ones, people can bring about the kind of change in their basic beliefs that will lead to positive changes in their mental functioning.

## *Evaluating Automatic Thoughts*

When we encounter a stressful event or problem, we have an immediate reaction. The reaction is often in the form of a thought, which we call an *automatic thought*. It's our first and immediate response to the situation. If you stick your finger into a flame, for instance, you'll say something like, "Ouch, that's hot," and you'll immediately get your finger out of there. (For more on automatic thoughts, see Chapter 2, "You Are What You Believe.")

Let's take the case of Mark, who is suffering from depression. He took a test and didn't do as well on it as he would have liked. His reaction when learning the test score was

> "Man, I really blew it."

accompanied by expressions of great disappointment and a lengthy period of sulking. Marie took the same test that Mark did and was also disappointed in her score. Her reaction was

> "Oh well, it's not the end of the world."

Marie committed herself to working hard so that she'd do better the next time, and then she started getting ready for her date.

Marie clearly does not have a problem in this area. Mark suffers from depression and may benefit from cognitive therapy, in which his therapist would train him to evaluate that automatic thought (I really blew it) and what it means; did he really blow it, or is something else going on?

Mark would be asked to think about the situation. He did poorly on a test. Okay. On a scale of 0 to 10, with 0 being not bad and 10 being awful, just how much did I mess things up for myself?

Once Mark had answered that, the therapist would evaluate his automatic thought further by asking questions such as these:

➤ You said you really blew it. Blew what? Even if you did badly on the test, how bad can it be?

➤ What's the worst thing that could happen as a result of not doing well?

➤ What impact is the test likely to have on your life a year or five years from now?

Or the therapist might ask these questions:

➤ What's the best thing that could result from doing poorly on the test?

➤ What's the minimum impact that doing poorly could have, or is there an opportunity for you to use the bad grade in a positive way?

After Mark answers the questions, the therapist will work with him on developing an alternative thought.

## Developing Alternative Automatic Thoughts

An alternative thought is one that's more in alignment with the actual impact of a negative experience than an automatic thought. An alternative statement for Mark might be

> "I really hoped to do better on the test, but at least now I have a better understanding of what tests in this course are like. Anyway, this is just one test, and it isn't going to significantly impact my life."

The important points to acknowledge when developing alternative thoughts are …

➤ I didn't do as well as I'd wanted.

➤ Some good may come from the experience.

➤ The situation isn't as bad as it could be.

Mark's therapist would ask him to form a new, alternative statement and say it out loud. Afterward, the therapist would have Mark, using the new statement, again rate the severity of the problem on a scale of 0 to 10.

Inevitably, after Mark reconsiders the situation and develops an alternative automatic thought, his disappointment level will go down and, with it, his whining and sulking. He will just take a deep breath and start preparing for his next test.

Chapter 22, "Changing What We Believe," gets into much more detail about changing automatic thoughts and behaviors. For now, here's a review of the steps to recognizing a problem and changing the automatic thought behind it into an alternative thought:

1. Identify the problem (in Mark's case, the problem is depression).

2. Ask yourself how often it bothers you.

3. Ask yourself how much distress it causes.

4. Ask yourself how much you want to change your reactions.

5. Identify a specific situation that exemplifies the problem, and provide your automatic thought and the emotion and behavior that accompanied it. (In Mark's case, the situation was the test, the automatic thought was *I blew it,* the emotion was disappointment, and the behavior was sulking.)

6. Evaluate your automatic thought; then, develop an alternative thought that will lead to new emotions and new behavior in response to the same circumstance.

# You Gotta Believe

Runners who believe they can run faster. Kids who believe they can climb higher. Sick people who believe they can heal faster. And … people who believe they can change their behavior. If you believe you can change your behavior, you have a much greater chance of success than someone who doesn't. We all can do more when we believe that we can.

When it comes to changing your behavior, the level of confidence you have in your ability to do so is crucial in determining your success. It is called *self-efficacy*, and it's extremely useful. For more on self-efficacy, see Chapter 12, "The All-Important Self-Esteem Factor."

If you're looking to change your behavior, ask yourself this question:

"How much do I believe cognitive therapy can help me?"

Now answer honestly, with 0 being not at all and 10 being a great deal.

Then ask yourself,

"How much do I think I can participate in cognitive therapy in order to have it make a change in my life?"

Respond using 0 as not at all and 10 as total partic-ipation. The higher your scores are on these ques-tions, the better chance you'll have of changing.

You gotta believe that you can do it if you expect to be successful in changing your behavior. Your therapist will guide you and direct you, but you're the one who can make it happen.

**Personality Parlance**

**Self-efficacy** is simply the belief that you have the ability to have an impact on the way that some-thing happens. It's extremely powerful and effective.

## Are We There Yet?

We've all heard about people like the guy who's been in therapy for 16 years and the woman who spends 3 mornings a week on her therapist's couch. There's no reason to think that if you choose to use cognitive therapy to change your behavior it's going to be a long, drawn-out process as it is for those in psychoanalysis.

No one can tell you exactly how long it will take for you to achieve the behavioral changes you're looking to make; it varies from person to person and is affected greatly by factors such as self-efficacy and the willingness to try.

You very well may be able to make the changes on your own, using the methods you'll find in this book and other books. Or you may want to look for a therapist to help you.

However you choose to go about developing alternative thoughts, beliefs, and behav-iors, you can expect to start seeing results on the very first day you decide to embark on cognitive therapy. That's not to say that your problem will be solved and your be-havior changed, but you'll feel better because you'll know that you've taken your first step toward change and you're working to get control of your life.

Cognitive therapy was developed as short-term therapy, not for long-term use. It's used successfully to treat many different problems in a short period of time, such as those we outlined in Chapter 13, "States of Being."

➤ Mood disorders

➤ Adjustment disorders

➤ Substance abuse

➤ Eating disorders

➤ Anxiety disorders

When these and other Axis I disorders are treated with cognitive therapy, we normally see results within three to six months.

Recent research also shows that cognitive therapy is useful in treating schizophrenia, a major mental disorder.

Cognitive therapy and schema-focused cognitive therapy (developed by Jeffery Young, Ph.D.) can be used to treat personality disorders, but the process takes longer than it does for Axis I disorders. Depending on the disorder and its severity, cognitive therapy treatment for a personality disorder could take one to three years or more depending on the severity of the problem.

**Personality Pointer**

To learn more about cognitive therapy and how it's used to treat personality disorders, check out *Reinventing Your Life,* by Jeffrey E. Young, Ph.D. and Janet S. Klosko, Ph.D.

Many factors will affect the rate at which you'll be able to change your beliefs and behaviors. If you're attempting to gauge how long your treatment may be, it will be helpful to consider these questions:

➤ How long have I had the problem?

Rate your answer from 0 to 10, with 0 being just started, 5 being less than a year, and 10 being many years.

➤ How severe is my problem?

Rate your answer from 0 to 10, with 0 being mild, 5 being moderate, and 10 being severe.

➤ How specific can I be about the problem?

Rate your answer from 0 to 10, with 0 being very specific, 5 being in general terms, and 10 being vague or uncertain.

➤ What is my confidence level in the treatment process?

Rate your answer from 0 to 10, with 0 being high confidence and 10 being no confidence.

➤ How great is my confidence in my ability to participate in treatment?

Rate your answer from 0 to 10, with 0 being high and 10 being no confidence.

➤ How serious are my medical problems?

Rate your answer from 0 to 10, with 0 being no problem and 10 being chronic problems.

➤ How serious are my social problems?

Rate your answer from 0 to 10, with 0 being no problems and 10 being long-standing ones.

If your scores fall into the 0-to-5 range, you're probably looking at fairly short-term treatment with a good chance for success.

If your scores are in the 5-to-10 range, your problem will be more difficult to treat and require longer treatment. There's no reason to believe, however, that your problem is unsolvable, no matter how high you scored on the questions.

Your willingness to work and your desire to help yourself mean a great deal and are big factors in your success. Believe that you can change, and you will.

**Personality Pointer**

Remember that once you begin developing alternative beliefs, you'll pave the way for more positive emotions, which will in turn support making the behavior changes you want to make.

## Check Yourself Out

Here are several questions to help you reflect on what you've read in this chapter, and perhaps to take the information a step or two farther in your own mind:

➤ Name one problem you've been experiencing.

➤ What stage of change are you in as far as addressing the problem?

➤ What is your automatic thought when you experience the problem?

➤ What alternative belief can you develop?

➤ How successful can you be at making changes?

You might benefit from discussing these questions with another person, or just thinking about them on your own.

## The Least You Need to Know

➤ Everyone has something they would like to change about themselves, but the people who are moved to change their beliefs and behaviors are those who are experiencing deep distress because of them.

➤ Although beliefs and behaviors may be firmly established, they can be changed with the proper techniques and work.

➤ The first step in changing beliefs and behavior is to identify the problem they're causing and evaluate the level of distress they're causing.

➤ There are five stages of change, and not everyone progresses through them at the same rate.

➤ Cognitive therapy is the basic tool used in changing beliefs and behavior.

➤ Cognitive therapy is designed as a short-term process, but various factors affect the amount of time needed to change beliefs and behavior.

# Changing What We Believe

---

### In This Chapter

➤ Learning the process of changing automatic thoughts

➤ Relieving anxiety with alternative automatic thoughts

➤ Changing automatic thoughts related to substance abuse

➤ Improving relationship problems with alternative automatic thoughts

➤ Developing alternative thoughts to stop obsessive-compulsive behavior

➤ Using new beliefs to conquer bulimic behavior

---

In Chapter 21, "Can a Leopard Change His Spots?" we gave you an example of an automatic thought problem that involved a poor test score and depression. Mark, who was suffering from depression, did poorly on a test and had the automatic thought, *I really blew it.*

Then we outlined the steps Mark had to go through to change that automatic thought and eventually end up with this alternative thought: *I really hoped to do better on the test, but at least now I have a better understanding of what tests in this course are like. Anyway, this is just one test, and it isn't going to significantly impact my life.*

In this chapter, we cover maladaptive automatic thoughts (those that are unsuited to the situation) in greater detail. We walk you through the process of reevaluating such thoughts and eventually changing them into alternative automatic thoughts.

We use examples, all based on actual cases, of people dealing with anxiety, substance abuse, relationship problems, obsessive-compulsive disorder, and anorexia/bulimia.

Here's the format for this chapter and the ones that follow: We present a scenario and tell you the automatic thoughts of the person involved. We identify the emotion the person feels, the behavior he or she displays, and the assumption the person makes about the scenario.

Then we present a series of questions a therapist actually would use to evaluate an automatic thought. We tell you about the alternative statement the patient comes up with to replace the automatic thought. Then we tell you how it leads to the formulation of an alternative automatic thought, as well as changes in the emotions and behavior of the individual.

If you're reading this chapter for self-help purposes, be sure to review the Cognitive Therapy for Change Worksheet at the end.

Before we start, let's just make sure that we're clear about what all these terms mean.

# What's That Mean?

Granted, all this talk about automatic thoughts, alternative statements, assumptions, behaviors, and emotions can get a little overwhelming.

Let's just have a quick look at what these things mean:

➤ **Automatic thoughts.** The immediate thought that pops into your mind in response to any sort of situation or event.

➤ **Emotions.** Feelings that occur along with the automatic thought.

➤ **Behaviors.** Actions you display in connection with the automatic thoughts.

➤ **Assumptions.** Descriptions of the conditions under which certain actions must be taken, usually in the format of, "If this happens, then that will happen."

➤ **Alternative statement (alternative automatic thought).** A new, more adaptable belief that's formed from consideration given to objective facts.

Okay. Now that we've got the terms down, let's see how a person can change automatic thoughts as they pertain to anxiety.

# Anxiety and Automatic Thoughts

In Chapter 2, "You Are What You Believe," we talked about the anxiety Larry had about making a presentation at work. Speaking in front of people is a common cause of anxiety.

Another situation that causes many people to be anxious is a job interview, and that's the scenario we deal with in this section.

Roger is preparing to interview for a job he desperately wants. He thinks that he's perfect for the position; it's just the type of job he's been waiting for. If he gets it, he'll head up an agency that he sincerely believes in, so he feels the job would be extremely rewarding. He also would make a lot more money than he makes now.

The interview is next week, and Roger's a nervous wreck. He's sure he won't be able to answer the questions the interviewers ask. He's afraid the interviewers won't like him. He's worried that he won't wear the right clothes, that he won't make a good impression, and so on and so forth. He's feeling very anxious and panicky. Roger's automatic thought is,

> *I'll never get the job.*

If Roger's working with a therapist, the therapist may ask the following questions. If you're using this chapter for self-help, ask yourself these questions and think about how you might answer them:

➤ How strongly do you believe that automatic thought?

Rate your answer on a scale of 0 to 10, with 0 being that you don't believe it at all and 10 being that you believe it completely. (Roger rates his belief at 8.)

➤ When you have this thought, how do you feel?

(Roger answers that he feels anxious.)

➤ How anxious are you?

Rate your answer on a scale of 0 to 10, with 0 being not very anxious and 10 being extremely anxious. (Roger rates his anxiety at 9.)

➤ What's your behavior like? What behavior is associated with your automatic thought?

(Roger says his behavior is irritable and impatient, and he's always pacing.)

We know that Roger wants this job very badly. He's tempted to cancel the interview, but he doesn't really want to do that. So he and his therapist sit down and evaluate Roger's automatic thought; they come up with the following observations and questions:

➤ The thought isn't based on any objective evidence that Roger won't get the job.

Nobody from the agency called him and told him he was out of the running. In fact, being chosen for an interview indicates that the agency is very interested in hiring Roger.

➤ The automatic thought is based on Roger's assumption that he can't present himself well, and his rule that he won't put himself on the spot or risk making a fool of himself.

The therapist asks Roger if it's really true that he can't present himself well. If so, he asks, how did Roger get as far along in his career as he has? How did he get through school, for that matter?

The therapist may point out that Roger's belief that he can't do very well may negatively affect his performance. By following his rule of not putting himself on the spot, Roger may have cheated himself out of many opportunities.

➤ After the therapist and Roger discuss those questions and observations, they come up with this alternative thought:

*I know there's stiff competition for this job, but I have a good chance just by the fact that I got the interview. And, if nothing else, this interview will be good experience and practice for interviews in the future.*

➤ The therapist asks Roger to identify the very worst and the very best thing that could happen.

Roger says, "I won't get the job, and I'll stay in the job I have. The best thing that could happen is I'll get the job and be very happy."

**Personality Pointer**

Remember that self-efficacy (believing that you can do something) is a big deal in accomplishing what you want to do. Generally, the more we think we can do, the more we're actually able to do.

Once Roger tries out his alternative automatic thought and identifies the worst and best possible scenarios, his anxiety level drops from 9 to 6. He's still anxious, but he is handling it better, which gives him a better chance of being successful at the interview.

## Substance Abuse and Automatic Thoughts

Substance abuse is a bit different from the other situations we discuss in this chapter, but it's still driven by automatic thoughts that need to be changed.

People in substance-abuse situations deal with the same factors as others: the automatic thought, the emotion, and the behavior. However, there's an extra step involved: acquiring the drugs or alcohol.

The scenario is that Tom is trying to stop abusing alcohol and marijuana.

He gets invited to go to a party with some friends, and his automatic thought is,

*Yes! I can get some relief and have fun.*

Tom's belief in that automatic thought, on a scale of 0 to 10, is 10. The emotion he's experiencing is craving, and he rates the craving at 10.

The preliminary action required is to go to the party, and the behavior is getting high.

Tom goes to the party, gets high, and wakes up the next day feeling upset and depressed about what he's done.

The assumption that Tom makes, related to his automatic thought, is that *If I can't handle things, I'll do whatever I have to do to get by.*

By doing whatever he has to do, of course, he means getting high. Doing so, however, makes Tom unhappy.

Tom and his therapist evaluate the situation and Tom's automatic thought *(Yes! I can get some relief and have fun.)* to see what he could do differently. They come up with the following observations and questions:

➤ What kind of relief do you get by getting high? If you get relief today, what about tomorrow?

   The therapist reminds Tom that relief provided by drugs is only temporary and asks him whether the relief he gets is short-term or long-term.

➤ What things do you need to get relief from? Is there another way to get relief from problems?

➤ What kinds of things have you tried in the past and found to be successful?

➤ Is drinking and using drugs the only way to have fun? What other ways could you have fun?

➤ The therapist asks what Tom thinks is the worst thing that may happen if he goes to the party.

   Tom says, "I could overdose and die; I could get into a car wreck; I could get arrested," and so forth.

➤ The therapist asks what Tom thinks is the worst thing that may happen if he doesn't go to the party.

   Tom answers, "I could go into withdrawal, but I've been there before, and I know there's help available if I need it. I know I'll have cravings, but I understand that cravings are temporary and will eventually go away."

Based on all those observations and questions, Tom and his therapist develop an alternative thought. Next time Tom's invited to a party, he'll say, "I'd really like to go to the party for some relief and fun, but that will be short-lived, and I'll feel like dirt in the morning. I'll be better off if I stay home with a safe friend."

Once Tom establishes his alternative belief, his emotion remains that of craving, but it's down from 10 to 5. His new behavior is to stay at home with a safe friend.

# A Relationship Problem and Automatic Thoughts

In this section, we look at a marriage in trouble. We get the individual perspectives of both the wife and the husband as they go through the process of examining their automatic thoughts and developing alternative thoughts or beliefs.

Joyce has been extremely angry at her husband, Robert, for a long time. The reason is that he doesn't help her with the housework, the kids, the cooking, or much of anything else. She keeps quiet about it, but one day she's had enough of it, and she loses it—screaming at him, making accusations, the works.

Instantly, she's mortified at what she's done. She's never yelled at Robert before, and she doesn't know what he'll do. He'll probably be angry with her, and he might slap her, or even worse, leave her.

Her automatic thought is,

> *Oh, I shouldn't have said anything. I should have kept my big mouth shut.*

On a scale of 0 to 10, she rates that belief at 10.

- ➤ The emotion Joyce feels is fear, of both her husband and other things, such as being left alone. She rates her fear at 9.
- ➤ Her behavior is to apologize to Robert and start cleaning the house from top to bottom.
- ➤ The assumption Joyce makes is that if she's in a relationship, she should take care of everything.

Robert's automatic thought after Joyce yells at him is,

> *Who does she think she is talking to me like that? She can't talk to me like that.*

On a scale of 0 to 10, he rates that belief at 10.

- ➤ Robert's emotion is outrage, which he rates at 9.
- ➤ Robert's behavior is to make strong retaliatory statements to his wife. In other words, he tells her in no uncertain terms to shut up and keep her place.
- ➤ His assumption is that if he's in a relationship, he had better be taken care of.

The therapist then works individually with Joyce and with Robert.

Joyce and her therapist evaluate the situation and look at Joyce's automatic thought (*I shouldn't have said anything. I should have kept my big mouth shut.*) to see what could be done differently. They come up with the following observations and questions:

- ➤ Joyce's automatic thought suggests that if she's in distress or needs something, she shouldn't talk about it. She should always be in a subordinate position.

   The therapist asks Joyce if this belief holds up to a common standard that one should never make one's thoughts and feelings known to others. In other words, he asks her if she thinks other people believe that they should never make their needs known or have their needs met.

➤ The therapist asks Joyce what she thinks is the worst thing that could happen as a result of her speaking up to her husband.

Joyce says, "My husband might leave me."

➤ The therapist asks Joyce what she thinks is the best thing that could happen as a result of her speaking up to her husband.

Joyce says, "Maybe I'll get his attention, and then we can talk about the situation."

➤ The therapist asks Joyce if she believes it's true that women shouldn't express their anger.

Joyce says, "It might be okay for other women to express their anger, but it's not okay for me."

Then Robert and the therapist evaluate Robert's automatic thought. *(Who does she think she is talking to me like that? She can't talk to me like that.)* They come up with the following observations and questions:

➤ The therapist asks Robert to think about whether Joyce is really out of line by expressing her feelings.

Robert says, "Yes, she is out of line."

➤ He asks if Robert really believes he's superior to his wife.

Robert would avoid the question and say, "I don't mean to say that I'm better than her, but, if it weren't for me, she would be nowhere and nobody."

➤ The therapist asks Robert what he sees as the worst thing that could happen if he continues to believe that Joyce can't talk to him about a problem.

Robert says, "I might alienate Joyce to the point where she'll get tired of taking care of me."

➤ The therapist asks Robert what he sees as the best thing that might happen if Robert continues to believe his automatic thought.

Robert answers, "The best possible thing that could happen would be what did happen. Joyce backed off, apologized, and cleaned the house."

Based on all those observations and questions, the couple and the therapist work to develop alternative beliefs for Joyce and Robert.

Joyce's alternative thought is,

> *I know I don't like to say anything, but I really do need some help with the house and the kids.*

Joyce rates her belief of that statement at 8. Her emotion of fear is replaced by a feeling of concern, and she says the level of it drops from 9 to 5.

Robert's alternative thought is,

> *I really don't like to do this stuff, but I can see she needs help with the house and the kids.*

He rates that belief at 6. Robert's new emotion, believe it or not, is humility, and he rates that at 5.

# Obsessive-Compulsive Disorder and Automatic Thoughts

Anna suffers from obsessive-compulsive disorder, and the scenario we're concerned with is that she's unable to stop repeating ritualistic prayers in her head or softly to herself.

Anna is afraid she's going crazy and won't be able to take care of her family. She worries that she'll lose her job and won't be able to function at a normal level if the prayers don't stop.

Though she wants the praying to stop, her automatic thought is,

> *I can't stop.*

On a scale of 0 to 10, she rates her belief in that thought at 10.

➤ Anna's emotion is fear—fear of losing her family and her job, fear of going crazy, and fear of having the prayers continue in her head forever. She rates the level of her fear at 8.5.

➤ Her behavior, as we know, is to repeat the ritualistic prayer.

➤ Her assumption is that, if she has bad thoughts, she needs to constantly ask for forgiveness. She's afraid that if she doesn't ask for forgiveness, something awful will happen to her.

Now bear in mind that Anna has no more bad thoughts than anyone else. But she's convinced that she does and that she needs forgiveness for those thoughts. The way to get it, she thinks, is through this prayer she perpetually repeats.

In an attempt to get Anna to change her automatic thought, Anna's therapist asks Anna the following questions:

➤ Is it really true that you can't stop saying these prayers?

Anna answers that she can't stop.

➤ What's the worst thing that might happen if you continue with the ritualistic behavior?

Anna answers that the worst thing would be that she won't be able to function, and she'll lose her family and her job.

➤ What's the best thing that might happen if you continue with the ritualistic behavior?

Anna says that the best thing would be to continue to function as she is, and eventually get tired of repeating the prayers and have them stop.

➤ What's the most likely thing that will happen?

Anna says the most likely thing is that she'll continue with the behavior, and it will somewhat affect her functioning, but not make her completely dysfunctional.

After thinking about it for a while, Anna comes up with this alternative statement:

> "I know it will be really scary to stop reciting the prayers, but nothing bad will happen for real if I do."

She rates her belief in that alternative statement at 4. Anna's new emotion still is fear, but it's gone down from 8.5 to 6.

Anna's new behavior is to recognize when she's about to start saying the ritualistic prayer, and to delay saying it for as long as she can. If she puts off reciting the prayer, and sees that nothing awful happens to her, her automatic thought and behavior aren't being reinforced, and the hope is that the behavior will eventually change.

**Personality Pointer**

Fear can decrease very quickly once an alternative thought is formulated and repeated. The level of fear can decrease from 10 to 4 or 5 immediately after someone first states and develops the alternative belief.

# Anorexia/Bulimia and Automatic Thoughts

Jeri is anorexic, and she engages in bulimic behavior. In other words, she eats and then makes herself vomit afterward.

It's a co-worker's birthday, and the gang from Jeri's office is going out for Italian food after work to celebrate. Jeri thinks all day about whether she should go and finally accepts the invitation. It's not that she doesn't want to be sociable, or that she doesn't like her co-workers. Eating, however, is a major issue for Jeri, and going out to dinner is very stressful.

Jeri and her friends get to the restaurant and order, and Jeri eats most of a small salad with no dressing and half a roll. Any reasonable standard would indicate that there's no way Jeri overate, but she's convinced that she did. Her automatic thought is,

*I feel like a stuffed pig.*

**Notes and Quotes**

More than five million Americans suffer from eating disorders, and about 1,000 people die each year from the effects of anorexia nervosa. Many more people suffer permanent physical damage from its effects. It's estimated that as many as 5 percent of all college women engage in bulimic behavior.

Jeri believes that thought on a level of 10. Her emotion, which she rates at 9, is a feeling of disgust with herself for what she perceives as overeating.

➤ Jeri's behavior is to purge.

➤ Her assumption is, *If I'm in a stressful situation, overeating will make it easier for me to handle.* She also assumes that if she overeats, she needs to purge so that she won't feel and look like a stuffed pig.

Note that Jeri's assumption is not unlike Tom's, except that he has a problem with drugs and alcohol instead of food. They both assume that by using something (either food or drugs and alcohol), they'll make themselves feel better. What they find out, of course, is that they feel even worse.

To help Jeri evaluate her automatic thought, her therapist asks these questions. Remember that if you're using this chapter for self-help, it's a good idea to ask yourself these questions:

➤ Are you really, literally, a stuffed pig?

Jeri answers that she's not, but she feels like one.

➤ How much overeating, by normal standards, actually occurred?

After thinking about it, Jeri admits that she never really overeats.

➤ If you don't purge, what's the worst thing that could happen?

Jeri says the worst thing would be that she'll feel stuffed forever and look like a pig.

➤ If you don't purge, what's the best thing that could happen?

Jeri answers that the best thing would be for the overstuffed feeling to go away on its own.

➤ Without purging, what's the most likely thing that will happen?

Jeri says it's most likely that the overstuffed feeling will last for 20 to 30 minutes and then go away.

Based on Jeri's answers, they come up with this alternative thought for Jeri to say the next time she feels like she ate too much:

"I feel too full and I don't like the feeling, but I know that it will pass in a short while, and I'll feel normal again."

Jeri believes the alternative statement on a level of 6, and her emotion, while it still is disgust, drops to a level of 4. Her new behavior is to delay purging and wait for the overstuffed feeling to pass.

If the scenarios in this chapter were useful to you and you're thinking about making a change in your automatic thoughts, use the following worksheet to get a sense of the process you'd be going through. The steps are similar to those in the preceding examples.

# Cognitive Therapy for Change Worksheet

This worksheet is designed to help you begin changing an automatic thought that's causing problems for you. Just answer the questions as honestly as you can. There is no comparison data or standard on which to interpret your ratings. They are meant to provide you with insight into your problem and guide you through the process of changing the automatic thought that's causing it.

And remember, don't expect your automatic thoughts to change overnight. They've probably been with you for a long time, and you'll need to train yourself to come up with alternative thoughts and beliefs.

1. What is the general problem that causes distress in your life?
2. How often does the problem bother you?

   0 _____ 10
   (infrequently   1-2x/wk   2-3x/wk   most days   every day)

3. How much distress does the problem cause you?

   0 _____ 10
   none      moderate      unbearable

4. How much do you want to change?

   0 _____ 10
   not at all      moderately      greatly

5. Name a specific situation in which the problem mentioned above occurred._____

6. What was your automatic thought?_____

7. What was your emotional response and its severity?
   Response:
   Severity:

   0 _____ 10
   not at all      very severe

8. What did you do (your behavior?)

*continues*

*continued*

9. How effective was your response (behavior)?

     0 _____ 10

     not at all   somewhat   moderately   mostly   completely

10. Ask yourself about your automatic thought:

     Is the thought really true? _____

     Does it hold true in all situations?_____

11. Ask yourself these questions about your situation: _____

     What's the worst thing that could happen? _____

     What's the best thing that could happen? _____

     What's the most likely thing to happen? _____

12. Write an alternative thought._____

13. What is your new emotion and how strong is it?

     Emotion:

     Severity:

     0 _____ 10

       none   mild   moderate   painful   unbearable

14. What is your new behavior?

     New behavior:

     Expected effectiveness:

     0 _____ 10

     none at all   some   moderate   mostly   completely

And Remember, don't expect your automatic thoughts to change overnight. They've probably been with you for a long time, and you'll need to train yourself to come up with alternative thoughts and beliefs.

# Check Yourself Out

Here are several questions to help you reflect on what you've read in this chapter, and perhaps to take the information a step or two farther in your own mind:

➤ How well do you understand the concepts discussed in this chapter?

➤ How much do you believe that this information can be beneficial to you?

➤ Did you respond to all the questions on the worksheet?

➤ How committed are you to making the change?

➤ How will you be different by using this information?

You might benefit from discussing these questions with another person, or just thinking about them on your own.

---

### The Least You Need to Know

➤ There's a specific process you can use to change your automatic thoughts and develop alternative thoughts.

➤ Changing your automatic thoughts can help you assume a more positive attitude and be more successful.

➤ People who are trying to quit abusing drugs and alcohol can benefit from developing alternative beliefs and thoughts.

➤ A therapist can walk you through the process of changing your automatic thoughts, or you can do it yourself.

➤ Developing alternative thoughts takes discipline and practice, but it can help you tremendously.

---

# Chapter 23

# Changing How We Behave

> ## In This Chapter
>
> ➤ Understanding behavior therapy
>
> ➤ Using relaxation techniques to relieve anxiety
>
> ➤ Learning to just say no
>
> ➤ Changing behavior to improve a relationship
>
> ➤ Coping with and changing obsessive-compulsive behavior
>
> ➤ Dealing with anorexia/bulimia

If you read Chapter 22, "Changing What We Believe," you learned that the process of changing automatic thoughts is not an easy thing to do, but it is possible, and the benefits of doing so can be great.

This chapter tells you how you can change your behavior.

While changing your automatic thoughts is a big step in changing your behavior, there are other, very practical things that you can do as well.

## Behavior Therapy

We use the same problems, characters, and scenarios in this chapter that we did in Chapter 22. Just in case you didn't read that chapter, or you don't remember the specifics of it, here's a refresher of the cast and their situations:

> ➤ **Anxiety.** Roger is preparing to interview for a job he desperately wants. He's extremely nervous and anxious, and afraid that he'll do everything wrong in the interview. He's worked on developing alternative thoughts, but he's still stressed out.

➤ **Substance abuse.** Tom is trying to stop abusing drugs and alcohol. He's sorely tempted to go to a party with his friends when invited, but he knows that if he does, he'll end up getting high. He's told himself that a better thing to do is to stay home with a safe friend, but he still really wants to go to the party.

➤ **Relationship problem.** Joyce is angry at Robert because he doesn't help her with the housework or the children. At one point, her anger gets the best of her and she lashes out verbally at Robert. Robert, who sees the home responsibilities as belonging to Joyce, is extremely offended by Joyce's behavior. Joyce apologizes to Robert and begins cleaning the house. They try to alter their automatic thoughts but are finding that old habits die hard.

➤ **Obsessive-compulsive disorder.** Anna feels compelled to recite ritualistic prayers over and over in her head or quietly to herself. The behavior is distressing to her, and she sometimes thinks she's going crazy. She wants to stop reciting the prayers, but she's convinced that she has bad thoughts, and that if she doesn't ask for forgiveness for those thoughts, something bad will happen to her. Her alternative thought is that she'll be okay—that nothing bad will happen. Still, the prayers continue.

➤ **Anorexia/Bulimia.** Jeri is anorexic and bulimic. She feels that she eats too much, even though she doesn't really eat much at all, and she purges after eating. Her alternative thought is that the feeling of being overfull, which she hates, will go away if she waits for 20 or 30 minutes, so she should delay purging and wait for that to happen.

Before we look at how Roger, Tom, Joyce and Robert, Anna, and Jeri can change the behavior that causes problems for them, a note about behavior therapy.

In the situations that follow, all of which are based on actual cases, you'll see some examples of behavior therapy. *Behavior therapy* is simply a process used to bring about desirable changes in the way a person behaves. This therapy may be used to get someone to stop smoking, or yelling at the kids, or reducing fears; it may also be effective in helping someone to be more assertive or more confident.

In earlier chapters we discussed the ideas of modeling behavior and reinforcing behavior. *Modeling behavior* is the display of a behavior that you want another person, often a child, to imitate. *Reinforcing behavior* is doing something to encourage a person to repeat certain behaviors. We usually think of reinforcement as involving praise or another kind of reward. These are two techniques used in behavior therapy.

**Personality Parlance**

**Behavior therapy** is a process used to help a person change his or her behavior in a positive manner. It has various steps and components.

Other techniques are based on the theory of *reciprocal inhibition,* which was first applied to the change of human behavior by Joseph Wolpe, M.D.

Wolpe says that you can't feel two competing feelings at the same time. You can't, for instance, feel both anxious and relaxed. In behavioral terms, this means that if you're in a situation that typically makes you anxious, you can train yourself to act like someone who feels relaxed. If you do that, you'll actually feel relaxed, even if you previously felt anxious in the same situation.

All right, keeping those techniques in mind, let's go back to Roger's anxiety problem and see how behavior therapy works for him.

# Roger Reduces His Anxiety Level

As you know, Roger is feeling very nervous about his upcoming job interview. Despite his alternative thought, he still is anxious.

## *Preparing for the Interview*

To further relieve Roger's anxiety, there are some things he can do to help himself prepare for the job interview. If he knows he's done as much preparation as he possibly can, he'll feel more relaxed and confident, and his anxiety level will drop.

As Roger sees it, there are two potential roadblocks to doing well in the job interview:

➤ He won't know what to say or how to act.

➤ He'll know what to say and how to act, but his anxiety level will be so high that he won't be able to do so properly.

**Personality Parlance**

**Reciprocal inhibition** is the theory that you can't have opposite feelings at the same time. If you can make yourself experience the desirable feeling (relaxation), you cannot feel the undesirable one (fear) simultaneously.

**Personality Pointer**

If you are concerned about a job interview, try reading *Power Interviews: Job-Winning Tactics from Fortune 500 Recruiters,* by Neil M. Yeager and Lee Hough. Or check out these web sites for good information and tips:

www.ocs.fas.harvard.edu/html/intview.html

www.gresumes.com/16tips.htm

So what can Roger do to solve these problems? He can learn how to act and what to say during the interview from the tons of books available on the subject. He can check the Internet sites that can tell him what to do, what to say, how to shake hands, what kind of socks to wear, and so forth.

Roger can ask a friend to give him a mock interview. He can talk to people who've been interviewed recently, plan exactly what he'll wear, prepare responses to anticipated questions, and decide exactly how much he'll share about his personal life.

Roger can make a list of the strengths he has that would make him a good candidate for the particular job. He can prepare the way he's going to tell the interviewer why he's excited about the opportunity, and what aspects of the job he can't wait to get started on.

### Don't Go There!

Don't worry unnecessarily about answering personal questions potential employers may ask you. They can't legally ask about personal matters and then use that information to discriminate against you. Some of the big taboos are marital and childbearing status, sexual orientation, religion, and cultural background.

### Personality Parlance

**Visualization** is simply the process of forming an image in your mind. Using all five of your senses to "visualize" the image will make it more real and effective. Visualization is used for many purposes.

After Roger gathers all the information and does his planning, he can practice his responses to the questions he'll be asked. Once he's done all that, Roger will be far more confident about the interview. He'll feel prepared, and his anxiety level will decrease. He'll be able to act like a relaxed person, which will help him feel like one.

## Using Relaxation Techniques

Even after Roger prepares himself to answer the interviewer's questions, he still feels anxious. To address the problem, he can give his full attention to practicing relaxation techniques.

He might consider yoga or tai chi to help him relax. Once he's achieved a state of relaxation, Roger might use *visualization*—a technique of imagining himself having a very successful job interview.

Roger shouldn't expect his relaxation techniques to work immediately; once he starts imagining the interview, he may feel himself getting anxious again. If that happens, he'll need to repeat the relaxation techniques until they take hold.

If Roger stays with it by practicing the interview and learning relaxation skills, he'll be able to relax enough to anticipate the job interview in a more positive way. He should do just fine.

## Tom Resists Temptation

Tom is again sorely tempted to go to a party with his friends, where he knows there will be booze and drugs. If he goes to the party, it's almost a sure bet that he'll get high—the exact behavior he's trying to avoid.

So how can Tom change his behavior and stay away from the party?

## Saying "No Thanks"

First Tom can learn how to say no when he's invited to a party where he'll be tempted to repeat his alcohol and drug use.

Sometimes people think they don't have the right to say no because they'll hurt somebody's feelings. It can be difficult, but assuming that Tom is—and considers himself to be—an equal to his friends, he has a perfect right to accept or reject their invitations. He just doesn't know how to do it because he hasn't practiced that behavior.

Here are some examples of how Tom might tell his friends that he's not going to the party:

**Personality Pointer**

Many people feel compelled to offer detailed explanations of why they say no. They feel as if they have to explain that their work situations are stressful, or that they have family obligations that won't allow them to participate. All they really have to say is, "Sorry, I don't want to. "

➤ "Thanks, but I already have other plans."

➤ "Thanks, but I really don't feel like it tonight."

➤ "Thanks, but I'm trying to cut back." (on drug and alcohol use)

Tom doesn't need an elaborate explanation or excuse for not going. All he really has to say is, "I don't want to."

## Dealing with Cravings

If Tom doesn't go to the party, it's important that he find alternative activities with "safe" people. Being with people who can show Tom how to have a great time without drugs and alcohol will help him tremendously. He might consider attending a self-help group, a sporting event, or an outdoor activity. It's important that he learn to participate in activities that don't involve drugs or booze.

Once Tom has saying "no" down, he may still have to deal with cravings. People handle cravings in different ways. Some prefer to be by themselves, while others like to talk about their cravings. Some people merely wait them out, not doing much of anything. Others might try the following options:

➤ Relaxation techniques

➤ Quiet activities, such as reading or listening to music

➤ Exercise, such as walking or jogging

To deal with difficult situations, such as cravings, Tom needs to plan ahead. If he thinks about what he'll do when the cravings occur, he can have a plan in place and be ready to implement it as soon as the cravings start. By doing this, he can resist other options, such as having a drink.

# Joyce and Robert Work on Their Relationship

Joyce and Robert have relationship problems. Joyce, after expressing anger at Robert for not helping her, immediately apologizes and resumes cleaning. The impression she gives is that she doesn't have the right to express anger.

Robert, even though he has moved from his original automatic thought to an alternative one (that he does need to help Joyce with household duties), has yet to learn how to listen and to respond appropriately to her complaints.

## Accepting and Expressing Anger

We know, of course, that everyone has a right to express their anger. Joyce first needs to understand that she's allowed to get angry, and then she needs to learn how to express that anger in an acceptable way.

**Don't Go There!**

Many people feel that anger is bad and should be suppressed. We know, however, that anger is natural, and to suppress it can actually be harmful. The trick isn't to suppress anger, it's to learn the proper way to express it.

Screaming and hurling accusations is not a productive way to express anger. Joyce needs to learn a way to do it that meets her needs but doesn't violate Robert's rights. To be able to do that, she needs to do some planning.

She should think about what she'll say if the same housework issue comes up again. It could be something like, "I'm feeling angry and upset because I have all this work to do. I really need some help." Ideally, Joyce would say this in a calm manner; she'll be better able to do that if she decides ahead of time what to say and how to say it.

If Joyce practices what she wants to say, she can focus on the tone of her voice, how she'll make eye contact, what her voice volume level should be, and so forth. Then, when she needs to address the matter with her husband, she'll be confident and prepared.

## Learning to Listen and Respond

At first Robert indicates through his outrage at Joyce's outburst that he believes she doesn't have the right to speak to him about the housework situation. He believes that it is Joyce's job to take care of the house, the kids, and him.

He then develops an alternative thought that acknowledges he needs to help Joyce. Now he needs to work on his willingness to listen to her and to respond in a more appropriate manner to her requests.

298

A problem here is that, when Joyce yelled at Robert, he didn't pick up on, or show that he cared about, her anger and frustration. He responded only to the tone of her voice, which made him angry and offended him.

To improve Robert's listening skills, and to help Joyce better deliver her message in an appropriate manner, the couple can practice talking and listening to each other. It works like this:

➤ Robert listens without interrupting while Joyce expresses her thoughts and feelings.

➤ When Joyce is finished speaking, Robert repeats back to her in his own words what she's said.

➤ If Robert has understood correctly, Joyce acknowledges that understanding.

➤ Then they switch roles, and Robert talks while Joyce listens.

Once Robert has learned to listen to what Joyce is telling him and not just to the tone of her voice, he can practice making appropriate responses.

If Joyce expresses anger, Robert might say something like, "I know you're very angry about this. Could we sit down and talk about it?"

Couples working on communication skills should practice first on small issues, such as taking out the trash. Once the skills are fine-tuned a bit, the couple will be better prepared to discuss important issues like their sex lives, parenting practices, or finances.

**Personality Pointer**

If you do the listening-and-repeating exercise, it's important that, when you express your understanding of what the other person said, you put it in your own words. If you simply parrot the other person's words, you'll fail to show that person that you fully understood what was said.

# Anna Works Through Obsessive-Compulsive Behavior

Anna still has that haunting ritualistic prayer in her head, and it's distressing her more and more. Obsessive-compulsive disorder exhibits other behaviors that involve external actions, such as hand-washing, recounting, and rechecking. In Anna's case, however, the behavior she needs to change is strictly internal—it's a dialog that goes on in her mind.

Even though Anna has developed an alternative belief (that she can delay the onset of the impulse to repeat the ritual praying), she still believes on some level that she's bad and needs to be forgiven, or that she needs to continue the prayer to avoid having something bad happen to her.

## Using Thought-Stopping to End a Behavior

To deal with these behaviors, Anna works toward the ultimate goal of eliminating the ritualistic behavior.

One way she can do this is to practice a technique called *thought-stopping.* Thought-stopping is just what its name implies. You simply stop a thought as it comes into your mind. You say to yourself "No." When Anna hears her own voice saying, "You've got to do a prayer now," she trains herself to answer "No."

**Personality Parlance**

**Thought-stopping** is a technique you use as soon as an unwanted thought comes into your mind: You stop it with a decisive "No." You must do this repeatedly in order for it to be effective.

Another thing that Anna could do is to wear a rubber band around her wrist. As soon as she hears the prayer starting in her head, she could snap the rubber band against her arm to interrupt the thought process.

At first, using the thought-stopping technique is likely to make Anna anxious, which may actually increase her urge to do the ritualistic prayer. After repeated use of the technique, however, her anxiety will lessen.

Anna, like many people, may be afraid to use the thought-stopping or rubber-band technique at first. That's because she still believes on some level that the prayer is necessary.

## Cutting Back on the Behavior

Even if Anna can't stop herself from doing the obsessive-compulsive behavior altogether, she can use some techniques to cut back on the behavior.

She can …

➤ Hold off praying until a certain time.

➤ Do the prayer only in certain places, like her bedroom or her car.

➤ Recite the prayer only at certain times, such as at noon and four o'clock.

These measures aren't meant to be permanent solutions—just means of eventually stopping the behavior. People who are able to control the behavior somewhat by doing it only in certain places or at specific times usually are able to eventually give it up completely.

Once Anna stops her obsessive-compulsive behavior, she may experience some anxiety as a result. If that happens, she may need to continue to use relaxation exercises. She can use actual relaxation techniques or simply go for a walk, take a bike ride, or engage in some other alternative activity.

# Jeri Delays Her Anorexic/Bulimic Behavior

Jeri is looking for ways to change her behavior of purging after she eats.

Her problem is that after eating, she feels overly full. She complains that she feels like a stuffed pig. We might be tempted to tell her not to eat so much, but remember that Jeri is anorexic and really doesn't eat much at all by reasonable standards. She perceives what she eats to be a lot, however. So instead of Jeri eating less so that she can avoid feeling overly full, she needs to learn to tolerate the feeling of fullness.

Jeri can't stop eating altogether—that simply isn't an option for her. She can't even cut down on her eating. As an anorexic, she's likely to already be eating dangerously little. What she must learn to do is to put up with the feeling of fullness, no matter how uncomfortable it is for her. Jeri needs to learn that if she can delay purging for a little while after eating, the feeling of being stuffed and overly full will go away.

If she's in a restaurant with her friends, she can excuse herself from the table when she's finished eating and take a short walk around the lobby or the parking lot. She should, at all costs, stay out of the bathroom and try to stay where there are other people around.

Once she gets used to the feeling of fullness and becomes confident that the feeling will pass with time, she'll become less dependent on purging.

As you can see, most behavioral change techniques are down-to-earth, common-sense suggestions. Of course, reading about making changes is easier than actually doing it. Changing your behavior, however, is entirely possible and quite likely if you're willing to work.

**Notes and Quotes**

As many as 5 percent of all U.S. college women engage in bulimic behavior.

# Behavior Change Worksheet

This worksheet is designed to help you identify specific behaviors and plan how to change them.

Try to fill out the worksheet completely, and give careful thought to your answers. There is no comparison data or standard on which to interpret your ratings. The worksheet is designed to help you begin changing a behavior that's troubling you or causing distress.

1. What is the specific behavior you want to change?
2. How often do you engage in the behavior?

   0 _____ 10

   infrequently   1-2x/wk   2-3x/wk   most days   every day
3. How much distress does the behavior cause you?

   0 _____ 10

   none        moderate        unbearable
4. How much do you want to change the behavior?

   0 _____ 10

   not at all        moderately        greatly
5. Name a specific situation in which the behavior mentioned above occurred.
6. What did you do?
7. What would work better in the same situation?
8. What do you need to learn in order to make things work better ?
9. What decisions do you need to make in regard to your behavior?
10. What materials, if any, do you need?
11. What other planning or preparation do you need to do in order to change the behavior?
12. How often will you practice the new behavior?
13. What will be an acceptable level of distress for you as you get used to your new behavior?

    0 _____ 10

    none   mild   moderate   painful   unbearable

# Check Yourself Out

Here are several questions to help you reflect on what you've read in this chapter, and perhaps to take the information a step or two farther in your own mind:

➤ Can you explain the connection between beliefs and behaviors?

➤ Why does acting like a relaxed person make you feel like a relaxed person?

➤ How important is it to practice new skills you are trying to learn?

➤ How could you benefit from listening more closely to others?

➤ How do you eventually want to act in a difficult situation?

You might benefit from discussing these questions with another person, or just thinking about them on your own.

**The Least You Need to Know**

➤ Developing alternative beliefs will help you if you're trying to change your behavior, but there are also other steps that you can take.

➤ Behavior therapy is a process used to change behavior. It involves techniques such as modeling behavior, reinforcing behavior, and techniques based on reciprocal inhibition.

➤ You can learn and practice relaxation techniques to help reduce your anxiety levels.

➤ You can develop communication skills to help make behavior changes in troubled relationships.

➤ Some people rely heavily on others when attempting to change their behavior, while others prefer to meet the challenge on their own.

➤ Behavioral changes aren't easy to accomplish, but they can greatly reduce distress levels and even sometimes improve the quality of life.

# Chapter 24

# Rewriting History

## In This Chapter

➤ Looking deeply within for core beliefs

➤ Understanding the difference between Axis I and Axis II disorders

➤ Knowing how core beliefs affect your sense of self

➤ Exploring the kinds of problems core beliefs can cause

➤ Developing alternative core beliefs to replace the negative ones

In Chapters 22, "Changing What We Believe," and 23, "Changing How We Behave," we examined processes and techniques for changing automatic thoughts and behaviors. We looked at examples based on real case histories to see how people can make such changes.

In this chapter, we take an in-depth look at core beliefs and why they are more difficult to change than our automatic thoughts or behaviors.

When you work to change automatic thoughts or behaviors, you work on problems that are troubling you at the time—in the present. These are called *Axis I problems*. If, however, an underlying personality disorder is associated with your current problem (an *Axis II problem*), changing your automatic thoughts and behaviors may only be effective in the short term; it would require changes in your core beliefs to achieve a long-term solution. Changing core beliefs is much more difficult, because they are deep-level beliefs formed during our developmental years. (See Chapter 2, "You Are What You Believe," for information about how core beliefs are formed.) By changing your core beliefs, you are, in effect, "changing history."

# Axis I and Axis II Revisited

Remember that five-tiered diagnostic tool from Chapter 13, "States of Being?" Axis I problems, called *presenting problems,* are the chief complaints people are experiencing in their present lives. They include mood disorders such as anxiety and depression.

The Axis II level includes personality disorders, such as paranoid, schizoid, antisocial, borderline, avoidant, and dependent disorders, among others. Except for major mental disorders, Axis I disorders normally are more treatable than Axis II. An Axis I disorder, however, such as anxiety, won't respond as quickly or as easily to treatment if the condition also involves an Axis II disorder. In fact, when people fail to respond to treatment for Axis I disorders, it is often a clue to professionals that an Axis II disorder may also be present.

To treat personality disorders or to change personality traits (Axis II), we need to deal with the underlying core beliefs.

# The Role of Core Beliefs

To explore how core beliefs can affect and complicate the treatment of Axis I disorders, we use the same people and problems in this chapter as we did in Chapters 22 and 23. We selected them because, in every case, their problems involve a personality disorder in addition to the presenting problem.

Before we get into the actual problems, though, let's revisit how core beliefs work (see Chapter 2 for a full discussion of core beliefs).

**Don't Go There!**

Don't fly into a panic thinking about something nasty you said to your child in a moment of anger. Statements need to be repeated over and over before they become part of the child's core belief. Telling your child a couple of times that he or she is lazy won't cause any lasting damage. If that's all you've done, you can relax.

People who grew up in maladaptive environments accept as true the terrible things that were said to them when they were small. Many of those things were said before the child had the ability to think abstractly or to interpret things figuratively. As a result, everything that was said to the child was concrete—everything had a literal meaning.

For instance, if Ray's dad tells him regularly when he's a small child that he's the stupidest, most worthless kid that ever lived, Ray will have the core belief of worthlessness, thanks to the early messages.

For that reason, harmful things that are said to a child are far more damaging than they would be if said to an adult. Many parents don't realize the impact their words have on their kids. If you tell kids that they're worthless, which is really nothing but a lie, they'll accept it as true.

Children take what's said to them literally. They then store these statements as facts in their schemas.

Thereafter, an individual's schema, or "What am I," is unable to assimilate any information to the contrary. That information must be accommodated elsewhere, outside the schema. The core belief, "I'm not good," rules, and only things that confirm that belief can be recognized by the schema.

Let's say that Shannon was told over and over again by her father that she was sloppy, ugly, fat, and that nobody will ever want her. All of that information, which as a child she believes completely, goes into her "What am I?" schema. Years later, Shannon meets John. John is crazy about her and tells her that he loves her and wants to marry her. Shannon can't assimilate John's compliments and affection into her "What am I?" schema. She tries to put them there, but deep down, she still believes the things her father told her. To accommodate the conflicting signals she gets from John, Shannon reacts with suspicion, thinking that John is trying to trick her or get something from her. After all, she's unlovable.

A therapist treating Shannon would first need to identify her core belief. To do that, the therapist would ask questions such as the following:

➤ As a child, you were told some hurtful things. On a scale of 0 to 10, how much do you believe the things you were told?

➤ Do you remember events during your life that seemed to confirm your core belief? On a scale of 0 to 10, how much do you believe them?

➤ What evidence do you have that contradicts your core beliefs?

Sometimes it's difficult to find evidence that contradicts your core belief, but it's really important to try to do so. Many people will say that they understand logically that their core beliefs aren't true, but they still feel in their gut that they are. That happens because they've repeated the core beliefs to themselves thousands of times. Repeating an alternative core belief just a few times won't knock a dent into those thousands of times.

After collecting and studying contradictory evidence, however, and repeating an alternative core belief a couple of thousand times, your gut will start to believe it. But before you have the alternative core belief down pat, you're likely to encounter some situations that will trigger your original core belief. When that happens, remind yourself that the original core belief is based on false, inaccurate information, and the alternative core belief is the one that's accurate and true.

**Personality Pointer**

If you're answering these questions as a self-help exercise, be aware that you may have trouble thinking of contradictory evidence. That's because that evidence of nice things that people have said about you and done for you, accomplishments you've earned, and so forth is stored someplace different than in your "What am I?" schema.

In a real sense, you can rewrite your history. People can't change things that were said to them as children—that's done. It's okay, though; you don't need to change the harmful things you heard as a child. Instead, you can change your understanding of those statements and events, and of what they mean to you. Changing those understandings can allow you to clear up the past and begin a new future.

Now let's see how Roger is doing.

# Getting to the Core of the Problem

Roger is extremely anxious and upset about an upcoming job interview, so he's working with his therapist. Roger's automatic thought about the interview and the job he wants is,

> *I won't get it.*

Roger's automatic thought is supported by his assumption that he can't present himself well to others. That assumption is supported by his core beliefs.

Roger's therapist has helped him reduce his anxiety level (Axis I), but the therapist suspects that Roger may also have an Axis II problem, which would involve his core beliefs. To find out more about Roger's core beliefs, the therapist looks more closely at the responses Roger gave to questions designed to evaluate the validity of his automatic thought. (See "Anxiety and Automatic Thoughts" in Chapter 22 for the therapist's questions and Roger's responses.) If the therapist can determine the origin of Roger's automatic thoughts, they can get to the core beliefs at the root of Roger's problems.

The conversation the therapist initiates with Roger might go something like this:

➤ Suppose that you don't get that job. What's that mean about you?

*That means I didn't earn it.*

➤ What does that mean—that you didn't earn it?

*I didn't work hard enough when I was in school.*

➤ What does that mean—that you didn't work hard enough in school?

*It means that I'm lazy and worthless.*

The fact that Roger thinks he's lazy and worthless opens a whole new dimension to his anxiety problem. His thought that he's lazy and worthless comes from an early maladaptive environment.

Roger grew up in a household where he was criticized for his lack of industry. He was told over and over that nobody would want to be around him because he was lazy and worthless.

**Notes and Quotes**

Most people can articulate the thoughts that relate to their core beliefs. They don't do it often because it's painful, and asking someone to remember extremely unpleasant life events can evoke very strong negative emotions. You shouldn't try to get someone to remember something awful if you're not trained to handle what could result. But when people are asked to relate their core beliefs in therapy, most get to those beliefs fairly quickly and easily.

Eventually Roger developed avoidant personality disorder, one of the disorders in the fearful behavior cluster, as discussed in Chapter 16, "Fearful Behaviors." Roger's job interview anxiety turned out to be just the tip of the iceberg. Anticipating the interview triggered memories in Roger of the worst experiences of his childhood.

Understanding what was really going on with Roger gave his therapist a much better handle on the anxiety problem, and they were then able to begin working on altering Roger's core belief.

# The Core Belief Factor in Substance Abuse

Back we go to our friend Tom, who's trying to quit abusing drugs and alcohol. The problem is, Tom's friends keep inviting him to parties, and Tom's automatic thought when asked is,

> *Yes! I can get relief and have some fun.*

Tom's automatic thought is supported by his assumption that if he can't handle things, he'll do whatever he can to feel better and get through. That, of course, means drinking and using drugs. (See "Substance Abuse and Automatic Thoughts" in Chapter 22.)

To learn more about Tom's automatic thoughts in relation to his core beliefs, his therapist initiates a conversation with him that goes something like this:

➤ What does that mean—you need relief?

*I was abused my whole life. Nobody ever loved me or ever will, and I can't do anything right.*

You'll notice that Tom's response is much more direct and to the point than Roger's is. This happens often with borderline personalities; they cut to the chase and go directly from their automatic thought to their core belief.

**Personality Parlance**

**Borderline personality disorder** is one of the disorders in the dramatic behaviors cluster. It's serious and disruptive, and the population who suffers from it has a high rate of suicide.

After working with Tom for a while, his therapist learns that Tom actually suffers from the serious condition of *borderline personality disorder* (Axis II). Because of Tom's core beliefs, he considers himself to be both unlovable and incompetent.

Tom had an abusive childhood, involving both physical and sexual abuse. His automatic thought reveals that he wants relief from the anguish of memories associated with the abuse. In addition, he is looking for relief from the core belief he internalized in his childhood. One question from the therapist often is enough to get from the automatic thought to the core belief. That's not, however, a typical response from people with personality disorders other than the borderline type.

## The Core Belief Factor in Relationship Problems

Joyce and Robert are having relationship problems. Joyce is angry at Robert because he doesn't help her around the house. When she loses her temper and yells at him for failing to do his part, Robert is shocked and outraged, and he tells her that she'd better keep her place if she knows what's good for her.

Joyce immediately backs down, apologizes, and goes back to cleaning the house and taking care of the kids.

Joyce's automatic thought following her blowup is,

> *Oh, I shouldn't have done that.*

This thought is based on her assumption that if she is in a relationship, she should take care of everything.

Robert's automatic thought after Joyce yells at him is,

> *Who does she think she is talking to me like that? She can't talk to me like that.*

His assumption is that Joyce should take care of him and meet all of his needs. (See "A Relationship Problem and Automatic Thoughts" in Chapter 22.) Some people find a person like Robert very difficult to take. In some ways, though, Joyce and Robert are a good fit.

Their therapist wants to find out more about their core beliefs and asks them some questions about their automatic thoughts. The therapist will use these thoughts as the route to their core beliefs and will ask Joyce something like this:

➤ What does that mean—that you shouldn't have said anything when you became angry?

*It means that I shouldn't rock the boat.*

➤ What does "not rock the boat" mean?

*He might leave me, and then I'd be left alone.*

➤ What would happen if you were left alone?

*I can't take care of myself.*

➤ What does it mean that you can't take care of yourself?

*I'm incompetent.*

The conversation between the therapist and Robert is similar:

➤ What does it mean about you that you can't understand that Joyce would say something like she did to you?

*People just can't talk to me like that.*

➤ What's that mean about you that people can't talk to you like that?

*Well, I'm just better than other people, and they can't talk to me like that.*

Both Joyce and Robert are suffering from personality disorders (Axis II). Joyce has *dependent personality disorder*, and Robert has *narcissistic personality disorder*.

Joyce is perfectly willing to idealize Robert, which feeds right into his narcissistic ways. To be idealized is exactly what he wants.

When Joyce was young, she was told repeatedly that she'd never make it on her own. She knew early on that she'd never be able to take care of herself. She knew that she'd better have somebody—preferably a man—take care of her and be there to help her. She believes that she's incompetent and unable to get by on her own.

When Joyce yelled at Robert and saw that he became outraged and angry toward her, she was terrified that he might leave her. That, to Joyce, is the worst thing that could happen. She must do anything she can to prevent it.

**Personality Parlance**

**Dependent personality disorder** is from the cluster of fearful behaviors, while **narcissistic personality disorder** is from the cluster of dramatic behaviors. The two disorders actually are a good complement to each other.

Robert, on the other hand, was doted upon when he was a child and made to believe that he was superior to everyone else, merely by the fact that he was around. He expects to be waited on because he deserves to be. He has a lot of trouble considering Joyce's feelings because he's so busy thinking about himself and his own feelings.

The problems that Joyce and Robert are experiencing are deeper than Axis I-type anxieties, which may have been more easily treated. The differences in their personalities also provide some insight into how Joyce and Robert became a couple in the first place.

Once therapists can understand where automatic thoughts come from, they can get a clear picture of what's really going on with a person. Automatic thoughts are almost always a product of people's core beliefs.

# The Core Belief Factor in Obsessive-Compulsive Disorder

Now we'll talk about Anna and the obsessive-compulsive disorder that causes her to relentlessly recite a ritualistic prayer.

The disorder, as you can imagine, is distressing to Anna, who fears that it will cause her to become completely dysfunctional, which would result in her losing her family and her job. Anna's automatic thought of

*I can't stop. I don't have control.*

is supported by her assumption that she requires forgiveness for bad thoughts that she has.

In reality, Anna doesn't have bad thoughts, but she thinks she does, and she's afraid that if she stops the praying, something very bad will happen to her. When she prays, she asks for forgiveness for being bad. (See "Obsessive-Compulsive Disorder and Automatic Thoughts" in Chapter 22.)

During therapy, Anna reveals that in her early environment, she was told she was defective. She wasn't good enough. She needed to work on improving herself. As a result, Anna developed the core belief of defectiveness. She is extremely anxious, and she uses the ritualistic prayer as a means of avoiding feeling bad about herself.

If Anna's therapist decides to further explore her automatic thoughts, the conversation would sound something like this:

➤ What does that mean—you can't stop reciting the prayer?

*I have to do that because of who I am.*

➤ What does that mean—"because of who you are?"

*I'm defective.*

Anna feels a deep shame about who she is. In her mind, she's not good—she's defective. By this point in her therapy, it's clear to the therapist that Anna suffers from obsessive-compulsive personality disorder. It's important to understand that there's a big difference between *obsessive-compulsive personality disorder* and *obsessive-compulsive disorder.*

The obsessive-compulsive personality order is an Axis II condition, and it's chronic and ongoing. It's part of the cluster of fearful behaviors, and it can be extremely disruptive and distressing.

Obsessive-compulsive disorder is an Axis I disorder and can be treated by dealing with Axis I issues, such as automatic thoughts and behaviors. It's an anxiety-based disorder and is a more temporary condition.

At this point, Anna needs to be treated for an Axis II disorder, with the hope of helping her develop an alternative core belief to replace her feelings of defectiveness.

**Personality Parlance**

Comparing **obsessive-compulsive personality disorder** and **obsessive-compulsive disorder** is like comparing a Ford with a Chevy. They're both automobiles; they're simply two different kinds. They both have obsessive and compulsive components, but otherwise, their diagnostic criteria are very different.

# Discovering the Core Belief Behind Anorexia/Bulimia

Jeri's behavioral problem is purging after she eats. After spending some time with Jeri, her therapist finds out that the underlying problem is dependent personality disorder. Jeri wants to stop her anorexic/bulimic cycle, but it's hard for her because of her automatic thoughts, her assumptions, and ultimately, her core beliefs.

When Jeri overeats, she hates the feeling of being overly full that results. (Remember that no one with reasonable standards would consider the amount of food she eats to be overeating. See "Obsessive-Compulsive Disorder and Automatic Thoughts" in Chapter 22.) Her automatic thought when she "overeats" is,

> *I feel like a stuffed pig.*

Because that feeling is very uncomfortable for her, she purges to rid herself of the sensation.

Jeri's therapist wants to find out the meaning behind her automatic thought. Their conversation goes something like this:

➤ What does that mean—you feel like a stuffed pig?

> *Well, I can't do anything right.*

➤ What does that mean—that you can't do anything right?

*Eating is the only thing I have any control over, and I can't even manage that. I don't have any control.*

➤ What's that mean—that you don't have any control?

*I'm helpless.*

From hearing that, the therapist understands Jeri's core belief and can diagnose the personality disorder. The therapist learns that when Jeri was a child, she was told that she couldn't do anything right, and that she would never be able to do anything right. She would always have to rely on others to do things for her. Those thoughts became Jeri's core belief and resulted in her feeling helpless and without control over her own life or anything else.

Core beliefs are deeply ingrained and difficult to change. People can be helped to develop alternative core beliefs, however, and if they're willing to work hard to incorporate their new beliefs, they can be treated successfully.

# Core Belief Worksheet

This worksheet is intended to help you learn more about your core beliefs. There is no comparison data or standard on which to interpret your ratings. If it interests you, take a few minutes to fill in the answers as completely and honestly as you can.

1. What is the general problem that causes distress in your life?

2. Name a specific situation in which the problem occurred.

3. What was your automatic thought at the time the problem occurred?

4. What assumptions do you have that support your automatic thoughts?

5. What's your core belief, or what does your automatic thought mean about you as a person? (Use the therapist/patient questions and answers as a guide to get your answer.)

6. Rate from 0 to 10 the level of unlovableness, incompetence, or some other negative feeling you think your core belief reflects.

7. List any emotions you feel may be associated with your core belief.

8. List any behaviors you feel are related to your core belief.

9. Formulate an alternative core belief.

10. Rate on a scale of 0 to 10 the level at which you believe your alternative core belief.

11. List any new emotions resulting from your alternative core belief.

12. List new behaviors that are a result of your alternative core belief.

13. How often will you practice your alternative core belief?

Changing core beliefs may be something you can do on your own, but it normally requires professional help. If you feel overwhelmed or unsure of what you're doing, don't hesitate to look for some guidance.

# Check Yourself Out

Here are several questions to help you reflect on what you've read in this chapter, and perhaps to take the information a step or two further in your own mind:

➤ How well do you understand the different layers of beliefs?

➤ Do you have any beliefs that you are unlovable or incompetent?

➤ How do your core beliefs affect your relationships with people?

➤ Does your alternative belief really work for you?

➤ Can you imagine yourself repeating your alternative belief regularly to replace the old belief?

You might benefit from discussing these questions with another person, or just thinking about them on your own.

---

### The Least You Need to Know

➤ While automatic thoughts and behaviors are at the surface of one's personality, core beliefs lie deep within.

➤ There's a world of difference between Axis I disorders, which are temporary, and Axis II disorders, which are enduring and harder to treat.

➤ Core beliefs, both positive and negative, have a huge impact on how we think of ourselves.

➤ Growing up in a maladaptive environment can result in negative core beliefs that will affect people for the rest of their lives.

➤ It's difficult but possible to develop an alternative core belief to replace the one that results in personality problems.

---

# Chapter 25

# Do Not Attempt to Do This at Home

## In This Chapter

➤ Understanding the difference between self-help and professional help

➤ Knowing when professional help is necessary

➤ Helping yourself while you're getting professional help

➤ Exploring the stigma associated with psychotherapy

➤ Finding a therapist you can work with

➤ Knowing when to move on

The earlier chapters in Part 6, "Personality and Change," provide a lot of information about self-help and offer suggestions for working through problems on your own. When you have a good understanding of personality and the potential problems associated with it, you can use that understanding to address thoughts and behaviors of your own that may be causing you concern or distress.

All of the techniques and suggestions offered in Chapters 22, 23, and 24 have been carefully and thoroughly researched, and are widely accepted and respected in the field of psychotherapy. In those chapters, we covered a broad range of personality factors and problems, staying within the bounds of what you, the reader, can reasonably do to work on your problems without professional help. You can address many issues on your own, such as changing automatic thoughts, behaviors, and even core beliefs. We've tried to give you the best tools possible to do that. However, there are limits as to how far you can—or should try—to go alone.

# Self-Help Only Goes So Far

In the earlier chapters in this section, we talk about problems that are mild and those that are serious, situations that are easy and those that are difficult. We never hesitate to offer suggestions for dealing with the situations we discuss, for self-help is a viable option. By no means have we addressed all the types of therapy available for personality problems, however, or all the means by which professional, trained therapists can effectively deal with problems too complex to be addressed by the layperson. Sometimes professional help is necessary.

Here are two examples of situations and problems you should never try to handle on your own:

➤ You're having thoughts of hurting yourself or someone else. If that's the case, you need professional help immediately. Call your local crisis intervention program—and don't wait. Your life, literally, is in the balance, and you need help right away.

➤ You've experienced problems for a long time and have tried to address them on your own. You've thought about getting professional help but never got around to it. If that's the case, it's time for you to call somebody. You're not being fair to yourself if you don't.

**Personality Pointer**

Don't hesitate to find other self-help materials that can be of use to you. Plenty are available in books and on the Internet. A great source is Drs. Jeffrey Young and Janet Klosko's book, *Reinventing Your Life.* Another excellent book is *Mind Over Mood,* by Dennis Greenberger, Ph.D., and Christine Padesky, Ph.D.

## Learning to Help Yourself

Even if you decide to get professional help, there are many things you can do to help yourself, both before and after therapy.

To give yourself some structure in your self-help, use the worksheets at the end of Chapters 22, 23, 24, and 27. Start with the Cognitive Therapy for Change Worksheet at the end of Chapter 22, "Changing What We Believe." Following the structure there will help you focus on important elements of change. The worksheet will help you address the problem that's specific to you, the amount of distress the problem causes you, and the level of control you think you have regarding the problem.

The Cognitive Therapy for Change Worksheet also will get you started in the change process by helping you evaluate your automatic thoughts. If you can do that, you're off to a great start.

After that, use the Behavior Change Worksheet at the end of Chapter 23, "Changing How We Behave." It will help you focus on behavioral aspects of your problems, such as abusing drugs or alcohol, or reciting a ritual prayer. It also can guide you in coming up with more adaptable, useful kinds of behaviors to replace your existing ones. It will help you plan and implement the changes as well.

The Core Belief Worksheet at the end of Chapter 24, "Rewriting History," provides a format for evaluating core beliefs. When you use it with the supporting information in the chapter, it can help you understand the connection between your automatic thoughts and your core beliefs, and direct you in developing an alternative core belief. If the problems you're addressing have roots beneath the surface of your personality, the Core Belief Worksheet is essential.

Using the Follow-Up Worksheet in Chapter 27, "Taking a Good, Long Look in Your Crystal Ball," will help you keep track of the progress you make— and continue to make.

When our states and situations improve, we have a strong tendency to forget the condition we were in when we first started the change process. We forget about the distress and pain we were experiencing when we decided to change, and we can become impatient with our progress. The Follow-Up Worksheet serves as a sort of diary for the change process.

The Worksheet will help you plan strategies that will enable you to stay on track after you've made successful changes.

Your process of self-help can be structured from beginning to end by following the formats on these worksheets.

See Appendix B, "Additional Resources," for books, Internet sites, and organizations we recommend.

**Don't Go There!**

If you use the Internet to find self-help materials, be careful. No doubt you know that although there's lots of good stuff to be found in cyberspace, there's also a lot of junk. Check to see who is sponsoring the site (an organization such as the American Psychological Association [APA], for example, or someone who simply has an interest?). If something doesn't look legitimate, ignore it.

## Knowing When You're in over Your Head

While we've made every attempt to cover the ground of personality profiling, there's no way this book can address *every* aspect of cognitive therapy. So don't assume that because you've read it, you can handle any problem you encounter. While most people get through their entire lives without requiring psychological help, some will not be able to work through their problems without the help of a trained therapist.

If you're experiencing any of the following situations, chances are you're in over your head and you need professional help:

➤ Things seem so overwhelming to you that you don't know where to start trying to make changes.

➤ You've tried for a while to make changes on your own but have been unsuccessful.

➤ Your level of distress keeps getting higher, not lower.

➤ Your problems are interfering with your ability to function normally at work, with your family, or in other areas of your life.

Remember that, while self-help is useful and valuable, it can't always be used as a substitute for professional therapy.

# Someone to Lean On

There's a lot more professional help available today than there was in the past, and people tend to seek it sooner than they used to. If you feel that you're experiencing problems that you can't handle yourself, don't hesitate to look for professional help. If you're employed, check your benefits package to see if it includes an employee assistance program. These programs have brief intervention plans available for free to many employed people.

**Personality Pointer**

Many insurance plans include psychological care, but most of it is on a limited basis or includes stipulations and restrictions. Check out your plan to see what it includes, but don't let lack of insurance prevent you from getting help that you really need.

If you're experiencing a true crisis—having thoughts of harming yourself or others, for example—call a local crisis office immediately. But you don't have to be experiencing a crisis to enlist professional help. If you're just starting a program of change, you may need guidance, support, and encouragement in the beginning. Perhaps you've been working on changing a belief or behavior and feel that you made good progress until recently, when you hit a plateau. Before you become discouraged and think about giving up, consider finding someone objective who can assess the situation and direct you in your journey.

A professional, trained cognitive therapist knows more about changing beliefs and behaviors than even the best-read self-help aficionados. When you need somebody who knows more about change than you do, go for a pro.

## *Why the Stigma of Getting Professional Help?*

We've come a long way, but there still is something of a stigma associated with psychological care. Some people more than others like to think of themselves as self-sufficient, self-reliant, and infallible. They tend to deny or ignore problems until they're in extreme distress and are reluctant to share their fears and problems, even with the people they're closest to. Others think of their mental health problems as dirty laundry they don't want anyone to see. It's important to remember, however, that few of us get through life without experiencing instances in which we need to get some help.

Another reason why the remnants of a stigma associated with psychotherapy remain is that many people still lack a good understanding of psychological problems and treatments. There are those who think that if they attempt to get help for even a mild psychological problem, they could end up in a state hospital. In reality, there's no more likelihood that someone with a mild case of depression will end up in a state hospital than there is that somebody with a headache will turn out to have a brain tumor.

Dozens of misconceptions about psychological problems prevent people who need help from seeking it. Here are just a few of those misconceptions:

➤ Psychological problems make you act strange or say inappropriate things at inappropriate times.

➤ People with psychological problems usually are homeless; they wear odd clothes and carry around all their belongings in shopping bags.

➤ People with psychological problems can't have jobs that entail any responsibility because they can't be depended on.

➤ People with psychological problems shouldn't have children because they will pass those problems on to their children.

➤ Psychological problems can't be fixed.

The list could go on and on. Many people don't understand psychological problems, and the air of secrecy that surrounds psychological treatment does little to improve matters.

Companies provide employee assistance programs for employees who need therapy, but nobody's allowed to divulge the identity of anyone who uses these programs. Why? Because if people couldn't consult a therapist without being assured of their privacy, far fewer people would do so.

A lot of people will pay for psychotherapy costs out of their own pockets so their co-workers don't find out from their benefits records that they're under the care of a therapist. They're afraid their position in the company may be jeopardized or they'll be denied health benefits in the future.

**Personality Pointer**

Even people accused of crimes and required to submit to psychological evaluations are concerned about other people's perceptions of their mental states. Many of them express the preference of being considered "a criminal" rather than a "crazy person."

There's even a real dichotomy among behavioral healthcare professionals themselves. Some healthcare professionals won't seek treatment for themselves—under any circumstances. On the other hand, many people who work in the addictions recovery field are themselves recovering and feel that their background enhances their credentials.

### Notes and Quotes

Licensed mental health professionals aren't legally allowed to acknowledge that they even know a person who's in their care. If Dr. Jones is treating Mark Smith and somebody asks the doctor whether he knows Mark, Jones isn't legally permitted to answer yes or no. Although it's important to respect privacy, it can have the unintended effect of keeping treatment clothed in secrecy and intrigue.

When, in addition to the secretive personal and social attitudes that prevail, therapists (unlike medical doctors and lawyers, for example) are not permitted even to admit that they know an individual, it is easy to see how the stigma surrounding psychotherapy is perpetuated.

The self-help book boom is probably due, at least in part, to people wanting psychological help but being unable to ignore the stigma and go for therapy. Attitudes toward mental healthcare, we hope, will continue to change as people learn more about mental health problems and treatments.

## What Kind of Folks Get Therapy?

Given all that talk about the stigma surrounding therapy, you have to wonder who in the world would ever make an appointment with a mental health professional.

When people reach a certain level of desperation, they forget about the stigma and phone for appointments. That doesn't mean that everybody who seeks therapy is ready to leap from the top of a 12-story building or drive their car off a cliff. It does mean, however, that most people who enter therapy are decidedly uncomfortable with a certain aspect of their lives, or with their lives in general.

Let's face it. For most of us, life is stressful. We have different kinds of stresses now than our parents and grandparents had, but life moves faster, and we set very high expectations for ourselves. There's tremendous pressure to meet or exceed societal expectations: bigger houses, trendier cars, better clothes, and the best colleges for our kids.

Unfortunately, all of those things come at a cost—and it's not just in dollars. To keep up with all these things, we need to move faster and work harder. We have less time to enjoy hobbies, play games with our kids, or read books for pleasure. As our lifestyles become increasingly stressful, more and more people are seeking treatment for anxiety and related problems.

What kind of folks get therapy? All kinds, and for all sorts of reasons. We can't help but think that, as we continue to move faster and faster as a society, the number of folks who seek therapy will continue to increase.

## There's No Shame in Seeking Help

There are many double standards regarding psychotherapy. A lot of people sympathize and say they think it's just fine for John or Mary or Ed or Suzie to get therapy. As for themselves, however, never in a thousand years would they be caught in a therapist's office.

In reality, there's no shame at all in seeking psychotherapy. Therapy has time and time again proven to be effective for mental health and substance-abuse disorders. When it comes down to the wire, the only person you need to resolve this issue with is yourself. If you feel you need professional help, you don't need permission or approval from anyone else.

Sometimes the "shame" you might feel about being in treatment is a treatment issue in itself. You can really do a number, beating yourself up mentally as you anguish over whether you should pick up the phone and make an appointment for therapy.

People who reconcile in their own minds that they're better off pursuing therapy avoid this inner conflict and put themselves on the road to better mental health.

**Notes and Quotes**

There's a movement underway by people who are looking to scale back and slow down. Popularly called the *Voluntary Simplicity* movement, those in it seek to trade in their fast-paced, stress-filled lives for simpler, quieter lifestyles. Check out www. simpleliving.com for more information.

# Finding the Right Therapist

Many folks who are seeking treatment for the first time don't know what to look for in a therapist. This problem certainly isn't unique to the field of mental health. People can have an equally difficult time finding lawyers, financial advisors, medical doctors, or automobile repair people.

Most people know they want a therapist who will be courteous and respectful toward them. They look for someone who complies with licensing and professional standards, and who has good training and experience in treating the type of problem that's troubling them.

If you'd like more information about a therapist you're thinking of seeing, you can call and ask to speak to the therapist for a few minutes. Most are willing to spend some time on the phone with potential clients to answer any questions they have.

**Don't Go There!**

Some people assume that anyone who goes for therapy is self-absorbed or doesn't have enough to do. Generalizations are dangerous: Unless you can see into somebody's head, you don't know what has occurred in that person's life or why he or she is seeking therapy.

Managed care companies these days have control over many referrals, so your choice of a therapist may be limited if it's paid for by your insurance. You can request a therapist with a certain type of training or background, however. For help in finding cognitive therapists, see Appendix B, "Additional Resources."

When you start therapy, feel free to talk to the therapist about diagnostic or treatment issues. Discuss fees, payment arrangements, appointments, and so forth with the office staff. Make sure you check on whether you'll be able to schedule your appointments for times that are convenient to you. Though most therapists offer hours to accommodate patients who work 9 to 5, some do not.

# When You and Your Shrink Don't See Eye to Eye

Some people never quite reach a comfort level with one another. Nobody really understands why this happens sometimes, but it does. If for some reason you feel uncomfortable with your therapist, you need to talk to him or her about it. Trust is extremely important; if it isn't there, you won't be able to work together successfully.

**Personality Pointer**

Your therapist should ask you regularly if he or she is doing anything that makes you feel uncomfortable, or if for any reason you're not satisfied with your treatment. Make sure that you're truthful. If not, the relationship won't work as well.

If you don't get along with your therapist, don't beat yourself up. You're certainly entitled to go elsewhere. These things happen, often without anybody being at fault.

In some cases, the therapist will recognize a problem with the relationship before the patient does and will ask if the patient wants to find a new doctor. At other times, the patient will be unhappy and reluctant to say anything; the therapist will recognize that and recommend that they end their relationship.

In order for your treatment to be as successful as possible, you and your therapist must have a trusting, mutually respectful relationship. If you don't, there's no need to cast blame or feel bad that things didn't work out. The important thing is to find someone you can work effectively with so that your treatments will be successful.

# Check Yourself Out

Here are several questions to help you reflect on what you've read in this chapter, and perhaps to take the information a step or two farther in your own mind:

➤ What are your thoughts about psychotherapy?

➤ If you had a problem, would you make changes on your own or seek professional assistance?

➤ What role would shame play in your decision about how to handle problems?

➤ What questions would you want to have answered by a therapist before scheduling an appointment?

➤ What things would you try on your own before going to a therapist?

You might benefit from discussing these questions with another person or just thinking about them on your own.

---

### The Least You Need to Know

➤ Self-help is beneficial and valuable in many instances, but it's not the same as getting professional help.

➤ If you have thoughts of hurting yourself or others, you feel completely overwhelmed, or you've tried to help yourself without success, it's time to look for professional help.

➤ There are things you can do to enhance and advance professional therapy to ensure that your treatment will be successful.

➤ Any stigmas associated with psychotherapy are primarily due to a general lack of understanding about the behavioral health area.

➤ It's important to find a therapist you feel comfortable with and will be able to work with.

➤ If your relationship with your therapist doesn't work out, you're free to find one who is better suited to your needs.

# Chapter 26

# Cheer Up, Will Ya?

## In This Chapter

➤ Understanding positive psychology

➤ Learning what the studies show

➤ Seeing the glass as half empty

➤ Learning to see the glass as half full

➤ Using cognitive, social, and spiritual techniques to improve your outlook on life

You've no doubt noticed that the world is full of all kinds of people, with all sorts of personalities. There are those who are happy to stop and chat when they pass you on the street, and those who act like they've never seen you before, even though you happen to be co-workers.

In the same vein, some folks always manage to acknowledge that there's some good in their lives, even when they're going through a particularly difficult time. Others, however, complain bitterly about their lot in life, despite the fact that they may have luxuries most of the world never dreams of.

Some people are optimists, while others are more pessimistic. To some, the glass is always half full and the sun is always rising. Others see the glass as half empty and the sun sinking into the horizon.

While we haven't figured out exactly why some people are so much more optimistic than others, there's an interesting area of psychology that focuses on positive thinking, happiness, and satisfaction. It's called positive psychology. Researchers in this area contend that those who aren't naturally optimistic can change their ways and join those who see the glass as half full. Let's take a closer look at the area of positive psychology, and you can make up your own mind about it.

# Positive Psychology

Lately there's been renewed interest in the field of *positive psychology,* and with good reason. From its beginnings in the 1920s elements of positive psychology have moved in and out of the spotlight; today's researchers recognize the importance it places on the relationship between good mental health and physical health. They've found that people who are happy and satisfied with their lives, and have hope for the future, are far less likely to suffer physical health problems than those who are unhappy, dissatisfied, and have a bleak outlook on what's to come.

While, in recent decades, much of the work in the field of psychology has focused on mental illnesses and their treatments, positive psychology looks at promoting general well-being and health, both mental and physical.

**Personality Parlance**

**Positive psychology** is an area of psychology that focuses on happiness, satisfaction, and hope, and is particularly interested in the link between mental and physical health. The area is attracting increasing interest.

# Everybody's Talking About It

A special January 2000 issue of *American Psychologist* focuses on positive psychology and the research done in that area. The subject of the special issue is *Happiness, Excellence, and Optimal Human Functioning.* Martin E.P. Seligman, one of the issue's guest editors, has done a good deal of work and written professional papers on the subject of positive psychology.

Seligman's article, "Selective Well-Being," tells of a study that he and researcher Gregory Buchanan conducted with two groups of students. One group attended a 16-hour workshop designed to alter negative thoughts. The other group, a control group, did not attend.

The students who attended the workshop were generally a pessimistic lot and, as a group, had a higher than average rate of depression. During the workshop, they learned to dispute their own chronic negative thoughts and were taught social and work skills that helped stave off depression.

Guess what? Eighteen months after that workshop, 22 percent of the students who participated had experienced depression. That sounds like a lot, but compare that number to 32 percent of the kids from the control group that didn't attend the workshop.

Seven percent of the workshop group had anxiety, compared to 15 percent in the control group. The students who attended the workshop also had fewer health problems during that 18 months, and when they didn't feel well, they saw doctors early on and avoided getting really sick.

Were the differences in well-being between these two groups related to the workshop? Seligman and Buchanan say yes.

### Notes and Quotes

Martin E.P. Seligman is well-known for the *Seligman Attributional Style Questionnaire (SASQ)*, a test used by companies and corporations to measure the optimism of employees and prospective employees, and to gauge how well they'll be able to function under pressure. Insurance industry management reviews of the SASQ report that salespeople who measured high for optimism sold 37 percent more insurance in a two-year period than those who didn't score high.

## Adapting Upward

In the same special issue of *American Psychologist,* Ed Diener, Ph.D., from the University of Illinois at Urbana-Champaign, refers to a study done by P. Brickman and D.T. Campbell in 1971. Brickman and Campbell reported on the *adaptation level theory,* which states that we quickly get used to, or adapt to, the level at which we function. Many people, the study reports, operate constantly on a "hedonic tread-mill"—that is, in their quest for pleasure, they move to, and quickly get used to new levels of accomplishments and possession.

To put that into plain English, consider this. Bob just got a big promotion at work, and he's thrilled to pieces. Talk about a raise! Bob's salary increases by more than a third, he gets an extra week of vacation, and—listen to this—a company car. He also gets a better office (with windows) and some nice perks like attending the winter conference that's always held someplace like Hawaii or Aruba.

Bob had his eye on the position for two years and really wanted it, so he has no doubt that he'll be happy and content in his new job for years to come.

Bob and his wife, Gina, celebrate the promotion in a fancy restaurant, where they start planning the cruise they'll take in the spring (after the winter conference) and talk about building a big home in the development that's under construction on the town's last bit of remaining farmland.

A few months later, Bob is griping about the many responsibilities and hassles of his new job. He's not satisfied with the company car because there are some new ones now that are nicer than the one he got. Gina is busily spending all of his raise and more, and plans for the new house have stalled due to a zoning issue.

Bob's thinking now that if he could just move one more rung up the ladder, things would be great for him at work. He sets his sights on the next level and begins plotting how he's going to get his next promotion.

## Adapting Downward

Bob's story is an example of one of the ways the adaptation theory works. There's another: People can adapt to misfortune.

When people first experience misfortune, it hits them hard, but they soon learn to adapt. At that point, whatever it is that made them unhappy doesn't have much of an effect anymore. Of course, the degree to which people adapt varies tremendously. We've known people who have lost a spouse and seemed only moderately affected; others never recover from the loss.

People can also adapt to less dramatic losses with a surprising degree of ease. While the correlation between attaining the basic necessities of life and being happy is great, it levels off after that. So if being rich or attractive doesn't necessarily make a person happier, neither will the loss of those qualities make a person unhappy for more than a short while.

**Personality Pointer**

Studies have conclusively shown that people without basic necessities (food, water, shelter, clothing) are happier when they get those things than they were without them. After that level, however, more material possessions don't correlate with an increased level of happiness. So if you think you're going to be happier when you get the Lexus, maybe you should reconsider.

## Happiness and Temperament

Think of the people you know who have a lot of money. Probably some of them are upbeat and happy, while others aren't. There are certainly many people who aren't considered attractive who are perfectly happy and content. They may wish they looked different, but they don't equate happiness with looking good. Health is another thing: Only when we lose it do most of us understand how precious it is.

Our temperaments can influence the sorts of things that make us happy. Someone who needs high sensation, for instance, is happiest on days when there's a lot going on—a lot of excitement. Those who prefer things quiet and low-key are happiest in a more subdued or restrained environment.

An article called *The Future of Optimism,* written by Christopher Peterson and also published in the January 2000 issue of *American Psychologist,* reported on a 1992 study conducted by Michael Scheier and Charles Carver, who studied a personality variable that they called *dispositional optimism.* They defined dispositional optimism as "the global expectation that good things will be plentiful in the future, and bad things scarce." Perhaps that is the attitude that has allowed humanity to endure and prevail, despite the great hardships and catastrophes of history—the sense that better things are ahead.

Scheier and Carver studied how people respond to the question of whether they believe their goals can be achieved, even when they see roadblocks ahead. If people are optimistic, the study concludes, they will continue to work toward their goals, despite the roadblocks. Pessimistic folks are more likely to throw in the towel. For that reason, Peterson says, "There is abundant reason to believe that optimism ... is useful to a person because positive expectations can be self fulfilling."

Still another article in the January issue of *American Psychologist,* this one called *The Funds, Friends and Faith of Happy People* and written by David Myers, says that people with particular personality traits who enjoy their work and leisure time, have close relationships, and have a degree of faith are generally happy people.

The point of citing all these studies is simply to make you aware of the significant amount of research and interest there is in the area of positive psychology. How it advances as the twenty-first century moves ahead will be something to watch.

**Personality Parlance**

**Dispositional optimism** is the general expectation of people everywhere that the future will be bright, with many more good things than bad.

# Born to Be a Pessimist

You've surely run into people along the way who seem destined to be eternally grouchy. Folks like this can be hard to live with, but the consequences of their grouchy personalities are even harder for them to take.

People with pessimistic outlooks are in for more than their share of trouble, according to studies conducted over the years. That doesn't mean they'll be educationally deprived, or less attractive (even though a permanent scowl isn't a good look for most people), or make less money. It does mean, however, that they may experience more health problems than optimistic people, and not heal as quickly when problems occur. Pessimistic people don't enjoy life as much as optimists, either.

Now, if that's not enough to make all those dyed-in-the-wool pessimists change their way of looking at the world, we don't know what is.

**Notes and Quotes**

Most of the results of these studies merely confirm what many people have thought or known for a long time: People who engage in meaningful activities, enjoy support from family and friends, and express hope about their future generally are happier and healthier than those who don't.

**331**

# Learning to Be an Optimist

The good news for all you pessimists out there is that you're not obligated to stay pessimistic for the rest of your life. Personality traits, including pessimism, are relatively enduring, but they're not set in stone. Research and studies show that pessimists can learn to be more optimistic.

To change pessimistic thinking into optimistic thinking (or at least into thinking that is less pessimistic), therapists use cognitive techniques that dispute chronic negative thoughts. They also teach social skills that assist in giving people more optimistic outlooks.

Just as with the other areas of change we discuss in earlier chapters, important factors to figure into the pessimistic-to-optimistic change process are *desire* and *self-efficacy*. The degree to which people desire to change their outlook, and their perceived level of control over the change, largely affect the actual rate of change.

Sharon has abused drugs and alcohol for years, and she suffers from depression. She also has attempted suicide several times.

If Sharon believes her life is worthless, that things are just too bad, and she's too far gone to be helped, there will be a self-fulfilling element to those beliefs. If, on the other hand, Sharon realizes that as long as she's alive there's no such thing as a point of no return, she may be able to benefit from her more positive outlook. That's not to say that thinking positively will turn Sharon's life into a stroll through the park. It will, however, give her a fighting chance to try to turn things around.

So how does Sharon—or anybody else—learn to be more optimistic? Let's look at some of the components involved.

## *Developing Positive Beliefs*

Way back in Chapter 2, "You Are What You Believe," we discuss the chapter title mostly in relation to problems. In fact, we spend the better part of this book talking about problems and how to fix them. Your beliefs, however, also can have a positive impact on your self-perception and how you navigate through life. Belief in yourself and in the people around you, your ability to function, your faith, and other factors all contribute to your well-being.

We spend a lot of time in this book discussing the negative side of personality— disorders, problems, quirks, and how to improve your personality, or to make yourself feel better by restructuring negative thoughts into more positive ones. That brings us to the topic of this section: developing positive beliefs.

If we don't naturally come up with positive beliefs, we need to learn how to develop and nurture them, and how to use them to our benefit.

Let's say that we hear Ron say, "Life is awful, and it's never going to get any better."

We can evaluate the merits of Ron's thought by asking him to rate the awfulness of his life on a scale of 0 to 10. We could acknowledge that every life includes problems and some pain, but that most people's lives also include qualities they enjoy and value. This will get him to really think about it, and he's likely to conclude that his life isn't really as unbearable as he's been thinking it is.

Here are some questions you could ask Ron to get him to consider his state:

➤ Exactly what about life is awful?

➤ Is there any part of your day that you find pleasant, fun, or enjoyable?

➤ Is there something you see or do that stimulates your interest?

➤ Are there any people you enjoy spending some time with?

➤ Do you look forward to any kinds of events or activities?

➤ Can you think of any way your life could be made more enjoyable or less awful?

➤ Are there any experiences you find rewarding or satisfying?

When most people stop to think about it, they conclude that life isn't really unbearable. Some people have even reported having positive experiences out of completely awful situations such as the early loss of both parents, childhood illnesses, and abusive backgrounds. They kept a thread of hope that things would get better, and that thread kept them going.

To say that your life will never get better can be the equivalent of locking yourself in a cage. It's not all that hard to convince yourself that life is crummy, nobody cares about you, it doesn't matter if you live or die—you get the picture. The real danger in that kind of thinking (along with making you completely miserable) is that, while you wallow in pessimism and misery, you may overlook qualities of it that have improved.

## Getting Social Support

Social support has proven to be an invaluable asset for people who are trying to improve their outlooks and generate positive thoughts. It doesn't have to be organized or formal; it can be just a few friends you enjoy spending time with. Different people have different needs, and they use support in various ways. For most people, having a small group of people to rely on is sufficient.

**Notes and Quotes**

People who overcome great difficulties while inspiring others, or those who positively lead and influence large numbers of people, are sometimes called *dynamic optimists*. People such as Mahatma Ghandi, Helen Keller, Magic Johnson, Christopher Reeve, Michael J. Fox, and Marie Curie are cited as having the quality of dynamic optimism.

Depending on the types of problems you experience and your specific needs and preferences, you might think about joining a formal or informal support group. Many churches and synagogues, community groups, schools, and social agencies offer support groups to help people deal with all kinds of problems.

Support groups deal with topics such as these:

➤ Divorce and separation

➤ Death and grieving

➤ Coping with caring for an elderly or sick loved one

➤ Dealing with a serious or chronic illness

➤ Overcoming addictions or dealing with addictions in others

➤ Parenting issues

➤ Issues of sexual orientation

➤ Aging

➤ Mental health issues

Many types of support groups are available. If you're interested in joining one but don't know how to find it, check the listings for human services agencies in your phone book, and look for information and referrals. Also see Appendix B, "Additional Resources," in this book.

Some people don't like support groups, and that's fine. Others swear by them. Regardless of where you find your social encouragement and support, keep in mind that it's generally better to rely on others for help than to try to handle all your problems by yourself.

**Don't Go There!**

Most support groups are well-run and structured, but there are some that inevitably turn into gripe-and-whine sessions. If you find yourself in one of those, don't hang around. They don't serve the purpose they're intended for, and they can actually end up making you feel worse instead of better.

## The Power of Spirituality

While the quest for spirituality has captivated many people in our society for some time, spirituality has received little attention from the area of psychology. Carl Jung focused on spirituality in his works, but other than that, there's been little study of it by psychologists. Perhaps it's because spirituality has so many implications and means so many things to so many people.

People in some self-help groups, such as Alcoholics Anonymous, talk of their relationships with "a higher power." What the higher power is, however, varies greatly from member to member. For some, the higher power is God. For others, it can be nature or the AA group itself. What we do know is that spirituality is clearly different from organized religion. It doesn't need to happen in a church, a synagogue, or a mosque. People report spiritual experiences while sitting quietly on the beach and watching the ocean. For others, holding a baby, standing on the top of a mountain, or listening to beautiful music are spiritual experiences.

Regardless of where spirituality comes from or what form it takes, it can give meaning to life and enhance the quality of life. Some people never miss a formal worship service, while others prefer to experience spirituality during a quiet walk in the woods.

Spirituality provides people with hope and gives them something to think about and look forward to.

**Personality Pointer**

For a listing of recently published, well-regarded books on a variety of spiritual issues, check out this site:

www.spiritualityhealth.com/spirit/books1999.html

## The Power of Visualization

*Visualization,* which is simply the practice of forming a mental image of something, is a technique used for all kinds of activities. It can be as basic as conjuring up an image of finding the best ice cream stand in the world on a hot, sunny day. Or it can be imagining where you'll be in life 5 or 10 years down the road.

Visualization can greatly affect your level of self-efficacy and the amount of control you perceive yourself to have over a particular situation.

Try going through these five steps of visualization:

1. Think about a problem that's caused distress in your life.

2. Think about your goal for the problem. How do you want to think about it and deal with it in the future?

3. Imagine that you have just done something that's hugely successful. Picture the scene and the people who are present. Listen to what they say and how enthusiastic they are. Experience the temperature and the smells in the air. Focus on the scene, and re-experience it as much as possible. Feel the pride you're experiencing.

4. Now imagine a time in the near future when you're dealing with your problem. Remember the sense of pride you felt when you visualized your success, and keep that pride with you now. Feel the pride of being successful, and use that feeling to help you deal with what's troubling you. Hold on to the feeling of pride until you've mastered the problem. Continue to feel the pride of your success.

5. Repeat the visualization exercise often. This will motivate you, increase your sense of control, and improve your outlook.

As you can see, there are various components to developing a more positive outlook and getting to be a more optimistic person. It can be done and most doctors and therapists think it's to your benefit to do it.

# Check Yourself Out

Here are several questions to help you reflect on what you've read in this chapter, and perhaps to take the information a step or two farther in your own mind:

➤ How much of the time is your thinking more positive than negative?

➤ How is your health affected by your thinking?

➤ Do you really believe that you can change your pessimistic thoughts?

➤ What do you want to be doing in five years? How can you use visualization to help yourself get there?

You might benefit from discussing these questions with another person or just thinking about them on your own.

---

### The Least You Need to Know

➤ There's renewed interest in the area of positive psychology, which focuses on positive thinking, happiness, and satisfaction.

➤ Studies on issues related to positive psychology conclude that optimistic people who enjoy and look forward to life are happier and healthier—both physically and mentally—than those who don't.

➤ Some people tend to have temperaments that are more pessimistic than others.

➤ Our temperaments tend to be pretty enduring, but a pessimist can work to become more optimistic.

➤ You can use cognitive, social, and spiritual techniques to increase your optimism and improve your outlook on life.

---

# Chapter 27

# Taking a Good, Long Look in Your Crystal Ball

## In This Chapter

➤ Assessing your present and your future

➤ Using a final review to help you assess your personality

➤ Understanding why people don't get help

➤ Looking at the positive aspects of life

➤ Enlisting the power of visualization

➤ Tracking your progress

Unless you're starting to read this book from the back, you've probably covered a lot of ground by this point. We've looked at personality from various angles.

We've talked about different theories of personality and about tests used for assessment purposes. We've explored personality traits and disorders, how your personality affects your career and your love life, and finally, how you can change parts of your personality that are causing problems or distress in your life.

One thing you should be aware of is the tendency that people just beginning to learn about psychology and personality have to diagnose themselves, their family, and their friends. If you've been thinking that you're probably suffering from two or three personality disorders and a couple of temporary states as well, don't despair. It's a natural thing to want to put your new knowledge to work. Just don't get carried away, and don't be too hard on yourself. You could have some of the characteristics of a personality or mood disorder without *having* a personality or mood disorder.

Everyone has a mixed bag of characteristics. As long as you are somewhere close to the middle of the continuum, you are in good shape. You shouldn't try to diagnose other people, either. If somebody has a problem with personality, it often becomes clear to the person in time.

What's in this book is, undoubtedly, a lot to digest. If you're having trouble remembering the difference between the social theory of personality and the humanistic theory, or avoidant and dependent personality disorders, don't despair. This last chapter serves as a review of some of the most important material covered in earlier chapters. It also includes some worksheets to help you evaluate your progress, see what you remember, and think about where you're going from here. To start, we're going to look at where you might be right now regarding your personality, and what you want for yourself in the future.

# Where Are You, and Where Are You Headed?

You may have missed this news flash: Nobody's perfect. Behaviors occur on continuums—not on an either/or basis. Some folks hang a little more toward the edges of the continuums than others, but we all share common experiences and problems in our lives.

When you stop to think about it, people are a lot more alike than they are different. We all come from the same evolutionary process, and we all live in the same general society. We all come into the world in generally the same fashion, we have our allotted number of years here, and we all die. We share many of the same instincts and the same emotions. We all laugh. We all feel pain and pleasure. We all cry.

**Personality Pointer**

We all have personality tendencies that fall into line with those of some of the personality disorders. Take a look at all the diagnostic criteria, and you're sure to see yourself in there somewhere. Don't worry, though; you're in good company, and having a couple of these tendencies is not a big problem.

Despite our similar backdrop, however, it's not an even playing field out there. Things happen to all of us in varying degrees, and those are the things that make us all unique individuals.

In our uniqueness, there are times when we clash with one another. The truth is that most of us get along most of the time, though, despite what we hear every day when we turn on the television news or pick up a newspaper. When you think about the vast amount of interaction people have every day, and how little of it ends up in conflict, you have to think that we're not doing all that bad.

Some aspects of our personalities can make it difficult to get along with others in some ways, though, or to cope with problems that occur.

If you're having problems, either with other people or within yourself, *don't, don't, please don't assume that you have a personality disorder.*

Many, many people have personality issues without having true disorders. The usual indicator for judging the seriousness of a problem is the level of distress you experience. People very rarely come for treatment announcing that they have a personality problem or disorder. They normally come for treatment because they feel depressed, or anxious, or have a relationship or substance-abuse problem, or something else that's troubling them. The degree to which personality contributes to creating or maintaining a level of distress varies from person to person.

What you'll find in the last section of this book will help you begin to address any problems that might be causing you distress. If you use the guidance and the worksheets wisely, you can get a lot of mileage out of them.

If you've tried self-help and your distress level hasn't gone down, or if you're frustrated or stuck on a long, high plateau, then you might want to contact a trained therapist. Resources for locating a cognitive therapist are provided in Appendix B, "Additional Resources."

Use your understanding of your personality to take a good, hard look into your future. Where do you see yourself going from here? Are you happy with your personality the way it is, or do some changes need to happen?

**Don't Go There!**

Don't assume that people who appear stoic and able to deal with anything always are. It's not unheard of, or even that unusual, for someone who keeps all of his or her pain and trouble inside, never giving any indication of distress, to experience sudden and profound problems—physical, mental, or both.

Do you see your personality carrying you far where your career is concerned? What about your personal life? Your love life? Are you happy with your relationships, or are they going nowhere and do they need some work?

Take a few minutes to fill out the following worksheet. There is no comparison data or standard on which to interpret your ratings. The worksheet is designed to help you get a clearer picture of where you are and where you're heading.

# Final Review Worksheet

## Final Review Worksheet

1. List the aspects of your personality you're most satisfied with.

_____     _____

_____     _____

_____     _____

*continues*

**339**

*continued*

2. List the behaviors you're most satisfied with.

_____     _____
_____     _____
_____     _____
_____     _____

3. List the aspect of your personality you feel could most use some improvement.

_____
_____

4. How much distress does this aspect of your personality create for you?

0 _____ 10
    none           moderate          unbearable

5. How much do you want to change this aspect of your personality?

0 _____ 10
    not at all        moderately        greatly

6. How much control over your ability to change do you think you have?

0 _____ 10
    none     a moderate amount   a great amount

7. This is what I'm going to do!

_____
_____

8. This is when I'm going to do it!

_____
_____

9. In one year, this is where I want to be concerning this issue:

_____
_____
_____

After you fill out the worksheet, spend some time thinking about how you'll achieve your goals, and formulate your one-year plan. You might want to jot down an outline on another piece of paper and store it along with the worksheet.

# Why Some People Avoid Getting Help

Maybe you've known somebody who obviously needed to get help, yet made one excuse after another for not doing it.

So why don't people who need help seek it? There are lots of reasons, and they vary greatly, depending on who you're talking to.

Some of the reasons people give are legitimate, while others are less convincing. Let's look at some of the most common reasons people avoid getting professional help when they need it:

➤ **They think treatment won't help.** Some people believe that they can't be helped. So what's the point of wasting the time and money to see someone?

Some people believe they can't be helped because they lack self-efficacy. They just can't imagine that their lives will improve or that they have sufficient power to change aspects of their lives.

## Notes and Quotes

Anyone who feels ashamed to seek therapy should know that millions of people around the world have had their conditions improve after treatment. About 17 million Americans suffer from depression in any one year; many of them seek professional help. As much as 20 percent of the population experiences personality disorders. Add in all the people who get treatment for other problems, and nobody who needs treatment should feel like they're alone or an outcast.

➤ **They feel ashamed for needing help.** Unfortunately, there is still a stigma concerning therapy, and derogatory statements sometimes pop up about people who look for help.

Another aspect of shame is that some people feel so awful about themselves that they fear a therapist will be horrified or disgusted by them. Interestingly, the people with the deepest levels of shame aren't those who have done the worst things. People who commit atrocities often feel a sense of righteousness about their actions. Those who feel deep shame feel it more so because of who they believe they are and what they've learned, than because of the things they've done. People who feel that way need to know that they'll be treated with respect and as worthwhile human beings.

➤ **They think the cost will be prohibitive.** Well, we're not going to tell you that therapists work for nothing. Therapists, like everyone else, need to be paid for their work. It's also true, unfortunately, that managed care and insurance companies have made it difficult for some people to get coverage for mental health services. The lack of funding to pay for healthcare generally, and mental health and substance-abuse care in particular, are hot topics.

Healthcare providers are working with patients to make it easier for them. Therapists sometimes offer sliding scales to make their costs more affordable to patients. Public money may be available in some cases.

You can't expect to get free treatment, but you usually can get help somehow if you need it. Check your phone directory for numbers for community mental health services that can answer your questions concerning payment for services.

Sure, there are many more reasons, but these are the ones we hear most often. The truth is that effective, affordable treatment is available to most people.

# What About the Positive Stuff?

As we discussed at length in Chapter 26, "Cheer Up, Will Ya?", there's renewed interest in the positive aspects of personality. Optimism and self-efficacy are standing out as factors that can positively affect our lives.

To reap the rewards of positive psychology, you may benefit by taking on a more positive belief system. We talked about the enduring patterns of personality traits, some of which are resistant to change and can create real challenges, but are not set in stone: We can learn to be optimistic if we really want to.

**Personality Pointer**

Pessimism has been identified as an important risk factor for mortality in cancer patients under the age of 60. Although it hasn't been shown conclusively that optimism makes cancer patients live longer, it's pretty clear that those with the most pessimistic attitudes die sooner.

We need to do a lot more work in the field of positive psychology, but research so far is encouraging. Studies have told us that we can accomplish two important things with powerful, positive thought:

➤ We can extend the length of our lives.

➤ We can improve the quality of our lives every day that we're here.

If we think in continuous terms, we can improve every aspect of our personalities. Chart your personality traits on a continuum, and work on improving the things you want to change—a little bit at a time. You won't move on the continuum from being completely shy to being completely aggressive, but you can nudge yourself up from being a 1 to being a 4.

*Visualization*—the practice of forming a mental image of something—can be a help in overcoming weaknesses and increasing your level of positive thinking.

A worksheet at the end of this chapter will help you improve your visualization techniques and move you toward your one-year goal.

Some people use positive thinking to better cope with challenges. Others use positive thinking because they feel the need to keep moving forward and to develop their full potential.

The next section gives you a guide to use as an aid for visualization. After that, a follow-up worksheet will help you determine how far you've come in your work to correct a behavior or change a belief.

If you're not ready to use the follow-up worksheet now, just remember that it's here, and use it after you've made more progress toward your one-year goal.

# A Visualization Guide

Visualization can greatly affect your level of self-efficacy and the amount of control you feel you have over a particular situation. Follow these steps:

**Notes and Quotes**

According to research by Martin E.P. Seligman, a renowned psychologist, professor, writer, and former president of the American Psychological Association, the main difference between optimists and pessimists is how they explain setbacks to themselves. Optimists tend to dismiss setbacks, while pessimists take them personally and look at them as permanent.

1. Visualize the greatest success you've ever had. This can be a real event or imagined. Picture the following:

   People who were there

   Things people said

   The atmosphere of the place

   The smells and sounds

   The emotions and sensations you're feeling

2. Now visualize yourself doing the things you need to do to accomplish your one-year goal.

3. Remember the feeling of success you felt in Step 1, and feel it each time during the year that you do something to move yourself toward your goal.

4. Imagine the great sense of accomplishment you'll feel one year from now as you reach your goal. Focus on the things you'll tell people about your accomplishments—who you'll tell, how you'll feel. Imagine the feelings and sensations of great success.

Have a pleasant journey!

# Follow-Up Worksheet

From time to time, it's a good idea to follow up on yourself and to chart your progress. This gives you an ongoing sense of where you are in relation to your goal.

You probably should do this exercise every two or three months during the year that you're working toward your goal.

---

## Follow-Up Worksheet

1. Original Problem: _____

   a. Level of distress when problem was first identified:

      0 _____10

        none         moderate        unbearable

   b. Level of distress at current time:

      0 _____ 10

        none         moderate        unbearable

2. How much did you want to change at the beginning of the one-year period?

      0 _____ 10

        not at all      moderately        greatly

3. How much do you want to continue with the changes or maintain the changes you've made at this point?

      0 _____ 10

        not at all      moderately        greatly

4. List your original automatic thought and mark on the continuum the level at which you believed the thought: _____

      0 _____ 10

        didn't believe  believed somewhat  believed completely

5. List your current automatic thought and mark on the continuum the level at which you believe the thought: _____

      0 _____ 10

        don't believe   believe somewhat   believe completely

6. List your original emotion and mark on the continuum the level at which you felt the emotion: _____

      0 _____ 10

        not at all      somewhat      very strongly

7. List your current emotion and mark on the continuum the level at which you feel the emotion: _____

      0 _____ 10

        not at all      somewhat      very strongly

---

8. List your original behavior and the level at which you believe it was functional:

_____

0 _____ 10

      not adaptive    somewhat adaptive    very functional

9. List your current behavior and the level at which you believe it is functional:

_____

0 _____ 10

      not adaptive    somewhat adaptive    very functional

10. List your original core beliefs and mark on the continuum the level at which you believed the thought: _____

0 _____ 10

    didn't believe   believed somewhat   believed completely

11. List your current core beliefs and mark on the continuum the level at which you believe the thought: _____

0 _____ 10

    don't believe   believe somewhat   believe completely

It's easy to lose track of the progress you've made if you don't chart it along the way. We sometimes need to look back at where we've come from to see how far we've progressed.

# Check Yourself Out

Here are several questions to help you reflect on what you've read in this book, and perhaps to take the information a step or two farther in your own mind:

➤ What have you learned about personality development by reading this book?

➤ What personal goals have you set for yourself?

➤ How much progress have you already made toward reaching your goals?

➤ How often will you continue to visualize your successes?

➤ How will you reward yourself as you achieve each step toward your goals?

You might benefit from discussing these questions with another person or just thinking about them on your own.

## The Least You Need to Know

➤ It's good every now and then to assess where you are, and to plan where you hope to be in a specific period of time.

➤ There are all kinds of reasons why people don't get help when they need it, but the most common are that they don't believe it will do any good, they're ashamed, or they think it will cost too much.

➤ Positive thoughts and optimism can benefit your personality and your life in many ways.

➤ Visualization is a powerful imagery tool used in many instances.

➤ It's important to track your progress and understand how far you've moved ahead toward your goal.

# Glossary

**action stage**   The fourth of the five stages of change, in which a person is actively working toward change.

**actualizing tendency**   The inherent desire and drive in all living things to develop to their fullest potential.

**addiction**   The state of being devoted to, or given up to, a particular practice or habit; disputed as to whether addiction is a disease or learned behavior.

**adjustment disorder**   A condition that occurs in response to an identifiable stressor and is evidenced by symptoms that may be emotional, behavioral, or both.

**alternative statement**   A new, more adaptable belief, formed from consideration given to objective facts.

**anal stage**   The second stage of development, from 18 months to four years of age, which focuses on expulsion and excrement and has the goal of successful potty-training.

**anorexia/bulimia**   A disorder involving food that is characterized by an aversion to food, obsession with weight loss, and purging after eating.

**antisocial personality disorder**   One of the dramatic behaviors, characterized by a pervasive pattern of disregard for and violation of the rights of others.

**anxiety disorder**   A condition that causes people to feel scared, uneasy, and distressed; if not treated, anxiety can be very disruptive and distressing.

**archetype**   A specific instinct that causes people to do something. For example, a mother archetype is a built-in tendency for a person to form relationships with mothering figures.

**automatic thoughts**   The very first thing that pops into your mind when you're confronted with an experience or problem.

**avoidant personality disorder**   One of the fearful behaviors, characterized by a persistent pattern of social inhibition, feelings of inadequacy, and hypersensitivity to negative evaluation.

**Axis I**   One of the five-tiered diagnostic tools used in assessing psychological problems and complaints. Lists the presenting problem or chief complaint, including mood disorders such an anxiety and depression.

**Axis II**   One of the five-tiered diagnostic tools used in assessing psychological problems and complaints. Lists personality disorders, such as paranoid, schizoid, antisocial, borderline, avoidant, dependent, and so forth.

**Axis III**   One of the five-tiered diagnostic tools used in assessing psychological problems and complaints. Lists any type of relevant medical conditions.

**Axis IV**   One of the five-tiered diagnostic tools used in assessing psychological problems and complaints. Lists social stressors, such as early childhood abuse, job loss, divorce, and so forth.

**Axis V**   One of the five-tiered diagnostic tools used in assessing psychological problems and complaints. Gives a numerical rating between 0 and 100 of how well a person is functioning.

**behavior therapy**   A process that uses various steps and components to help people change their behavior in a positive manner.

**behaviorist**   A person who believes in and practices the learning theory of personality.

**behaviors**   Actions displayed by people in connection with their automatic thoughts.

**beliefs**   Links between biological instincts and the environment.

**bipolar disorder**   A mood disorder characterized by extreme shifts between depression and manic phases.

**biopsychosocial characteristics**   Characteristics influenced by biology, psychological factors, and social factors.

**borderline personality disorder**   One of the dramatic behaviors, characterized by a pervasive pattern of instability of interpersonal relationships, self-image, emotions, and marked impulsiveness.

**classical conditioning**   A conditioned response to a conditioned stimulus; the process of learning behavior.

**cognitive distortion**   A means of maintaining schemas, in which people hold on to faulty thinking because it works within their schema.

**cognitive therapy**   The most widely researched form of psychotherapy, which teaches patients to recognize and change maladaptive thought patterns.

**collective unconscious**   A reservoir of everything human that has been passed down from generations, including biology, knowledge, instincts, and so forth.

**connectionism**   The theory that says learning is the connection between a certain stimulus and a certain response.

**conscious**   The part of your mind you are fully aware of.

**constructivist**   Someone who subscribes to and practices the constructivist theory.

**constructivist theory**   A theory of personality stating that psychological processes (thoughts, feelings, and behaviors) are formed according to how people anticipate events.

**contemplation**   The second of the five stages of change, during which people believe they may have a problem.

**core beliefs**   Basic beliefs formed at a very early age, based on the messages and signals received.

**defense mechanism**   A device used by the ego to block out conflict between the id and the superego.

**delusional beliefs**   Beliefs that are based on suspicion and distrust, but not on any evidence.

**denial**   A defense mechanism that forces a desire, wish, or memory into the unconscious mind so that it does not have to be dealt with.

**dependent personality disorder**   One of the fearful behaviors, characterized by a pervasive and excessive need to be taken care of that leads to submissive and clinging behavior and fear of separation.

**depression**   A psychological condition that changes how people think and feel, and also affects social behavior and the sense of physical well-being.

**developmentalist**   Someone who believes in and subscribes to the developmentalist theory.

**developmentalist theory**   A theory of personality that asserts that different stages of growth and change occur in response to cognitive and maturation issues.

**dramatic behavior**   A cluster of personality disorders that includes antisocial, borderline, histrionic, and narcissistic.

**eccentric behavior**   A cluster of personality disorders, including paranoid, schizoid, and schizotypal.

**ego**   A defense mechanism that's partly conscious and contains the capabilities to calculate, reason, and plan.

**emotions**   Feelings that occur along with an automatic thought.

**environment**   The people, things, and circumstances that surround you; all the factors of your surroundings.

**existentialism**   A school of thought that believes each person exists as an individual and must make his or her own purpose in a purposeless world, while focusing on the importance of free will.

**face validity**   The degree to which a question on a psychological test can be directly and easily related to the characteristic or problem the test is intended to evaluate.

**factor analysis**   A complex statistical procedure in which large numbers of objects, traits, and so on are classified and put together into larger categories.

**fearful behavior**   A cluster of personality disorders that includes avoidant, dependent, and obsessive-compulsive.

**genital stage**   The fifth and final stage of development, from puberty on, which has the goal of resolving one's sexual identity.

**histrionic personality disorder**   One of the dramatic behaviors, characterized by a pervasive pattern of excessive emotionality and attention seeking.

**humanist**   Someone who subscribes to and believes in the humanistic theory of personality.

**humanistic theory**   A theory of personality that emphasizes the uniqueness of the individual and recognizes people as being self-directed toward personal growth, which eventually results in self-actualization.

**id**   The unconscious part of the mind that consists of natural instincts, urges, and drives that are repressed.

**ideal self**   The person you think you should be, based on the expectations of society, family, and peers; may vary greatly from the real self.

**identification**   To take on the characteristics of someone else (say "What would Mom do?") and rely on those characteristics instead of following your urges.

**impulse control disorder**   A disorder characterized by an urge to do something harmful to oneself or others.

**individual psychology**   A type of psychology that says each individual should be viewed as a whole person, rather than a compilation of parts.

**infatuation**   A strong attraction to another person, heightened by real or perceived common goals and fantasies; often referred to as *love at first sight*.

**intellectualization**   The process of separating emotion from memory; sometimes done unconsciously as a means of avoiding painful feelings or memories

**intuiting**   Using intuition to organize complex information. Intuiting is based on feeling, as opposed to thinking, which is based on logical, rational thought.

**Keirsey Temperament Sorter**   A personality test often used to determine career aptitude.

**latency period**   The fourth stage of development, beginning from seven years old to puberty; there is no particular focus or goal during this stage.

**learning theory**   A theory of personality that says behavior is not genetic or due to anything in our unconscious mind, but to what we learn.

**maintenance**   The fifth of the five stages of change, in which a person works to maintain change.

**Millon Clinical Multiaxial Inventory**   A widely used psychological test written by Dr. Theodore Millon to determine personality disorders.

**mind reading**   A cognitive distortion in which one person assumes he or she knows what the other is thinking, even though there has been no discussion about the thoughts.

**Minnesota Multiphasic Personality Inventory**   The oldest and most-researched personality test, first developed in 1943. It is set up in a true/false format, with 567 questions.

**modeling**   When a person observes another person's particular behavior and then repeats the observed behavior.

**Montessori education**   A method of education based on the observations and discoveries of Dr. Maria Montessori, designed to help every child reach his or her fullest potential.

**morphology**   A theory that states that people's temperament is dependent on the form and shape of their bodies.

**narcissistic personality disorder**   One of the dramatic behaviors, characterized by a pervasive pattern of grandiosity, need for admiration, and lack of empathy.

**negative reinforcement**   The practice of removing a reinforcer and, by doing so, increasing the likelihood of a particular response.

**Neo-Freudian theories**   Theories of personality that deal with topics such as the human tendency to strive for perfection, birth order, and neurosis; also known as *social theories*.

**obsessive-compulsive disorder**   An anxiety-based, temporary condition that is classified as an Axis I disorder and can be treated by dealing with Axis I issues, such as automatic thoughts and behaviors.

**obsessive-compulsive personality disorder**   One of the fearful behaviors, characterized by a pervasive preoccupation with orderliness, perfectionism, and mental and interpersonal control at the expense of flexibility, openness, and efficiency.

**operant conditioning**   A method of reinforcing behavior by presenting a stimulus following a response.

**oral stage**   The first stage of development, from birth until about 18 months, which centers on the mouth and has the goal of successful weaning.

**panic disorder**   A condition in which a person suffers from panic attacks, or intense and sudden feelings of fear.

**paranoid personality disorder**   One of the eccentric behaviors cluster, characterized by suspiciousness or mistrust that is highly exaggerated or completely unfounded and unwarranted.

**personality**   The traits, qualities, and attitudes that make a person unique; the relatively fixed parts of what and who a person is.

**phallic stage**   The third stage of development, from four to seven years of age, which focuses on sexual organs and has the goal of resolving one's sexual relationship with his or her parents.

**phrenology**   A theory that claims the shape and size of a person's head accounts for mental abilities and personal characteristics.

**positive psychology**   An area of psychology that focuses on happiness, satisfaction, and hope; particularly interested in the link between mental and physical health.

**positive reinforcement**   A reward given for a particular behavioral response.

**preconscious**   The part of the mind that can recall data without much trouble; the thoughts and memories there are easily accessible.

**precontemplation**   The first of the five stages of change, during which a person has no idea that there is a problem and has no plans to make a change.

**preparation**   The third of the five stages of change, in which a person intends to take action toward change.

**projection**   Attributing your own drives and impulses to another person, or recognizing undesirable characteristics in someone else, but not in yourself.

**projective tests**   Tests that do not rely on true and false or multiple-choice questions, but require test takers to reveal what they see or think.

**psychoanalysis**   A form of therapy that depends largely on looking at a person's past to uncover the source of a current problem.

**psychodynamic theory**   A theory of personality based on the findings of Sigmund Freud and the idea of the unconscious mind.

**psychosis**   A breaking with reality that can be as mild as disorganized thinking or as serious as uncontrolled and dangerous aggression.

**punishment**   A type of reinforcement that induces pain or humiliation in the belief that it will suppress a behavior.

**rationalization**   The practice of making up excuses for unacceptable thoughts, ideas, or behaviors.

**reaction formation**   The process of hiding unacceptable behavior and displaying its opposite behavior, such as hugging and kissing someone with whom you're very angry.

**reciprocal inhibition**   A theory that says people can't have opposite feelings at the same time and that if they can make themselves experience desirable feelings, the undesirable ones will be eliminated.

**regression**   The process of going back to an earlier stage of development.

**reinforcement**   Repetition of what people say, or constancy within the environment.

**reliability**   The quality of a psychological test that ensures basically the same results from the same group of people every time they take the test.

**repression**   The state of pushing a desire, wish, or memory down so deep into the unconscious mind that you no longer have any conscious memory of it.

**Rorschach test**   A widely used psychological test that consists of a series of ink blots, developed by Herman Rorschach in 1921.

**schizoid personality disorder**   One of the eccentric behaviors cluster, characterized by a strong and constant pattern of detachment from social relationships and difficulty in interpersonal relationships, and caused by the inability to effectively experience and express emotions.

**schizotypal personality disorder**   The most serious of the eccentric behaviors cluster, evidenced by great discomfort with close relationships, as well as oddness and eccentricities of behavior and thinking.

**scientific method**   A formal testing process used to study behavior and other concepts.

**self-actualization**   The process of fully becoming yourself and completely fulfilling your inner drives.

**self-archetype**   A drive to become perfect—to resolve and integrate all parts of the personality.

**self-efficacy**   The belief that you have some control over your life, and that your actions and accomplishments will affect the direction and path of your life.

**self-esteem**   Your own measure of what you think of yourself; your opinion of yourself.

**self-fulfilling prophecy**   An expectation or prediction that comes to pass primarily because a person has expected or predicted it.

**self-rating**   A process in which people being evaluated are asked to rate themselves on a scale of 0 to 10, in order to give the therapist an idea of their state of mind and how they view themselves.

**sensing**   Obtaining information through the senses—sight, hearing, smell, taste, and touch.

**social theories**   Theories of personality that deal with topics such as the human tendency to strive for perfection, birth order, and neurosis; also known as *Neo-Freudian theories.*

**Stanford-Binet Intelligence Tests**   Developed in 1910 to measure verbal and nonverbal areas of development, mathematical reasoning, and short-term memory. The test was named for Alfred Binet, a French psychologist.

**state**   A temporary condition of one's personality, similar to a mood.

**sublimation**   To change an unacceptable drive into a more socially acceptable behavior.

**superego**   The connection between the id and ego that serves as the mind's link to reality and society. It describes what we come to believe as right and wrong.

**temperament**   The fixed, enduring, biological part of one's personality or disposition.

**theory**   A thought or idea supported by facts and data collected by a formal testing process called the *scientific method.*

**thought-stopping**   A technique used for behavior modification. As soon as an unwanted thought comes into the mind, the person stops it with a decisive "No."

**traits**   Characteristics, such as shyness, thought to be biological and that contribute to the temperament of a person.

**unconscious**   The part of the mind that's not easily accessible, including memories, biological instincts, and motivations for physical needs.

**validity**   The quality of a psychological test that ensures that the test measures what it's supposed to measure.

**visualization**   A technique used for various purposes, such as relaxation or to improve self-image, that concentrates on forming an image in the mind.

**Wechsler Adult Intelligence Scale (WAIS)**   A widely used intelligence test written by David Wechsler and introduced in 1939.

# Additional Resources

This appendix lists additional resources—books, periodicals, Internet sites, and agencies—that can give you more information on personality, psychology, and psychological problems.

## Books

Acocella, Joan Ross. *Creating Hysteria: Women and Multiple Personality Disorder.* Jossey-Bass Publishers, Inc., 1999.

Adderholdt-Elliott, Miriam, Jan Goldberg, and Caroline Price. *Perfectionism: What's Bad About Being Too Good?* Free Spirit Publishing, 1999.

Alderman, Ph.D., Tracy, and Karen Marshall. *Amongst Ourselves: A Self-Help Guide to Living With Dissociative Identity Disorder.* New Harbinger Publications, 1998.

Baron, Renee, and Elizabeth Wagele. *Are You My Type, Am I Yours?: Relationships Made Easy Through The Enneagram.* Harper San Francisco, 1997.

Berens, Linda V., and Nario Nardi. *The 16 Personality Types, Descriptions for Self-Discovery.* Telos Publications, 1999.

Berent, Jonathan, and Amy Lemley. *Beyond Shyness: How to Conquer Social Anxieties.* Simon & Schuster Trade, 1994.

Black, Donald W., and C. Lindon Larson. *Bad Boys, Bad Men: Confronting Antisocial Personality Disorder.* Oxford University Press, 1999, 2000.

Briggs Myers, Isabel, with Peter B. Myers. *Gifts Differing: Understanding Personality Type.* Davies-Black Publishing, 1995.

Butcher, James Neal. *A Beginner's Guide to the MMPI-2.* The American Psychological Association, 1999.

Casey, Joan Frances, with Lynn Wilson. *The Flock: The Autobiography of a Multiple Personality.* Fawcett Book Group, 1992.

Cline, Jean Darby. *Silencing the Voices: One Woman's Triumph Over Multiple Personality Disorder.* Berkeley Publishing Group, 1997.

Cooper, Terry D. *Accepting the Troll Underneath the Bridge: Overcoming Our Self-Doubts.* Paulist Press, 1996.

Coren, Stanley. *Why We Love the Dogs We Do: How to Find the Dog That Matches Your Personality.* Simon & Schuster Trade, 2000.

Covy, Stephen R. *Living the 7 Habits: The Courage to Change.* Simon & Schuster Trade Paperbacks, 2000.

Dickson, Heather, ed. *Pocket Personality Quiz.* Lagoon Books, 2000.

Dimitrius, Ph.D., Jo-Ellan, and Mark Mazzarella. *Reading People: How to Understand People and Predict Their Behavior—Anytime, Anyplace.* Random House, 1999.

Editors of *Teen* and *All About You* magazines. *Reveal the Real You: 20 Cool Quizzes All About You.* Troll Assoc., 1999 (for ages 9-12).

Elster, Jon. *Addiction: Entries and Exits.* Russell Sage Foundation, 1999.

———. *Strong Feelings: Emotion, Addiction, and Human Behavior.* MIT Press, 1999.

Ford Thornton, Mellissa. *Eclipses: Behind the Borderline Personality Disorder.* Monte Sano Publishing, 1997.

Fromm, Eric. *Anatomy of Human Destructiveness.* Henry Holt, 1992.

Golomb, Elan. *Trapped in the Mirror: Adult Children of Narcissistic Parents in Their Struggle for Self.* William Morrow & Company, 1995.

Hall, Calvin Springer, with John Campbell and Gardner Lindzey. *Theories of Personality.* John Wiley & Sons, Inc., 1997.

Hare, Robert D. *Without Conscience: The Disturbing World of the Psychopaths Among Us.* Guilford Press, 1999.

Horney, M.D., Karen. *The Neurotic Personality of Our Time.* WW Norton, 1993.

Janda, Louis H. *Career Tests: 25 Revealing Self-Tests to Help You Find and Succeed at the Perfect Career.* Adams Media Corporation, 1999.

———. *The Psychologist's Book of Self-Tests: 25 Love, Sex, Intelligence, Career, and Personality Tests Developed by Professionals to Reveal the Real You.* Perigee Press, 1996.

Keirsey, David W., and Marilyn Bates. *Please Understand Me: Character and Temperament Types.* Prometheus Books, 1985.

Kincher, Jonni. *Psychology for Kids: 40 Fun Tests That Help You Learn About Yourself.* Free Spirit Publications, 1995 (for ages 9–12).

————. *Psychology for Kids II: 40 Fun Experiments That Help You Learn About Others.* Free Spirit Publications, 1998 (for ages 9–12).

Kreisman, M.D., Jerold J., and Hal Straus. *I Hate You—Don't Leave Me: Understanding the Borderline Personality.* Avon, 1991.

Kroeger, Otto, with Janet M. Thuesen. *Type Talk at Work: How the 16 Personality Types Determine Your Success on the Job.* Dell Publishing Company, Inc., 1994.

————. *Type Talk: The 16 Personality Types That Determine How We Live, Love, and Work.* Dell Publishing Company, Inc., 1989.

Littauer, Florence. *Personality Plus.* Revell, Fleming H. Company, 1992.

————. *Personality Plus: How to Understand Others by Understanding Yourself.* Fleming H. Revell Co., 1992.

Littauer, Florence, and Marita Littauer. *Getting Along With Almost Anybody: The Complete Personality Book.* Fleming H. Revell Co., 1998.

Littauer, Fred, and Florence Littauer. *Why Do I Feel the Way I Do?* Baker Book House Company, 1998.

Lowen, Alexander. *Narcissism.* Simon & Schuster, 1997.

Lubinski, David John, and Rene V. Dawis. *Assessing Individual Differences in Human Behavior: New Concepts, Methods, and Findings.* Consulting Psychologists Press, 1995.

Magid, Ken, and Carole A. McKelvey. *High Risk: Children Without a Conscience.* Bantam Books, 1989.

Mallinger, Allan E., and Jeannette Dewyze. *Too Perfect: When Being in Control Gets Out of Control.* Fawcett Book Group, 2000.

Martin, Paul, and Patrick Bateson. *Design for a Life: How Behavior and Personality Develop.* Simon & Schuster, 2000.

Maslow, Abraham H. *Toward a Psychology of Being.* John Wiley & Sons, Inc., 1998.

Maslow, Abraham Harold, James Fadiman, and Robert Frager. *Motivation and Personality.* Addison Wesley Educational Publishers, 1976.

Mason, Paul T., Randi Kreger, and Larry J. Siever. *Stop Walking on Eggshells; Coping When Someone You Care about Has Borderline Personality Disorder.* New Harbinger Publications, 1998.

Masterson, James F. *The Search for the Real Self: Unmasking the Personality Disorders of Our Age.* The Free Press, 1990.

Millon, Theodore, and Roger Davis. *Personality Disorders in Modern Life.* John Wiley & Sons, Inc., 1999.

Moskovitz, Richard A. *The Lost in the Mirror: An Inside Look at Borderline Personality Disorder.* Taylor Publishing Company, 1996.

Myss, Caroline. *Why People Don't Heal and How They Can.* Crown Publishing Group, 1998.

Nakken, Craig. *The Addictive Personality: Understanding the Addictive Process and Compulsive Behavior.* Hazelden Education Information, 1996.

Oldham, John M., and Lois B. Morris. *The New Personality Self-Portrait: Why You Think, Work, Love and Act the Way You Do.* Bantam Doubleday Dell Publishing Group, 1991.

Quenk, Naomi L. *Beside Ourselves: Our Hidden Personality in Everyday Life.* Davies-Black Publishing, 1993.

Ramirez Basco, Monica. *Never Good Enough; How to Use Perfectionism to Your Advantage Without Letting It Ruin Your Life.* Simon & Schuster, 2000.

Rank, Otto, Charles Francis Atkinson, and Anais Nin. *Art and Artist: Creative Urge and Personality Development.* W.W. Norton and Company, 1989.

Rathus, Spencer A., and Jeffrey S. Nevi. *Adjustment and Growth: The Challenges of Life.* HBJ College and School Division, 1999.

Riso, Don Richard, and Russ Hudson. *Understanding the Enneagram: The Practical Guide to Personality Types.* Houghton Mifflin Company, 2000.

———. *Personality Types.* Houghton Mifflin Company, 1996.

Ross, Colin A. *Dissociative Identity Disorder: Diagnosis, Clinical Features, and Treatment of Multiple Personality.* John Wiley & Sons, Inc., 1996.

Rusk, Tom, and Randy Read. *I Want to Change, But I Don't Know How.* The Putnam Publishing Group, 1979.

Santoro, Ph.D., Joseph, and Ronald Cohen, Ph.D. *The Angry Heart: Overcoming Borderline and Addictive Disorders: An Interactive Self-Help Guide.* New Harbinger Publications, 1997.

Sulloway, Frank J. *Born to Rebel: Birth Order, Family Dynamics, & Creative Lives.* Random House, 1997.

Thomson, Lenore. *Personality Type: An Owner's Manual.* Shambhala Publications, 1998.

Tieger, Paul D., and Barbara Barron-Tieger. *Do What You Are: Discover the Perfect Career for You Through the Secrets of Personality Type.* Little, Brown and Company, 1995.

———. *Just Your Type: Create the Relationship You've Always Wanted Using the Secrets of Personality Type.* Little, Brown & Company, 1999.

Turner, Diane, and Thelma Greco. *The Personality Compass: A New Way to Understand People.* Barnes and Noble Books, 1999.

Twerski, Abraham J. *Addictive Thinking: Understanding Self-Deception.* Hazelden Information & Educational Services, 1997.

Twerski, Abraham J., and Craig Nakken. *Addictive Thinking and the Addictive Personality.* Fine Communications, 1999.

Wheelis, Allen. *How People Change.* Harper Trade, 1974.

Wolman, Benjamin B. *Antisocial Behavior: Personality Disorders from Hostility to Homicide.* Prometheus Books, 1999.

Wright, William. *Born That Way: Genes, Behavior, Personality.* Routledge, 1999.

Young, Jeffrey E. *Cognitive Therapy for Personality Disorders: A Schema-Focused Approach.* Professional Resource Exchange, 1999.

# Periodical

*Psychology Today*
49 E. 21st St.
New York, NY 10010
1-800-234-8361

This popular magazine presents information from the latest research in psychology in a readable, understandable manner, making it useful to people in their everyday lives. Check it out on the Internet at www.psychologytoday.com.

# Web Sites

### All About You
www.outofservice.com/you

*Includes a personality test developed by a psychologist at U.C. Berkley. Asks you questions about yourself and encourages you to answer the same questions about another person, preferably a sibling, for research purposes.*

### The American Psychological Society
www.apa.org

*Loaded with information for professionals and people who are just looking for information about hundreds of issues related to psychology.*

### Ansir
www.ansir.com/ansirforone

*Billed as the Web's toughest but most accurate personality test, this can provide insights into how you think, work, and love.*

### Blots
www.geocities.com/HotSprings/6502.Blots.html

*Determine your personality by interpreting ink blots on this Web site. Asks for your first name and e-mail address, but providing the address is optional.*

**BPD Central**
www.bpdcentral.com

*A collection of resources for people who care about someone who suffers from borderline personality disorder.*

**BrainTainment Center**
www.members.tripod.com

*Offers a 36-question, five-minute IQ test and some personality tests.*

**CCS Publishing**
www.ccspublishing.com

*Provides information about various personality disorders and the latest treatments available.*

**Color Quiz**
www.colorquiz.com

*A five-minute personality test based on research by color psychologists around the world.*

**Concerned Counseling**
www.concernedcounseling.com

*Offers lots of information about psychological issues, including personality disorders. Provides symptoms of disorders and links to other sites.*

**Dr. Ivan's Depressional Central**
www.psycom.net

*A central clearinghouse for all kinds of information on different types of depressive disorders and treatments for people suffering from depression. The site also contains information on other personality disorders.*

**Greater Hampton Roads**
www.greaterhamptonroads.com

*Includes employment, personality, and IQ tests, and the Motivational Style Profile.*

**The Keirsey Temperament Sorter**
www.keirsey.com

*A test based on the Myers-Briggs Type Indicator. It measures four main attributes: extroversion-introversion, sensing-intuition, thinking-feeling, and judging-perceiving. It tells you which of one of 16 types you are, based on your answers.*

**The KNOWZONE**
www.webhome.idirect.com

*Offers personality tests, information about psychology and personality, and links to other sites.*

**The Lighter Side of Psychology**
www.users.erols.com/geary/psychology

*Comic strips, links to similar sites, and jokes such as "How many psychologists does it take to change a light bulb? Just one, but the bulb has to be ready to change."*

**Mental Health Net**
www.mentalhelp.net

*A big, comprehensive guide to mental health issues, with lots of links to other sites.*

**Mentalhealth Internet Resources**
www.mirconnect.com

*Offers a glossary of terms concerning personality disorders and other mental health issues.*

**Personality and IQ Tests**
www.davideck.com

*Easy-to-take personality and IQ tests.*

**Personality Online**
www.spods.net/personality/index.php3

*A site with personality tests and information concerning various personality-related topics.*

**The Personality Page Library**
www.personalitypage.com

*Recommends books related to personality, and gives you information about how to buy them.*

**Personality Test**
www.cs.ucr.edu

*Gives you a free analysis of your personality, based on which of nine images you select.*

**Personality Test**
www.ullazang.com

*Determines your personality by asking you to click on the shapes you find most appealing.*

**Personality Tests**
www.2h.com/Tests/personality.phtml

*More than 50 tests to assess IQ, personality, and entrepreneurial possibilities.*

**Personality: What Makes Us Who We Are?**
www.learner.org/exhibits/personality

*Lots of photos illustrate personality-related issues such as behavior, genetics, human nature, and thoughts and feelings.*

**Planet Wally**

www.gunnar.com/gwally/tests/personality2.html

*A fun, four-question test that you can take yourself or do with your friends to determine your personality type.*

**The Profiler Personality Test**

www.od-online.com

*A professional personality assessment designed by psychologists to help you realize your full potential.*

**Psych Central**

www.psychcentral.com

*A site dealing with issues ranging from the use of St. John's Wort to Internet addiction. It's the site of Dr. John Grohol, a popular author on mental health issues.*

**PsychCrawler**

www.psychcrawler.com

*Provides access to many sites dealing with psychology and personality.*

**Shakey**

www.shakey.net

*A directory helps you find information on any personality disorder or other mental health issue.*

**Survivor Art Gallery**

www.multiple-personality.com/gallery.13.htm

*This site displays art by people who have survived child abuse. It also gives you information about multiple personalities.*

**WAYPAGES**

www.plgrm.com

*Gives you information about personality disorders and tells you where to find more news and information.*

**The Webhouse**

www.thewebhouse.net

*Offers questionnaires, quizzes, personality tests, and online personal ads.*

**Worldbiz**

www.worldbiz.net

*Offers information and resources for people who care about someone who suffers from borderline personality disorder.*

# Agencies

## *The Academy of Cognitive Therapy*

(An international listing of certified cognitive therapists, designed to assist patients in finding a qualified therapist in their area)

**GSB Building, City Line and Belmont Avenues, Suite 700**
Bala Cynwyd, PA 19004-1610
610-6643020 (Phone)
610-664-4437 (Fax)
www.academyofct.org

**The Beck Institute for Cognitive Therapy and Research**
GSB Building, City Line and Belmont Avenues, Suite 700
Bala Cynwyd, PA 19004-1610
610-6643020 (Phone)
610-664-4437 (Fax)
www.beckinstitute.org/

**Cognitive Therapy Centers of New York and Connecticut**
120 E. 56th Street, Suite 530
New York, NY 10022
212-588-1998
www.schematherapy.com

**San Francisco Bay Area Center for Cognitive Therapy**
5435 College Avenue
Oakland, CA 94618
510-652-4455

**Center for Cognitive Therapy**
University of Pennsylvania
3600 Market Street, 8th Floor
Philadelphia, PA 19104-2649
215-898-4100
www.med.upenn.edu/psychct/edu

# Index